CAN THESE BONES LIVE?

T0385874

Cultural Memory
in
the
Present

Mieke Bal and Hent de Vries, Editors

CAN THESE BONES LIVE?

Translation, Survival, and Cultural Memory

Bella Brodzki

STANFORD UNIVERSITY PRESS

STANFORD, CALIFORNIA

2007

Stanford University Press
Stanford, California

© 2007 by the Board of Trustees of the
Leland Stanford Junior University.

Published with the assistance of the Faculty Publication Fund
at Sarah Lawrence College.

Printed and bound by CPI Group (UK) Ltd, Croydon, CR0 4YY

Library of Congress Cataloging-in-Publication Data
Brodzki, Bella.
 Can these bones live? : translation, survival, and cultural memory / Bella Brodzki.
    p. cm.—(Cultural memory in the present)
 Includes bibliographical references and index.
 ISBN 978-0-8047-5541-2 (cloth : alk. paper)—ISBN 978-0-8047-5542-9 (pbk. :
alk. paper)
 1. Translating and interpreting. 2. Translating and interpreting—Social aspects.
I. Title.

PN241.B67 2007
418'.02—dc22   2006100034

Typeset by Classic Typography in 11/13.5 Adobe Garamond.

Contents

Acknowledgments

Although this project was crystallized in the late 1990s, *Can These Bones Live?* draws on a set of intersecting themes that have preoccupied me for much of my writing and teaching career. I am grateful to my students at Sarah Lawrence College, whose enduring intellectual vitality never ceases to inspire and challenge me. Many of the ideas presented here were developed in dialogue with them. Colleagues, both former and current, have stimulated my thinking and enriched my understanding of translation as a kind of interdisciplinary exchange. I thank in this regard Regina Arnold, Melvin Bukiet, Robert Desjarlais, Tara Fitzpatrick, Deborah Hertz, Daniel Kaiser, Angela Moger, Gilberto Perez, Gina Philogene, Shahnaz Rouse, Lyde Sizer, Frederick Smoler, Malcolm Turvey, Marina Vitkin, Peter Whitely, and Charles Zerner. I am also grateful to Roland Dollinger, Margery Franklin, Melissa Frazier, Mary Morris, Maria Negroni, Joan Peters, and (especially) Barbara Schecter, all of whom read portions of the manuscript and offered very helpful criticism. I owe very special thanks to Arnold Krupat, my faculty don, whose scholarly example and generosity of spirit have been invaluable at many crucial stages in the writing of this book.

My work has been sustained in various ways by Ulrich Baer, Chagit Deitz, Stephen Feinstein, Karen Gantz-Zahler, Sandor Goodhart, Anne-Marie Levine, Michael Levine, Suzanne Jill Levine, Judith Misrahi-Barak, Gila Safran Naveh, Anna Orofiamma, Anne Paupert, Kathleen Ross, Annie Saulnier, Ada Savin, L. B. Thomp, and Yves Zeidenberg. Collaborating with Jeremy Varon on a related project has been deeply meaningful to me.

I have presented different arguments and analyses, at various stages, to audiences at national and international conferences and colloquia and at universities in the United States and abroad. I am grateful for those opportunities and invitations; they have been instrumental to the evolution of this book.

I am grateful as well to Claire Landiss, who was my research assistant at the inception of this project, and to Jennie Panchy and James Gibbons, whose editorial finesse significantly improved the manuscript. I would also like to express my thanks to my current research assistant, Luiza Flynn-Goodlett, whose unflagging energy, goodwill, and technical skills enabled me to get through the final hurdles. From the launching of *Can These Bones Live?* as a book to the execution of its final pages, Ramiza Koya has played an essential role in every aspect of the enterprise. I cannot thank her enough. Margaret Higonnet, Marianne Hirsch, Françoise Lionnet, Ronnie Scharfman, Julia Watson, and Louise Yelin have provoked, encouraged, and nourished me throughout this endeavor. I owe them a profound debt.

This book would not have been possible without the love and savoir faire of my husband, Henry Issenberg. I am infinitely grateful also to my son, Sasha Issenberg, and daughter, Sarina Issenberg, for their capacity to retranslate the world for me in their own remarkable fashions. They remind me daily that intergenerational transmission moves in two directions.

I thank Dr. Jeffrey Schultz and Dr. Alan Friedman for affording me the acuity to see this book to completion.

I thank Rosemary Weeks, faculty secretary, for her help in the last stages of preparation. I have been the beneficiary of patient and thorough assistance from the staff of the Esther Raushenbush Library at Sarah Lawrence College: Charling Fagan, Janet Alexander, Judy Kicinski, Emily Drabinski, Jenni McFadden, and Geoffrey Danisher. No investigative problem or research question of mine was either too small or too elusive to pursue.

My research was supported by Sarah Lawrence College in the form of a Hewlitt-Mellon Faculty Development Grant, which provided release time from teaching in 2001, and a sabbatical leave in 2002. I was able to extend that leave with the generous aid in 2003–4 of a National Endowment for the Humanities Fellowship, which provided me with a year of uninterrupted time for research and writing.

I would like to thank my expert *PMLA* readers, Eva Tanor Banet and Lawrence Venuti, whose earlier critiques had a catalytic effect on my understanding of the field of translation studies. I am grateful to David Damrosch, external reader for Stanford University Press, who made incisive comments and suggestions, and to Norris Pope, Mariana Raykov, and

Angie Michaelis for all their efforts on my behalf. Peter Dreyer did a meticulous job of copyediting.

I thank Ammann Verlag for permission to publish Wulf Kirsten's poem "Bleak Site: A Triptych," from Kirsten's collection *Erdlebenbilder: Gedichte aus fünfzig Jahren, 1954–2004* (Zurich: Ammann, 2004), in my Chapter 4, and Sabine Dollinger for translating the poem into English.

Portions of this book have been previously published and appear here in extended and substantially revised form. Permission to reprint is gratefully acknowledged.

"Nomadism and the Texualization of Memory in André Schwarz-Bart's *A Woman Named Solitude*," *Yale French Studies* 82–83 (1993). Reprinted courtesy *Yale French Studies*. Reworked in Chapter 2.

"Changing Masters: Gender, Genre, and the Discourses of Slavery," in *Borderwork: Feminist Engagements with Comparative Literature*, ed. Margaret R. Higonnet (Ithaca, N.Y.: Cornell University Press, 1994). Reprinted courtesy Cornell University Press. Reworked in Chapter 2.

"History, Cultural Memory, and the Tasks of Translation in T. Obinkaram Echewa's *I Saw the Sky Catch Fire*," *PMLA* 114, no. 2 (1999). Reprinted courtesy Modern Language Association. Reworked in Chapter 3.

"Trauma Inherited, Trauma Reclaimed: *Chamberet: Recollections from an Ordinary Childhood*," *Yale Journal of Criticism* 14, no. 1 (2001). Reprinted courtesy Johns Hopkins University Press. Reworked in Chapter 3.

"Reading Himself and Others: Philip Roth's *The Professor of Desire*," in *Profils américains: Philip Roth*, ed. Ada Savin and Paule Lévy (Montpellier: Centre d'études et de recherches sur la culture et la littérature américaines, Université Paul-Valéry, Montpellier III, 2002). Reprinted courtesy Université Paul-Valéry, Montpellier III. Reworked in Chapter 1.

"Race, Slavery and 'The Law of Genre' in Charles Johnson's *Oxherding Tale*," in *Revisiting Slave Narratives/Les avatars contemporains des récits d'esclaves*, ed. Judith Misrahi-Barak (Montpellier: Centre d'études et de recherches sur les pays du Commonwealth, Université Paul-Valéry, Montpellier III, 2005). Reprinted courtesy Université Paul-Valéry, Montpellier III. Reworked in Chapter 2.

Abbreviations

AA   Cynthia Ozick, *Art and Ardor: Essays* (New York: Knopf, 1983)

AFS   Jorge Semprún, *Communism in Spain in the Franco Era: The Autobiography of Federico Sanchez*, trans. Helen R. Lane (Brighton, Eng.: Harvester Press, 1980)

LJ   André Schwarz-Bart, *Le dernier des Justes* (Paris: Seuil, 1959), trans. Stephen Becker as *The Last of the Just* (New York: Atheneum, 1960)

LL   Jorge Semprún, *Literature or Life*, trans. Linda Coverdale (New York: Viking Penguin, 1997)

LV   Jorge Semprún, *The Long Voyage*, trans. Richard Seaver (New York: Grove Press, 1964)

PCE   Partido Comunista Español

PSWC   David Brion Davis, *The Problem of Slavery in Western Culture* (Ithaca, N.Y.: Cornell University Press, 1966)

CAN THESE BONES LIVE?

Introduction

> The hand of the Lord came upon me. He took me out by the spirit of the Lord and set me down in the valley. It was full of bones. He led me all around them; there were very many of them spread over the valley, and they were very dry. He said to me, "O mortal, can these bones live?"
> —Ezekiel 37:1–6

> For in its afterlife—which could not be called that if it were not a transformation and a renewal of something living—the original undergoes a change.
> —Walter Benjamin, "The Task of the Translator"

> I think of us as interpreters of the skeleton's language.
> —Clea Koff, *The Bone Woman: A Forensic Anthropologist's Search for Truth in the Mass Graves of Rwanda, Bosnia, Croatia, and Kosovo*

We are in the midst of a widespread rethinking of translation. This moment, not unlike the linguistic turn of the 1970s, signals a rise in translative consciousness everywhere in the humanities, but especially in comparative literature studies.[1] Such changes in awareness and appreciation of translation can be linked to paradigm shifts in critical and cultural theory across disciplines. The recent shifts in translation theory, as well as the rise in translation studies generally, are informed by and have benefited in different degrees from deconstruction, psychoanalysis, gender studies, and postcolonial studies, as does my own approach in the staging of translation in this book.[2]

My understanding of translation is indebted to Walter Benjamin's essay "The Task of the Translator," written in 1923, which prefaces his translation of Baudelaire's *Tableaux parisiens*.[3] In this remarkably generative text, Benjamin posits that translation is a redemptive mode that ensures the survival, the living on, of an individual text or cultural narrative, albeit in a revised or altered form. Jacques Derrida's elaborations of Benjamin's view of translation as survival in "Living On: Border Lines," *The Ear of the Other: Otobiography, Transference, Translation*, and "Des Tours de Babel" have marked me no less than Benjamin's essay has.[4] In these three interrelated texts, Derrida stakes a claim to a particular philosophical inheritance, asserting that the scene of translation is inscribed "within a scene of inheritance" and arguing that Benjamin's notion of translation as survival, whether in the sense of *Überleben* (outliving, outlasting) or *Fortleben* (living on, sur-viving), is to be understood as implying, not the extension of life, but an infusion, a transfusion, of otherness: "The work does not simply live longer, it lives more and better, beyond the means of its author."[5] Benjamin, Derrida, and others who have followed in their wake have forged my view of translation as a kind of critical and dynamic displacement: in an act of identification that is not imitation, translation hearkens back to the original or source text and elicits what might otherwise remain recessed or unarticulated, enabling the source text to live beyond itself, to exceed its own limitations.

Translations do not belong to a separate sphere of literary production (or as some would say, reproduction) but are embedded in an extensive social and political network of language relations, cultural practices, and perspectives. Translations are subject to and reflective of external conditions of reception and specific literary-historical contexts that are themselves always changing. Just as it has become impossible, for example, to explore authorship, agency, subjectivity, performativity, multiculturalism, postcolonialism, transnationalism, diasporic literacy, and technological literacy without considering the impact of gender as an intersecting category of analysis, so should it be inconceivable to overlook translation's integral role in every discursive field. More than ever, translation is now understood to be a politics as well as a poetics, an ethics as well as an aesthetics. Translation is no longer seen to involve only narrowly circumscribed technical procedures of specialized or local interest, but rather to underwrite all cultural transactions, from the most benign to the most venal. It is the purpose of this book to show how these broader conceptions of translation are embedded in the practice of translating itself.

Although the way was richly paved in the 1980s by such provocative collections as *Difference in Translation*, edited by Joseph Graham (1985), the 1990s was the boom decade for translation studies. At the start of this new century, all indicators point to the subject of translation and its globalized frames of reference as central to the work of scholars and students of the humanities across traditional disciplinary boundaries.[6] In the constantly reconfigured fields of comparative literature and cultural studies, questions of translation have inflected the most compelling and consequential debates on every facet of identity and representation, including how these fields define themselves, protect their borders, and justify their existence as distinct(ive) disciplines. J. Hillis Miller identifies "the question of translation as the central problematic in comparative literature."[7] In alignment with this position, I intend this study as a contribution to current efforts to situate translation within comparative literature studies, thus invigorating comparative literature in the process. As a comparatist, I find it nearly impossible to think along a single linguistic, national, or disciplinary line; at the same time, I believe that we must continue to foreground the specificity of individual languages and their literary and cultural productions whenever possible. At the nexus of the comparative literature project—indeed, of every project that thinks about its "others"—translation is the mode by which various discourses read each other, locate their commonalities, and name their differences.[8]

*

It was while teaching Maxine Hong Kingston's *The Woman Warrior*, a language-obsessed memoir of growing up Chinese-American, that I recognized that I had found a literary paradigm for Benjamin's theory of translation as afterlife.[9] Kingston's widely taught, much anthologized, highly mediated rendering of her mother's confusing, contradictory "talk story" encompasses translation on multiple levels. But what resonates so profoundly in the Benjaminian sense is Kingston's self-attribution as an "outlaw knot-maker" (190), a mythopoeic storyteller, who, through an act of imaginative identification with the dead, creates a textual memorial on her own terms and in her own right. *The Woman Warrior* is a fantastic cosmic drama played out within the parameters of an immigrant family, a parable about the fundamental ambiguity and violence of translation and its power to betray, disarm, and transform inherited, reified cultural scripts.

The concluding line of Kingston's book is "it translated well," which must be understood to mean that her mother's "talk story," despite its opacity and equivocalness, has been rendered usable, is deemed "translatable." Book in hand, the reader may never have questioned the original's translatability. Still, it can never be assumed. Moreover, although *The Woman Warrior*'s act of translation marks an act of poetic recovery, it does not achieve cultural communion or synthesis with the source narrative, even as it transmits more than specific content or subject matter. Rather, à la Benjamin, this translation signifies a life-sustaining act, a life-empowering moment shared between two generations in an ongoing process of carrying over the past into the present. Both languages—the Chinese of "impossible dreams" and the English of "waking life normal"—remain present in this transaction, in which coincidence of meaning is not attained; Babelian confusion will not be overcome and contradiction will not be resolved to the advantage of one or the other. The last section, "Eighteen Songs for a Barbarian Reed Pipe," confirms translation as the medium by which the viability of cultural forms throughout history has been tested through such exchange, indeed, often in brutal confrontation with others. From these clashes and rifts, traditions are revised, conceptual boundaries are inevitably expanded, and new art forms emerge, producing cultural change. Kingston's translative performance in *The Woman Warrior*—an example of this very phenomenon—has itself redefined the genre of autobiography and reconfigured the world literary canon.

As is clear in *The Woman Warrior*, translation is an intercultural as well as a translingual phenomenon, a transcultural as well as an interlingual process. It involves the transfer of a narrative or text from one signifying form to another, the transporting of texts from one historical context to another, and the tracking of the migration of meanings from one cultural space to another. Because translation is a movement never fully achieved, both *trans*, meaning "across," and *inter*, meaning "between," are crucial to an understanding of the breadth of the workings of translation. We are most accustomed to thinking of translation as an empirical linguistic maneuver, but excavating or unearthing burial sites or ruins in order to reconstruct traces of the physical and textual past in a new context is also a mode of translation, just as resurrecting a memory or interpreting a dream are acts of translation.[10] In the process of being transferred from one realm or condition to another, the source event or idea is necessarily reconfigured; the result of translation is that the original, also inaccessible, is no longer an original per se; it is a pretext whose identity has been redefined.

The significance of this point as an idea, and its implications for understanding the relationship between survival and cultural memory, will be reiterated throughout this study. Even if, hypothetically, it were possible to excavate a body, a text, a narrative, an image, or even a memory intact, the necessarily delayed, translated context of such an excavation would be transformed in the interval between the moment of production and the moment of its translation.[11] As Benjamin states in the sixth of his eighteen "Theses on the Philosophy of History," a testament written not long before his suicide in 1940 in Port Bou at the French-Spanish border, as he fled the Nazis:

> To articulate the past historically does not mean to recognize it "the way it actually was" (Ranke). It means to seize hold of a memory as it flashes up at a moment of danger. Historical materialism wishes to retain that image of the past which unexpectedly appears to man singled out by history at a moment of danger. The danger affects both the content of the tradition and its receivers. The same threat hangs over both: that of becoming a tool of the ruling classes. In every era the attempt must be made anew to wrest tradition away from a conformism that is about to overpower it.[12]

This is memory resurrected and reconstructed in the breach, rescued from the breach. Benjamin conceives of remembrance as a corrective flash of insight that emerges in times of crisis, and in response to political and cultural persecution, to the threat of erasure of the voices of resistance, disruption, and heterogeneity by totalitarian regimes. Arguably, the idea that a seamless continuity of the past exists or should be desired could itself be taken as a sign of crisis (of conscience): a deliberate or enforced concealment or forgetting that requires redress. Recent accounts by forensic anthropologists who have retrieved, extricated, identified, and reconstituted the corporeal evidence of mass slaughter, on behalf of those who mourn the victims and to promote social justice, explain how the reading of human remains can "give a voice to people silenced . . . to people suppressed in the most final way: murdered and put into clandestine graves." But before bodily remains can be read, they claim an irrefutable form of evidence. Clyde Snow explains: "Bones . . . are often our last and best witnesses: they never lie, and they never forget."[13]

I proceed, then, by linking translation to a concept of survival—"survival" as a cultural practice and symbolic action, and above all as a process that extends life, but one that also prolongs the meaning traces of death-in-life, life after death, and life after life. Both bodies and texts harbor the prospect of living on in their own remarkable ways.[14] Echoing the haunting, unanswerable question about the possibility of resurrection in the biblical book of Ezekiel, my title *Can These Bones Live?* seeks to affirm survival's ongoing poetic and political significance and rhetorical power. Despite its usual connotations, prophetic speech is not only annunciatory; it involves recovery, too, which is another kind of revelation. To cross the threshold from life to death and from death to afterlife is *to be translated, to be in translation*. Translation is the mode through which what is dead, disappeared, forgotten, buried, or suppressed overcomes its determined fate by being borne (and thus born anew) to other contexts across time and space, as famously asserted by Salman Rushdie: "I, too, am a translated man. I have been borne across. It is generally believed that something is always lost in translation; I cling to the notion . . . that something can also be gained."[15]

This project presumes what Richard Terdiman calls "the memory crisis": the cultural stress or perturbation that is marked by a loss of faith in one's own inheritance.[16] Whereas Terdiman's *Present Past* concentrates on the period from 1789 to 1920 ("the long nineteenth century"), my historical frame is the second half of the twentieth century and the advent of the twenty-first. I connect the current obsession with memory—its functions, institutions, and productions—to the redemptive work of translation. Through the act of translation, remnants and fragments are inscribed—reclaimed and reconstituted as a narrative—and then recollected collectively; that is, altered and reinscribed into a history that also undergoes alteration, transformation, in the process. *Can These Bones Live?* aspires to be testimony to the power and persistence of cultural memory as a challenge to the degradation of both matter and discourse.

*

That translation is both a self-reflexive feature intrinsic to writing and an extrinsic operation performed on a text is not news to writers. Throughout literary history, authors have always aspired to reach constituencies beyond their own linguistic borders and historical moment. It is not hyperbolic to say that the history of literature is to a determining extent the history of literary translation—or, perhaps, the history of *translated* literature. In most cases, the translation history of a particular writer's oeuvre or even of a single literary work has had a make-or-break effect on its canonical status in and outside its own literary tradition; that is, on what gets read and taught around the globe. Having said that, in David Damrosch's analysis of what defines world literature, for example, translatability remains a crucial variable. Though, of course, translatability is not a direct index of value; it indicates a trait, a capacity for both retention and renovation, across time and space.

In contrast to even the most distinguished works of national and re-gional literature, Damrosch contends that "world literature is writing that gains in translation." "World" literature is another way of saying literature that has been translated. Reading a text, he explains, "in the elliptical space of world literature" inevitably involves some decontextualizing, but the payoff occurs when "stylistic losses are offset by an expansion in depth as they increase their range . . . , when there is a *heightening* of the naturally creative interaction between reader and text": the result of "translating it out of its home culture and into a new and broader context."[17] Ironically, however, translation's role in making possible the global circulation and ex-change of texts, resulting in the "deepening, heightening, and broadening" of intercultural understanding, is not necessarily appreciated.

The paradox is acute: the more translation is celebrated as being per-vasive, as well as necessary to overall cultural development, interdependency, and exchange (i.e., expansion), and is thus often described in economic terms, the more its material dimensions are usually overlooked. In *The Trans-lator's Invisibility*, Lawrence Venuti decries the devalued status and activity of translation, especially in Anglo-American culture, arguing that the standard ideal of transparent translation effectively "conceals the numerous conditions under which the translation is made, starting with the translator's crucial intervention in the foreign text. The more fluent the translation, the more invisible the translator."[18] The invisibility of the translator is not a metaphor, as any glance at a cover of a translated book will show. Rarely is the name of the translator on the cover, although the edition is obviously not in the orig-inal language; often, the translator's name cannot even be found on the title page and is not included with other essential bibliographical information. It is not difficult to conclude that many cultural biases still abound in this do-main, including a mystification of the authorial or creative process as di-vinely inspired, and the concomitant belief that only the original is truly in-scribed, whereas the translation is merely transcribed, and thus not really worthy of separate mention. The original is acclaimed as a work of art; the translation is viewed as a technical product.

In translation studies, the postcolonial lens has focused lately on the connection between the translator's "invisibility" and the putative traditional bias toward "transparency" in translation. These metaphors are closely related and worth reflecting upon, inasmuch as they refer to a condition in which the hand of the translator is not evident or one that consciously obscures the translator's machinations or effects; as such, the translator is "invisible," absent, nonexistent, even when translation is known to have occurred. As Ralph Ellison taught us, to be considered "invisible," or to be rendered or desired as such by others, is a gross insult; but it also provides the greatest margin for movement, especially of the subversive kind. "Transparency" can be understood to function in at least two contradictory ways: (1) as being so insignificant or devalued as to be virtually invisible to others, hence effectively clandestine; or (2) as engaging in such open operations that the methods are laid bare and are thus perceptible to all. Translation's paradoxical posture and position—at once acknowledged as pervasive, while effectively ignored, or alternately, purposefully cloaked in subterfuge—reflect a strange cultural ambivalence.

Although I certainly advocate directing greater critical attention to the marginalized status of the translator, I am not at all convinced that a materialist critique of translation should, therefore, necessarily promote or valorize a particular translation technique, whether domesticating (favoring the target language or culture) or estranging (favoring the source language of target). I tend to support the notion that translation, being generally inseparable from language use, is context-dependent or case-specific. For example, if translation's traditionally subordinate status is a function of the valorizing of the original at the expense of the "copy" or "reproduction," would not a strategy or technique that favors the original appear to reinforce that very bias? Not always, it turns out. Venuti links the material invisibility of the translator to an expressed, canonical translation strategy that strives to obscure that a text has, in fact, been translated. In such a case, it is the original that is effaced, or domesticated, to facilitate the reception of the translation by masking what would look strange and making it sound familiar to the target reader. In Venuti's view, then, "fluency," "transparency," and "invisibility" are critically interrelated: "A fluent translation strategy produces the effect of transparency by foregrounding the conceptual signified and minimizing any disruptive play of signifiers, pursuing linear syntax, univocal meaning, current usage, linguistic consistency. . . . The production of a transparent discourse inevitably contributes to the cultural marginality and economic exploitation that translators suffer everywhere today."[19]

Venuti's point that linguistic and cultural dominance are, characteristically, signaled by an implicit, if not declared, preference for "transparency" is almost incontestable in the case of English-language translation. Should we therefore generalize, however, that transparency and the suppression of linguistic difference *always* masks or protects an asymmetric linguistic transaction, or, if they do, that the asymmetry is always the same? If such asymmetry is endemic to the translation enterprise, is it "inevitable" that the target language is always exercising power? What about cases in which both are minority languages? What other ideological positions lurk behind various translation techniques? These important questions about translation practice demonstrate how techniques of translation and their theoretical frameworks are interconnected; those who focus on one must engage the other.

*

A *New Yorker* cartoon by Matthew Diffee shows a casually dressed, somewhat annoyed-looking man speaking into a telephone receiver. In his other hand, he holds a book, his finger marking the page he was reading when his private space was invaded by an unwanted phone call. "I'm sorry— you have the wrong language," he says, in a play on words that illustrates both the need for translation and its putative impossibility. What is comical about the response is that it is said to someone who presumably won't understand it. Moreover, it is implied that having the wrong language or the wrong number amount to the same thing.

The cartoon character's response illustrates the disjunction between the basic goal of every telephonic call—to communicate something—and a higher ideal of meaningfulness. What, moreover, are the possible political implications of "having the wrong language"? A nativist knowledge-power nexus is reflected in the evident monolingualism of the man on the phone. Any foreign speaker's voice on the other end of the line, it seems, could have provoked this guarded, self-protective, somewhat hostile response to the possibility of translation.

So, what really hangs in the balance? That translation is a function of every cognitive and communicative operation, that every exchange (and non-exchange) has the transforming potential of a fateful encounter. We can postulate that one side or the other inevitably has the "wrong language," but a connection can, and must, be made from the space of difference. Can we afford not to make the effort? Diffee's cartoon illustrates the role translation plays in every aspect of cultural politics, in every facet of our survival.

The principal concern of this book is not the comical underside of translation, but rather its underlying gravity. It would be difficult to overstate the role of translation in shaping history, culture, and memory. It is

"I'm sorry—you have the wrong language."

FIGURE 1. Matthew Diffee, New Yorker Cartoon. © 2002 New Yorker Magazine.

imperative, I believe, especially given the current international political climate, in which relations with the Other are so volatile, that concentrated interest and material resources be directed toward recognizing the crucial role of translation in culture, of translation *as* culture. This is more than an academic matter. At the same time, however, it is one thing to make rhetorical claims about the (over)determinacy of translation in our lives and in the lives of future generations, and another to show how and why being more attentive to the fundamental, though intricate and often elusive, workings of translation can crucially benefit interpreters of the humanities. My aim is the latter, but I doubt whether the demonstration can be effective without the assertion. We are utterly dependent on translation, but that does not mean that we respect the enterprise or want to think too much about how it gets done. It bears repeating, I believe, that there is translation because there are different languages, and that this multilingualism is a gift, rather than a necessary (or natural) evil best defended with reductive instrumentalism and resignation. Because translation is a shared commodity whose value is not equally distributed, its labor must be recognized to ensure both quality and fairness; it cannot be consigned only to bureaucrats, "experts," or custodial others.

As subjects in a multicultural, polyglot, transnational, and intertextual universe, all of us "live in translation," but we also occupy that space differently, depending on our linguistic capital and the status of our language(s) in rapidly changing historical, political, and geographic contexts. We also occupy that space more or less self-consciously, and are more or less deluded by what passes as transparency in our communicative encounters around the globe.[20] The specific asymmetric relations that currently incorporate translation into globalization (call it "linguistic outsourcing") mean that non-native speakers of English are expected to fulfill most of the translating demands in the world. The refusal to translate that both literally and figuratively characterizes most Anglophones' cultural comportment bespeaks a sense of power and privilege and has devastating consequences for everyone. As the study of foreign languages declines in the United States and English increasingly becomes the dominant global language, despite having fewer native speakers than Chinese, Hindi, and Spanish, we ignore the impact of unidirectional translation and mistranslation in international relations, mass tourism, science, and technology at incalculable cost. Although I do not address these concerns directly here, I conceive of this critical project as being wedded to them. We need to encourage, simultaneously, on two fronts, both the study of foreign languages and the study of translation, because—of course—they are not mutually exclusive, but mutually reinforcing.

*

Can These Bones Live? employs an eclectic critical approach; when I privilege a particular theoretical approach or interpretive strategy, I do so in response to what the literary texts themselves elicit or dictate. I prefer not to impose a unifying theoretical idiom on any of the critical language(s) that the texts I analyze may speak. Although I refer broadly to various translating strategies and currents in translation theory, I do not focus on the problem of translation practice as a procedure or technique; nor do I compare the virtues and vicissitudes of specific literary translations. Instead, each chapter demonstrates or illustrates different, intersecting ways by which we can identify translation's critical performance in literature, culture, and history.

This book brings together and juxtaposes a diverse collection of twentieth-century literary texts, both fictional and autobiographical, in which translation performs overtly and covertly—as an intensive structuring and thematic device within a narrative, and as a coextensive process of transporting and transposing meanings, both vertically and horizontally, within the same language, as well as across different languages, cultures, genres, and modes of artistic expression. Each chapter examines a discrete example of a different translation effect or protocol, beginning with a rather circumscribed literary thematic that radiates out toward the interpenetrating planes of history and culture.

My first two chapters focus, respectively, on translation as a mode of literary renewal and cross-cultural elixir, and on the thorny politics of translating an original literary and historical experience in relation to ongoing debates on race, gender, representation, and canonicity. Chapter 1, "Figuring Translation: Lovers, Traitors, and Cultural Mediators," opens the book with a discussion of the notable emergence of practicing translators as characters in fiction, and the theoretical and practical impact of this phenomenon, in texts by Cynthia Ozick, Italo Calvino, Barbara Wilson, and Philip Roth. A certain, unmistakable anxiety about the vital, instrumental role that translation plays in literary and material culture can be gleaned from these authors' critical positioning of an elusive, estranged, erotic, and enigmatic figure in narratives about all manner of circulation, transmission, and exchange. Ultimately, I argue, translation itself figures for a hermeneutics of reading that is inseparable from matters of life and death.

Chapter 2, "Genre and Genealogy: The Slave Narrative Translated Otherwise and Elsewhere," explores how literary and historical narratives of and about slavery, especially as deviations from the legacy of the "original" (prototypical) American slave-narrative model, are revised, challenged, and enriched through acts of generic translation. Read together, the novels by Charles Johnson, Buchi Emecheta, and André Schwartz-Bart globalize, denationalize, and particularize the brutality and injustice of slavery as a singular catastrophic event, enabling the slave narrative to exceed its genealogical and geographical boundaries. Translation's interrogative impact defamiliarizes genre's seamless relation to canon-formation, authorship, period, and literary movement. By reading genre through the lens of translation, I propose, all our methods of literary classification are subject to critical review and are reinvigorated as a result.

The third and fourth chapters are explicitly concerned with cultural memory and survival, conceived as acts of translation, and autobiography as a memorialist practice.[21] Chapter 3, "Scenes of Inheritance: Intergenerational Transmission and Imperiled Narratives," most directly engages Walter Benjamin's model of, as well as Jacques Derrida's commentaries on, translation: translation as enabling, indeed ensuring, the survival, the living *on*, the living *beyond*, of the original. Here the reader will encounter most directly Benjamin's materialist and mystical view of translation as ushering in the afterlife of texts, endowing them with a place for posterity. I examine this structural problematic—which I characterize as the intergenerational, interlingual, transcultural transmission of endangered knowledge—in two familially framed texts: a French Holocaust child survivor narrative by Claude Morhange-Bégué and a Nigerian postcolonial novel by T. Obinkaram Echewa, both of which are rooted in political and historical catastrophe. In and through (the space of) thick translation from orality to textuality, both works grant a second life to an original story whose altered form is always a belated reparation, a reconfiguration, and a remembrance of what would otherwise be forever lost. Because translation enacts and reenacts the dynamic of identity and alterity by pairing a source language or text or genre with a target one, or one generation with the one that precedes/succeeds it, it forces the question of the relation between what something "is" and what it "does." This process enables these texts to become more fully realized—not through replication, but through reciprocity, complementarity, and supplementarity.

Chapter 4 links the tasks of translation to autobiography, the work of mourning, and the challenges of ongoing survival in the political and intellectual career and testimonial corpus of the bilingual Spanish writer Jorge Semprún. Semprún's experiences as an exile from Spain after the Spanish Civil War, a member of the French Resistance, an internee in Buchenwald, and a militant in the Spanish Communist Party following World War II have compelled him to revisit and recontextualize the interconnections among language, nation, history, memory, and loss over the course of a lifetime. Disputing the normative pieties, Semprún does not question the capacity of narrative to translate catastrophic experience; at the same time he demystifies the consoling idea of the narrative cure, while continuing throughout his long and rich career to write. Indeed, each Semprúnian text constitutes a cultural memory-site, in which mourning is the purposeful, insistent faculty for remembering precisely what has been systematically, selectively suppressed or erased from collective memory. While I certainly advocate a reading of Semprún's story for its own sake, my proposition in this chapter is that his life narrative is a potent rearticulation of mourning's relation to cultural survival. For Semprún the memorialist, writing as a form of mourning takes the subjective refusal to relinquish a connection to the dead and binds it to another category of intersubjective, historical loss: the narrative of shared struggle and belief in the Marxist promise of emancipation. Above all, in translating the past, Semprún laments a world of lost political ideals, lost ethical possibilities, and particular failures of the spirit.

Ultimately, this book endorses a view of translation as transfigurative in every aspect of human production, but, as it moves beyond its conclusion, it rests on a formidable instance of untranslatability. In the Epilogue, "'The home of the photograph is the cemetery': A Second-Generation Holocaust Narrative," I re-member the historical, political, literary, and psychoanalytic dimensions of intercultural translation and intergenerational transmission in a personal narrative.

*

Translation is effected whenever we "think globally while acting locally," whenever, in discursive terms, we think of one entity in terms of another, while minding the temporal, spatial, and conceptual gap between them—

that is, between the irreducible particular and the false universal. Thinking of translation as a cognitive faculty or a transcultural orientation, as well as a linguistic, textual, or aesthetic strategy, foregrounds the mutability, intertextuality, and alterity inherent in every literary event. But we also need to remember that translation is the process through which elements from traditional interpretive frameworks are preserved and conserved, sometimes by another name, under a different cover. That is to say, being attuned to the currents of translation in our discursive and cultural lives demands a more rigorous and sustained attention to specificity and singularity. Culture is adaptable, shifting, syncretic; its work, therefore, is inseparable from the relational dynamic that is translation. In the following pages, I identify translation as a literary theme, a critical practice, a medium of intergenerational transmission and intercultural exchange, and a mode of memorialization. I hope that readers will be convinced, as I am, that so pervasive and expansive a model belongs, not at the margins of our cultural consciousness, but at the forefront.

1

Figuring Translation

LOVERS, TRAITORS, AND CULTURAL MEDIATORS

> When borders gain a paradoxical centrality, margins, edges and lines of
> communication emerge as complex maps and histories.
> —James Clifford, *Routes: Travel and Translation in the Late Twentieth Century*

Translators have been instrumental agents in the advancement of culture throughout history. In the words of two historians of translation, the
function of these "unassuming artisans of communication" has included
such far-reaching and transformative roles as "inventing alphabets, enriching languages, encouraging the emergence of national literatures, dissemi-
nating technical and scientific knowledge, propagating religions, and writing dictionaries."[1] Because translation is a multifaceted operation, whose
effects are pervasive but whose mechanisms have been largely ignored until recently, I begin by looking at representations of the translator in literature. I focus specifically on four modern or contemporary fictional texts in
which translation figures prominently as trope, metatextual theme, organizing principle, or the basis for a set of stylistic effects within the narrative. Why should it be considered more than a curiosity or merely an authorial conceit when a translator is a fictional character and engaged quite
visibly in the material as well as the intellectual travails of translating in a
literary text? What might a contemporary author seek to convey about
reading and writing as a broader project in the world by bringing the act
of translation and the role of the translator out from the shadows and from
behind the scenes to center stage? Why portray a translator as integral to
the literary plot or make a translator the center of intrigue, and not a sup-

plement or stand-in for the main event? And how can translation theory benefit from the many trenchant insights into translation practice these representations provide?

By featuring characters who are practicing translators, these narratives foreground reading and writing as issues of reception, transmission, and circulation, while also employing translation as a metaphor for extraliterary shifts in the international cultural, political, and economic spheres. Of course, sudden scrutiny of those who had previously been inhibited by or prohibited from performing publicly may show the displacement of a site of transgression rather than a revalorization of the practice. But since my overall point is that the translator under erasure has always been indispensable to cultural production and renewal, this investigation is less concerned with the particular slant of figuration—whether the image of the translator is corrupting or curative, or, more interestingly, both—than with (the work of) the translator being endowed with cultural significance at all.

In the four literary portraits discussed here, translators act primarily as vehicular beings, functioning as mediators or couriers transporting and circulating cultural knowledge and values from one site to another, as importers and exporters, even as power brokers. They alter the terms of every exchange; it is their task to articulate what others choose to ignore or cannot address. Because of their translingualism, sense of displacement, and intercultural experience, translators occupy a privileged position precisely because, typically, they are marginalized figures; because of their rare knowledge, they bring a heightened, more self-conscious perspective to both their own language and culture and that of the authors they translate. The translator's perspective diffuses any single point of view or reference: at minimum, the translator has double vision. In the space of translation, linguistic or cultural differences do not fuse or converge; they confront each other and compete for influence and possession—foreignizing or domesticating—of the Other and over the Other. What is, of course, most perceptible in a text that figures translation are the registered points of contact in the linguistic, discursive, and cultural encounter: generative and redemptive, resistant or collaborative, violent and appropriative. And yet the space and history of translation also include the conjunction or exchange that did not take place: missed encounters leave their ghostly reverberations, reminders of the not-yet-happened.

This chapter deals with Cynthia Ozick's novella "Envy; or, Yiddish in America" (1969), Italo Calvino's *If on a winter's night a traveler* (1979), Barbara Wilson's *Gaudí Afternoon* (1990), and Philip Roth's *The Professor of Desire* (1977). I have selected these texts, two by women and two by men, featuring two female and two male translators, because by making visible the role of the translator as figure and cultural mediator, each calls attention in a different way to translation as a potent transforming, transfusing, libidinal force. None of these translators—male or female—accepts the traditionally gendered idea that the position of the translator is a "feminized" one; none is self-effacing, submissive, or faithful to the authorizing regime of the original. On the contrary, these translators are covert or overt insubordinates, power brokers in their own minds. Whatever facets in particular these writers may highlight, together they pointedly represent translational processes as impossible to dissociate from social, cultural, and physical matters of life and death.[2]

My extended argument is that the heavy burden attached to the tasks of translation—nothing less than survival through intercultural and intergenerational transmission/commission—is fundamentally erotic, both in its narrow, commonsense meaning and in the overarching sense of that word. In "Envy," a young female translator is targeted by an aging, unsuccessful, legacy-less Yiddish writer who seeks generativity and a place in history, which now seem unattainable. Her refusal to translate him condemns him to the fate he most fears: oblivion. The devious and elusive translator in *If on a winter's night a traveler* is practiced in the arts of dissimulation and manipulation, but his textual machinations are ultimately celebrated as essential components of an infinite, life-promoting narrative process. The freewheeling lesbian translator in *Gaudí Afternoon* deploys translation as the signifier for all operations of displacement and defamiliarization—sexual, linguistic, cultural, and political. In *The Professor of Desire*, the translator is a middle-aged Czech who challenges the personal and intellectual obsessions of a morbid, narcissistic American professor by offering an alternative political model of desire. In these examples, translation is depicted as an especially intensive kind of reading experience—a kind of reading in extremis or erotics of reading, a kind of reading that one never does alone.

The Tongue of the (M)Other: Cynthia Ozick's "Envy; or Yiddish in America"

> The capacity to give and to preserve life is felt as the greatest gift
> and therefore creativeness becomes the deepest cause for envy.
> —Melanie Klein, "Envy and Gratitude"

The manic vitriol that drives Ozick's story "Envy; or, Yiddish in America" is only hinted at in the title's cunning conjunction "or" and in the line it draws, the unsettling limits it imposes, and the unfriendly wall the title erects between what precedes the semicolon and what follows it. While "or" most often suggests interchangeability or equivalence across inevitable difference, as in the putative goal of translation ("in *x* language, it can be said this way, *or* in *y* language, it can be said that way"), here positing symmetry or reciprocity is precisely not the point: there is no equivalence. This title obscures its object, telling us only that context is all. What might the condition or experience of envy have to do with the status of a dying diasporic language? Might it be some bittersweet Jewish joke? "What's envy? You want to know what envy is? Envy is Yiddish in America."

The greenhorn widower and poet Hershele Edelshtein lives in a chronic state of want. Peripatetic performer of misplaced elegies, he struggles pathetically, if valiantly, to peddle his wares all around New York, still feeling out of place after being in the United States for forty years: "He traveled from borough to borough, suburb to suburb, mourning in English the death of Yiddish" (43). Estranged in the unforgiving assimilationist cultural landscape of postwar American Jewish life, he is exiled from his shtetl origins, just like his mother tongue (*mamaloshen*), Yiddish, whose tragic destiny he wholly identifies with. Both are anachronisms; due to ignorance and neglect, neither has the audience it deserves. Both are on the decline, perhaps on their way to extinction, and worse— oblivion. Edelshtein is on a one-man crusade to rescue Yiddish and its rich literary tradition—and, not so incidentally, his own four-volume corpus of rather mediocre love poems—from that fate.[3] Both the satirical bite and the gravitas of this story derive from the asymmetry between the petulant, self-important, self-appointed savior's often mortifying efforts to memorialize Yiddish and the fathomless impoverishment the language has suffered, between Edelshtein's self-serving mission and the nature of the crime that was committed, both real and symbolic, when Yiddish was "lost, murdered" in the Holocaust (42). The narrator makes the consciousness of Edelshtein accessible through free, indirect discourse, the character's unexpressed ruminations often running in this direction: "Of what other language can it be said that it died a sudden and definite death, in a given decade, on a given piece of soil?" (42).

Mourning Yiddish is Edelshtein's subject, indeed his raison d'être. In his binary universe, opposites always obtain—between Jews and Gentiles, but, more acutely, between Jewish writers and readers from the Old Country who harbor in their hearts a primal attachment to his brand of *yiddishkeit* and those born in America (or worse, Americanized Jews), who react with shame or disdain whenever sounds of Yiddish happen to penetrate their midst. Their ears, deaf to the language of their parents and ancestors, want to hear only English, choosing the ethos and aesthetics of "Western Civilization" over their own tribal legacy. If the performative dimension of Edelshtein's estranged condition has caustic poignancy, it is because he is childless as well as audience-less; he belongs to a vanishing species whose final days can be marked only by his own grief-stricken address: "To speak of Yiddish was to preside over a funeral" (43). To speak *of* Yiddish—Ozick tells us by way of Edelshtein's pathos, nostalgia, and despair—is to speak of and to an absence, to be witness to a language and a world that were silenced, that died a catastrophic death. The precariousness of Edelshtein's historical position as a native speaker and writer of Yiddish is overdetermined, because he stands in a synecdochal relationship to Yiddish, itself a synecdoche for the Jewish people—a people whose religion and culture has depended for its survival for millennia on the transmission of oral traditions and a body of texts, on the force of collective memory. Now, Ozick's story asks its readers: under such debased conditions, reduced to pantomime and shtick, what is the future of Yiddish, this once vibrant exilic language, after—if not beyond—the Holocaust?[4] Indeed, should the fate of Yiddish literature hang on the unremarkable career of one sentimental poet? Can the inevitable rupture of Yiddish from its origins be incorporated, and, if so, how, and in what form? How will it matter? Who will decide if Yiddish can live on in America?

Wanted: A Translator

Although Edelshtein moves as a kind of ghost or revenant among the living, he is not terribly preoccupied with concerns of an existential or ontological nature himself. He is mostly preoccupied with his own marginalization, possessing an intuitive sense that life's value lies not in biology but in history. If, in this regard, Edelshtein is ravaged by sadness, he is also propelled and sustained by rage—or, more precisely, by unbridled envy of a rival Yiddish writer of stories, Yankel Ostrover. Ostrover, as "a modern," has succeeded in all the ways that Edelshtein has failed. Far from presiding "over a funeral," he has created a small but thriving publishing entourage and has found "American, national, and international" fame in the process. To what does he owe his success? "Ostrover's glory was exactly in this: that he required translators" (47). "Requiring translators" means that, although Ostrover writes only in Yiddish, he has escaped the linguistic ghetto that would surely have meant cultural death and is on his way to achieving immortality on the world stage.[5] The mystery of how Ostrover, in singular fashion, has managed to reach this pinnacle denied to Edelshtein, as well as his fellow unsung Yiddishists, maddens Edelshtein almost as much as the void left by the Holocaust itself.

In fact, Edelshtein's vanity threatens to obscure the difference between petty narcissism and collective atrocity, diminishing his symbolic stature while raising the tragicomic stakes of his endeavor. While plots and intrigues based on real and imagined literary rivalries are not new in fiction, what makes Ozick's story so unusual and seemingly ironic is its conceit that what counts most for a writer is having a translator; everything else is irrelevant. With this as a point of departure, the action involves a neglected writer's immodest quest to obtain one. Edelshtein, Ozick's obsessed and embittered protagonist, fastens on the intrinsic, if not determining, connection between translatability and fame. As Benjamin puts it,

Translatability is an essential quality of certain works, which is not to say that it is essential that they be translated; it means rather that a specific significance inherent in the original manifests itself in its translatability. . . . The history of the great works of art tells us about their antecedents, their realization in the age of the artist, their potentially eternal afterlife in succeeding generations. Where this last manifests itself, it is called fame. (71)

Edelshtein's all-consuming envy and sense of personal victimization are certainly extreme: there is surely no direct and inverse correlation between

Edelshtein's pain and Ostrover's gain. And yet Edelstein ascertains correctly that in a tight market, Ostrover has cultural currency and he doesn't. Moreover, Ostrover's rewards will yield immense dividends. The success he enjoys today—in translation—will not only inscribe him in the book of Yiddish literary life, it will also ensure him a unique space in the world's cultural memory, that is, not only help reclaim the past but also endow him with a future.

Why only Ostrover? Ostrover should be the only one? Everyone else sentenced to darkness, Ostrover alone saved? Ostrover the survivor? As if hidden in the attic like that child. *His* diary, so to speak, the only documentation of what was. Like Ringelblum of Warsaw. Ostrover was to be the only evidence that there was once a Yiddish tongue, a Yiddish literature? And all the others lost? Lost. Drowned. Snuffed out. Under the earth. As if never. (5)

Why is Ostrover worthy of a translator, and, therefore, of redemption, of remembrance? The question eats away at every fiber of Edelshtein's being. Neither special talent nor virtue explains or accounts for Ostrover's position in what is, for all intents and purposes, the Yiddish canon. In fact, although it might seem counterintuitive, both Benjamin and Derrida posit that it is precisely a structural fault in the original that calls for its translation; but how that call is answered, and its implications for literary history and cultural memory, cannot be measured in terms of a lifetime. As indicative as translatability may be of the cultural politics of a particular historical moment, it is, in fact, a suprahistorical phenomenon.

"Envy" situates translation as a series of displacements at the center of some of the more sordid and desperate aspects of human interaction. Both in its execution and its effects, translation is shown to be an instrument of power, perhaps exercised most when withheld. In Ozick's depiction, translation plays for the highest stakes, even in its most pitiful and demeaning manifestations. This important point is part of a larger argument that translation is one of the most highly performative aspects of culture: by extending and expanding existing assumptions and frames of reference, especially by putting on the line the viability or incontrovertibility of assumptions about transmission and succession, translation offers a psychodynamic model of literary and cultural history.

"Envy" can also be read, indeed has been read, as commentary on and assessment of the contested terrain of Yiddish American literature and literary relations and the status of Jews in American culture nearly a quarter of a century after the Holocaust. Ozick's novella first appeared in 1969

in *Commentary*; its dismal and acerbic appraisal of the fortunes of transplanted Yiddish localizes translation into English—in America—as perhaps the only key to its survival into the twenty-first century. Since nearly
half the Jews in the world today—and not only as a result of the Holocaust—call English their mother tongue, Ozick's assessment of the situation can be judged to be both a pragmatic and creative response to Yiddish
no longer being the lingua franca of the Jewish Diaspora. Yet Ozick's depiction of "Yiddish in America"—deterritorialized and newly historicized
as a language in peril—reveals, ironically, that its prospects are not as dire
as Edelshtein believes, his own apparently doomed career notwithstanding.
It also underscores the idea, as Benjamin presumes and Derrida makes explicit, that "after Babel," translation and exile have always gone hand in
hand: "This story [of Babel] recounts, among other things, the origin of
the confusion of tongues, the irreducible multiplicity of idioms, the necessary and impossible task of translation, its necessity as impossibility."[6]

Ozick has often been characterized as a moralist who also happens to
be a supreme stylist. While a certain ambivalence regarding the unequivocal relationship between Jewish content and linguistic form pervades this
story, Ozick does not appear to be wedded to the notion that Yiddish is the
only medium capable of transmitting specific Jewish content (obviously
not, since she wrote this story in English). The universalist/particularist
debate played out in the narrative seems to privilege the universalist or assimilationist paradigm, which is at the heart of the Jewish struggle for
identity as cultural survival. Thus, while Edelshtein disparages other Jewish
writers in America, whatever their idiom, he never questions the premise
that if Yiddish is to have a post-Holocaust future, a future that survives
both the survivors and the dead, then that future lies in translation. Be-
moaning his own situation, he welcomes the translation of Yiddish, understanding full well that it poses neither a betrayal nor a threat to Yiddish
in the original. Instead, as a means of restoration after magnificent loss,
translation offers real salvation, an afterlife.

Without ever citing Ozick, Irving Howe confirms this view in *World
of Our Fathers* in his rendering of the plight of Yiddish literature after the
Holocaust.

It did not help, for the thinning ranks of Yiddish poets and novelists, that the world
catastrophe of the Jews coincided with a visible disintegration of their own culture
in America[. . . .] A number of the Yiddish writers sought consolation, perhaps

even dreamed innocently of a literary resurrection, in the prospect of having their work translated into English. If it had happened to Asch in the thirties, and was happening to Isaac Bashevis Singer in the fifties and sixties, why not to them? Alas, they failed to understand that some edict of fate, or whim of taste, allows only one Yiddish writer at a time to be popular with American readers. There was a growing amount of translation in the fifties and sixties, some of it accomplished; yet no one could suppose that this brought about a genuine revival of Yiddish literature.[7]

Howe refers to Jacob Glatshtein, a writer "hardly known outside the Yiddish perimeter," whom most critics consider to be Ozick's model for Edelshtein, when he asks sardonically, "What does it mean to be a poet of an abandoned culture? It means that I have to be aware of Auden but Auden need never to have heard of me."[8]

In 1970, shortly after "Envy" appeared, Ozick delivered a talk in Israel entitled "Toward a New Yiddish" as part of a series of intellectual dialogues between Jewish Americans and Israelis. She later included it in her essay collection *Art and Ardor*, published in 1983 (cited below as *AA*). Ozick explains in a note that not only was it conceived as a reply to George Steiner (the author of the famed hermeneutic study of translation *After Babel*), but that she is "no longer greatly attached to its conclusions."[9] As in "Envy," Ozick's theme is Jewish cultural and artistic regeneration. Whence will it come? Ozick engages the perennial debates of Jewish parochialism versus universalism, tribalism versus the Diaspora, and proceeds from the premise that we must look to America as the source of the next Jewish culture in exile. In "Envy," her concern had been the future of Yiddish as the vessel of and the vehicle for the transmission of a certain Jewish experience and sensibility, with translation into English proffered as the way out of the historical impasse. With her decidedly non-diasporic, Israeli interlocutors, however, she bypasses translation altogether and turns to what she terms "the new Yiddish." She expects this self-referential language, spoken and written for and among Jews, to be what she calls "liturgical" in orientation; but, at the same time, this "new Yiddish," like the "old Yiddish," "will be in possession of a significant literature capable of every conceivable resonance" (*AA*, 174). Ozick asks rhetorically, "Who will invent this language?" Her answer is that she is already speaking it. English, she argues, is capacious enough to perform like "the old Yiddish"; indeed, it is currently doing so, the result of which, she imagines, will be a renewal of Jewish culture in a novel but ultimately productive setting.

"New Yiddish," she continues, will have a distinct advantage over "old Yiddish" because it will be indigenous, the desirable visionary instrument of its time and place.

Thirteen years after delivering her talk in Israel, Ozick chose to include the essay in *Art and Ardor* but modified her programmatic approach a bit. As she puts it, "For one thing, I no longer believe that the project of fashioning a Diaspora literary culture, in the broadest *belles-lettres* sense, can be answered by any theory of an indispensable language—i.e., the Judaization of a single language used by large populations of Jews" (*AA*, 152). I have dwelled on Ozick's characterization of English as the "new Yiddish," because it seems a strange displacement of the Yiddish question so soon after the publication of "Envy; or, Yiddish in America." To valorize English's replacement of Yiddish as the new idiom of Jews in the Diaspora is, on the one hand, to de-essentialize the connection between language and identity in the manner, for example, of Benjamin and Derrida. At the same time, Ozick is committed to an ideal of Jewish content—a body of knowledge, a set of ideas and values, and a sensibility—both universal and universalizable because "Judaized" and, therefore, separable from any particular linguistic mode or form, whether it be "old Yiddish," "new Yiddish," or some heretofore unnamed diasporic tongue. Ozick's eulogy for Yiddish in translation was premature, as her own experience as a translator suggests.

That contradiction is, nonetheless, a kind of continuity crucial to historical consciousness. One sign that Yiddish is surviving, on its own terms, is evident in the appearance in 2000 of an essay by Katherine Hellerstein on feminist translations of Yiddish poetry.[10] Hellerstein focuses on her own practice as a translator of Yiddish poetry by women, part of an ambitious, variegated project begun in 1985. Her claim that the greatest prospects for the renewal of Yiddish literature lie in translation corresponds to Derrida's notion of translation as a process of transformation and revitalization. Not only does she introduce previously unpublished Yiddish women poets into the canon, but she also situates translation in the context of feminist discourse and presents it as a mode of female agency alongside that of female authorship. So strong is Hellerstein's stress on the feminist perspective she brings to her practice as a translator of Yiddish that the Yiddishist Anita Norich, in a response appended to Hellerstein's essay, is prompted to redress what she perceives to be an imbalance of presentation in relation to the cultural politics of Yiddish.

The positions of Hellerstein and Norich bear on my reading of "Envy," not only because they provoke new interpretive possibilities for this text—which savagely and poignantly wrestles with the problem of Jewish literary survival in the shadow of the Holocaust—but also because they show through their own interrogations that the status of Yiddish in translation remains relevant and resonant at the beginning of the twenty-first century.

Norich's response engages "the cultural politics of Yiddish translation" in a specifically Benjaminian way, arguing that, after the Holocaust, "translation is also an act of resistance to history." And, although she concurs with the urgency of the task besetting Yiddish translators, she delineates the challenges in singular fashion, especially in relation to canon formation, refuting the usual defensive posture that identifies Yiddish with insularity and parochialism: "Every writer of Yiddish, and almost every reader as well, has always been multilingual," she writes. Always nomadic and borderless, "modern Yiddish . . . has been a cosmopolitan, international, multilingual culture," thus perhaps, ironically, making it "peculiarly adaptive to translation."

Norich's insistence that Yiddish's permeability brings together differences contrasts starkly with Edelshtein's pronouncement that Yiddish is fundamentally untranslatable:

The gait, the prance, the hobble, of Yiddish is not the same as the gait of English. A big headache for a translator probably. . . . *Mamaloshen* doesn't produce *Wastelands*. No alienation, no nihilism, no dadaism. With all the suffering no smashing! No incoherence! . . . The same Biblical figure, with exactly the same history, once he puts on a name from King James, comes out a different person! Life, history, hope, tragedy, they don't come out even.[11]

Debates about linguistic inadequation and Jewish identity aside, Edelshtein is a cultural materialist who subscribes to the "translation is survival" school in its most base form. However shortsighted and limited his view of most kinds of human relations, Edelshtein seeks the (M)Other/daughter who will affirm and extend his existence through her (re)generative capacities. She will be the supplement to his lack, just as language needs translation to more fully be itself. Ozick's story, with its allegorical overtones, is structured in traditionally gendered terms, but, in fact, it assigns determining agency to Hannah, a twenty-three-year-old American woman. In pursuit of her, Edelshtein shows that he is a very nimble, if

ultimately impotent, rhetorician whose declamatory repertoire leans heavily toward invective, confession, deceit, flattery, and self-pity, and ends in
his acknowledged exploitation of Holocaust imagery to gain sympathy for
his personal plight. But Hannah contemptuously resists Edelshtein's furi-
ous, manipulative patriarchal entreaties that she serve as his translator, his
"goddess Futura."[12] He will die with no progeny.

In the story, Edelshtein's writes a desperate letter late at night from
the home of his friends and literary colleagues Baumzweig and his wife,
Paula. As Ozick's psychodrama fleshes out Benjamin and Derrida's abstract, depersonalized conceptions of (the role) of the translator, the psychoanalytic implications of Edelshtein's rather seamy and pathetic proposition to Hannah come even more to the fore.[13] Despite his overweening
emphasis on her procreative powers, Edelshtein claims—in the epistolary
follow-up to their first meeting, in which she had expressed surprise that
he was still alive and recited to him by heart lines from his poems taught
her by her grandfather—not to remember what the young female translator looks like. For him, she is but a vessel of transmission, a mode of conveyance for his aspirations toward authorial immortality, and, not so incidentally, entitled to none of her own. What higher purpose could she fulfill
for her tribe, and thus for humanity, than to bring new life and the
promise of an afterlife to this withering language and literature? Biology
and history get intertwined, and the metaphora of translation is literalized
in Edelshtein's vain efforts to rouse her to translate him as he finds himself
aroused by the species-perpetuating potential she embodies. Through her,
he will be transformed: "I discover in myself an unwillingness to despise
survival. . . . The *sound* of a dead language on a live girl's *tongue*! . . . Grow
old in Yiddish, Hannah, and *carry* fathers and uncles into the future with
you!" (74; emphases added).

Then at one point in the pleading of his case, Edelshtein's addressee—
"you"—seems to shift almost imperceptibly from Hannah to Yiddish itself. In that apostrophic address, desire turns to desperation as he exhorts
the "tattered, withered" language to secure its destiny and seek its redemption through translation, which, he now contends, may be no "choice"
at all.

Yiddish, I call on you to choose! Yiddish! Choose death or death. Which is to say,
death through forgetting or death through translation. Who will redeem you? What
act of salvation will restore you? All you can hope for, you tattered, you withered, is

translation in America! Hannah, you have a strong mouth, made to *carry* the future. (74–75; emphasis added)

Here the possibility of a language "living on" through or despite the inevitable loss produced and signified by translation is characterized as another form of death, less grave, perhaps, than oblivion, but a death all the same. And yet the message is clear: the situation is dire. In personifying the language, in conflating the egocentric and the ethnocentric, Edelshtein becomes his own addressee: he and Yiddish, both enfeebled, have no other recourse than to yield to translation and, for better or worse, succumb, submit to the force of female generativity, if they are to live on.

This double imperative, then, to call and be called (on), is presented in the form of a demand, a mandate—in other words, a task (*Aufgabe*). What is the nature of the task, and whose task is it to take on? While Yiddish in America appears to be the object in this passage and in this text, the drama pivots on the unconsummated relationship between the ever-receding, unretrievable past and the potentially amnesiac, always-emergent future. Edelshtein breaks off the last line of the letter, its strangeness permanently suspended, and addresses Hannah again directly: "Hannah, you have a strong *mouth*, made to *carry* the future" (emphases added). Edelshtein's metalinguistic appeal, in which *mouth* and *carry* are the operative terms of transitivity, perform an entire theory of intergenerational transmission as cultural survival. Indeed, there is something perfectly appropriate, if profoundly unexpected, about Edelshtein's displacement of the vehicle or mode of conveyance from the female *womb* to the seemingly ungendered *mouth*. What survives in and through translation into the future? Says Edelshtein, "If not the thicket of lamentation itself, then the language on which it rode" (74).

What is so startling about this very Benjaminian image of translation is that it does not isolate or privilege the question of meaning. Despite the crucial significance of remembrance in Jewish tradition, Ozick's dramatic depiction of the link between translation and cultural memory stresses, along with Derrida, that the issue is not the mere transmission of communicable, least of all, essential content or information, but rather a structure that is "the relation of life to sur-vival."[14] This structure of relation also refers to the kinship, but not the likeness, among languages, which is the essence of translatability. The kinship among languages is what calls forth translation in the first place. By bypassing content per se, while insisting that translation itself is a form, Benjamin and Derrida displace the distinction between form and content that is considered to be translation's main concern, emphasizing instead the act of communication, of transmission across time and space, that challenges linguistic estrangement.

If, as allegorized in this story, Edelshtein is the past and Hannah the future, Edelshtein the figure of exile and Hannah the figure of redemption, Edelshtein the parochial and Hannah the universal, and, as Benjamin and Derrida both assert, a contract of mutual claim and debt structures their relation, what are we to make of their final, ugly misalliance? Having wandered the bitterly cold nocturnal streets until he tracks her down at her sick uncle's sad, reeking one-room apartment, Edelshtein tries—first by appealing to Hannah's honor and pride, then by inducing paternal guilt, and finally by an offer of compensation—to wring a commitment from her. All of Edelshtein's messianic hopes resound in his "bereaved" entreaty: "Translate me, lift me out of the ghetto, it's my life that's hanging on you!" (94). She is immune to the stigmata of death he tries to impose on her; it is Hannah's ultimate dismissal of him and the Yiddish of his kind in America that prompts him to hit her, symbolically as well as literally, in the mouth. To her, the intergenerational contract is a burden she wants to be rid of; she is not in the least flattered or moved by his proposal. She wants to live on her own terms, not to be appropriated for his ends; thus, even violence doesn't affect her. Indeed, in a reversal of the clichés usually directed at translators and critics, she accuses him of being a "vampire, parasite, cannibal, bloodsucker"; but more mortifying than all these invectives is her desolate admission of boredom, the insult that finally sends him away: "You don't interest me. I would have to be interested" (98–99). This conclusive rejection seals Edelshtein's fate; he is declared "untranslatable" and left to the vagaries of a brutal and indifferent universe.

Sarah Blacher Cohen contends that this final confrontation, in which Edelshtein and Hannah virtually annihilate each other, nonetheless produces an "epiphany" that secures his sense of Jewish identity, over and against "self-hatred" and the desire for "worldly fame," although his "optimistic vision" does not prevail.[15] Edelshtein leaves this hothouse scene for the life of the street: the bright, kinetic imagery of the "full day" that greets him might suggest, as a kind of objective correlative, both intellectual lucidity and spiritual enlightenment. In my view, however, Edelshtein's change of heart regarding the nature of his Jewish identity—that "the ghetto was the real world, and the outside world only a ghetto" (96)—resembles less an epiphany than a reaction formation along the lines of Sartre's notion that Jewish identity is to some extent determined or partly constituted by its negative Other, anti-Semitism. Indeed, to unpack the wrenching, absurd, almost surreal hysteria of the story's ending that immediately follows his departure from the scene with Hannah, it is necessary briefly to consider the possibility that without anti-Semites, there would be no Jews. In Edelshtein's psycho-Babelian, monological narrative, his interlocutor, a ranting, disembodied voice on the other end of the telephone wire, spits out the slurs that have dogged Jews for centuries. It is quite likely, of course, that the paranoid, delusional "voice" is Edelshtein's own. No matter, in this case, whether the anti-Semitic evangelist is real or imagined: to each his own scapegoat. What does matter is how with comic savagery Edelshtein blames all the world's ills—and most pointedly, his own inability to find a translator—on the forces throughout history that have conspired to exclude Jews from the realm of promise and fulfillment. Ozick's desperate protagonist's obsessional paranoia is perfectly distilled in the discursive brilliance of this scene. "Edelshtein shouted into the telephone, 'Amalekite! Titus! Nazi! The whole world is infected by you anti-Semites! On account of you children become corrupted! On account of you I lost everything, my whole life! On account of you I have no translator!'" (100).

The Readers' Romance: Italo Calvino's *If on a winter's night a traveler*

> Why does it disturb us that Don Quixote be a reader of the *Quixote* and Hamlet a spectator of *Hamlet*? I believe I have found the reason: these inversions suggest that if the characters of a fictional work can be readers and spectators, we, its readers or spectators, can be fictitious.
> —Jorge Luis Borges, "Partial Magic of the Quixote"

The translator Ermes Marana makes a relatively late appearance in Italo Calvino's novel *If on a winter's night a traveler*, and his reputation as a furtive and nefarious being has long been uncontested in the narrative. Thus, it comes as somewhat of a subtle surprise when his function as a character is revealed to be integral to every aspect of the plot and to the novel's metatextual design. The design itself reveals an extensive web of interconnectedness among reading, writing, and translation, without which, of course, there would be no literature. As with all literature, this novel is propelled by the drive for narrative. As various readers in the novel, in one epigrammatic formulation or another, attempt to explain their preference for certain kinds of narratives and why fiction, especially, is so enthralling, the novel makes the unequivocal claim that narrative is a metonym for the human condition: "the ultimate meaning to which all stories refer has two faces: the continuity of life, the inevitability of death" (259). Nonetheless, Calvino maintains a crucial, wry distinction between those who have an existential commitment to fiction for its own pleasure-giving, life-enhancing sake and the functionalists, ideologues, and exegetes who traffic in literary academic commerce for other ends. Because genuinely passionate, persistent readers are rare and valuable, Calvino seems to suggest, bibliomania and scopophilia go together. If part of the pleasure derived from reading books is actually tactile, involving the handling, fondling, folding, pleating, bending, even cutting of their pages, what could be more erotic than watching someone else holding and being captivated by a book you yourself cannot touch?

This novel is an intricately constructed, polymorphous, fragmented metanarrative through which the basic elements of classical and contemporary romance commingle and leave their traces through implication and complementarity of prior inscriptions and unfulfilled longing. The novel is a love story about reading books—books as material, physical, fetishized aesthetic, sensual, spiritual objects—and about the lengths to which obsessive readers will go to capture and sustain what always exhilarates and eludes them: the Ultimate book, the Ideal reading experience. Because the reader outside the text is projected through structures of address to be somewhat jaded and yet easily aroused, the text itself must be endlessly performative and permutative, adeptly employing the same techniques of seduction, suspense, and satisfaction that it repeatedly—but always in different fashion—parodies at every critical and stylistic turn.[16] In an interview, Calvino—the author outside the text who does indeed exist—admitted that his relationship to his reader has a sadomasochistic edge, that it is his authorial prerogative to play with his readers by luring them in, deluding them into thinking they have agency, and then frustrating them by consistently exercising control over their responses. Soliciting the reader outside the text to play and work simultaneously, Calvino inscribes and

parodies the literary critical/theoretical and philosophical discourses of
hermeneutics, Marxism, phenomenology, semiotics, structuralism, deconstruction, narratology, and psychoanalysis.

Readerly Relations

What also makes *If on a winter's night* a romance is that the continu-
ous (diachronic) love story—the (male) Reader's plot that crosscuts the
truncated (synchronic) ten chapters—showcases a Hero who embarks on
a quest for his (female) object of desire, Ludmilla, and whose perspective
is challenged and pursuit frustrated by other would-be suitors and claims
for Ludmilla's attention. All their entanglements precipitate a series of intriguing and provocative scenarios and prolong the desire for (more) narrative, reinforcing one notion: the equation of reading and (heterosexual)
romance. All the intrigues result, predictably, in the requisite happy ending: Reader and Reader reading in a "great double bed [that] receives
[their] parallel readings" (260). This is predictable, not only because the final scene of conjugal harmony that closes the novel seals the Romantic
plot, but also because it is already proleptically inscribed when the Readers
consummate their relationship in one of the earlier chapters:

Ludmilla, now you are being read. Your body is being subjected to a systematic
reading . . . and all the signs that are on the frontier between you and usage and
habits and memory and prehistory and fashion, all codes, all the poor alphabets by
which one human being believes at certain moments that he is reading another human being. . . . The Other Reader is now reviewing your body as if skimming the
index. . . . Meanwhile, from the satisfaction you receive from her way of reading
you, from the textual quotations of your physical objectivity, you begin to harbor
a doubt: that she is not reading you, single and whole as you are, but using you,
using fragments of you detached from the context to construct for herself a ghostly
partner . . . and what she is deciphering is the apocryphal visitor, not you. . . .
Already, in the confused improvisation of the first encounter, the possible future of
a cohabitation is read. . . . But do not wax ironic about this prospect of conjugal
harmony: what happier image of a couple could you set against it? (156–57)

If Calvino's Reader enjoys likening the body to a text and the decoding habits
of lovers to those of readers, he is quick to assert that ardent readers are
not necessarily naive or innocent ones. Indeed, in a text so self-consciously

cosmopolitan and cultivated in its literariness, impure motives (having nothing to do with carnal desire) constitute the greatest danger, because they compromise the integrity of the reading experience by foreclosing the process of surrender to the open-ended possibilities of pleasure. Thus, the only operative question is *how* one reads; and if one reads programmatically, cynically, or dispassionately, then that, Calvino suggests, is the kiss of death for fiction. Ludmilla, the Other Reader, is by any measure, the Ideal Reader; her desire that fiction both fill the lack and point to what is always still missing in the world inevitably puts the Author's imperious and totalizing impulses in check.[17] Ludmilla is she for whom "[r]eading means stripping herself of every purpose, every foregone conclusion, to be ready to catch a voice that makes itself heard when you least expect it, a voice that comes from an unknown source, from somewhere beyond the book, beyond the author, beyond the conventions of writing: from the unsaid, from what the world has not yet said about itself and does not have the words to say" (239). Ludmilla is represented as an object of desire and mystery within a nexus of readerly relations. The vectors of identification among all the various reader positions are drawn schematically along traditional gender lines (male subject–female object), such that every other reader who reads Ludmilla as a text, including the reader outside the text, is constructed de facto as male. But, since almost every kind of imaginable critical reading practice and subject position is parodied in this postmodern, self-ironic approach to textuality, why should a simple feminist critique be exempt? Calvino's representations of gender are not simple; indeed, the blurring of binary oppositions—surface/depth and activity/passivity—exercises a feminist critical function. The desires and motivations of the three principal male characters—the Reader, the Author, and the Translator— are presented as unmediated expressions of their psyches, while "the elusive feminine presence" is often invoked referentially or through citation or paraphrase. Even when Ludmilla declares her own reading preferences directly and repeatedly—"The novels that attract me most are . . . "—her complex approach to reading cannot be rendered or satisfied in a single formulation. If her reading tastes and practices are uncontainable and repeatedly represented as elusive and ineffable, as both infinitely receptive and impenetrable, her status as Ideal Reader is fixed in place by its overt opposition to her twisted sister, the academic militant feminist Lotaria. Whereas Ludmilla reads for pleasure, Lotaria reads to analyze, dissect, criticize, debate.

She is introduced to the Reader as the leader of a university seminar, which both the Reader and Ludmilla are auditing in hopes of finding the novel they were reading. It turns out to be neither book they sought—it is neither *Outside the town of Malbork* nor *If on a winter's night a traveler*, the interpolated opening chapters of which alternate with the Readers' plot.

Since the plot unfolding in the numbered chapters that we are reading along with the Readers is structured as an open-ended search for a potentially infinite series of stories, the lines of readerly affiliation are resolutely drawn when, as the Reader relates, Lotaria preempts the reading experience by making student assignments, rather than the reading of the book, the first order of class business: some of these must "underline the reflections of production methods, others the processes of reification, others the sublimation of repression, others the sexual semantic codes, others the metalanguage of the body, the transgression of roles, in politics and in private life" (75). In pursuit of the always-interrupted, ever-missing, incomplete manuscript, the reader-outside-the-text is set up to "sympathize" with the two Readers, who are on the side of literature for its own sake, and to regard Lotaria, who subjects the text to her own ruthless ideological and theoretical operations and trains her minions to do likewise, with self-conscious suspicion. Unlike Ludmilla, for whom literature is always a surprise, Lotaria always finds what she is looking for. To the Reader's dismay, the students provide formulaic anti-humanist—indeed, dehumanized—responses to Lotharia's theoretical call, consisting of "general concepts" rather than those elements that render the book's texture: "events, characters, setting, impressions" (91). The book—which is to say, every book—is literally and figuratively "lacerated" in the service of Marxist, Freudian, semiotic, structuralist, feminist analysis, while the Reader, falling ever more in love with Ludmilla, admits that, like her, he also dreams of "rediscovering a condition of natural reading, innocent, primitive" (92).

But what are we to think about Ludmilla when, "on principle," she refuses to visit a publishing house with the Reader because, as she explains, "There is a boundary line: on one side are those who make books, on the other those who read them" (93)? As Teresa de Lauretis points out, Lotaria, in her role and demeanor as the pen/knife-wielding penetrator of texts, is depicted as a sexual threat, a castrating critic, the negative image of Woman, while Ludmilla is idealized as eternally feminine (permanently uninscribed) and, therefore, categorically disempowered as an agent in the cultural sphere.[18] While I do not disagree on one level with this interpretation, I would argue that neither of these polarized, gendered representations of reading are to be taken at face value. Although Calvino's caricature of Lotaria makes her something of a monster (de Lauretis refers to her as an "android"), I wonder if the caricatured portrait of the denatured academic is any less extreme than the organic, inviolate reader who, undoubtedly, knows more than she lets on about the dangers of corruptibility. She knows enough to avoid the moneylenders in the temple. Although it may seem that the Reader—in a sentimental alliance with Ludmilla—longs for the return of "natural, innocent, primitive" reading practices, if such a position were anything other than rhetorical in *If on a winter's night a traveler*, Calvino himself would have virtually no readers.

In every sense, the object of the novel's gaze is Ludmilla, who blurs the boundary between outside and inside, between form and content. She is never so desirable to the other characters as when she is reading. With the exception of the Reader, who eventually succeeds in reading *with* Ludmilla for life, the male spectators in this narrative ache to possess her, to possess the book, and, ultimately, to replace the book, that is to *be* the one and only book she is reading, now and for all time. Because reading is a true leap of faith, much of the frenetic action of *If on a winter's night* revolves around solving a hermeneutic mystery that is never directed toward deciphering the already expressed, but is always about the not yet written: "Reading is going toward something that is about to be, and no one knows yet what it will be" (72).

Lectus Interruptus

And yet, while this celebration of reading and the Book may privilege the extra-referential and with near-mystical fervor extol the inexhaustibility of the imagination and the ideal of the ineffable, the world in which *If on a winter's night a traveler* operates is, unambiguously, the material world. Literary creation and the commercial demands of the publishing industry coexist in this rendering of a global literary marketplace. There are cherished values to protect and a valiant battle to be waged, and there is no question about who are the victors; but the Ideal Reader is ultimately immune (or inviolate) to all attempts to either undermine or appropriate her literary experience. As the Reader puts it, as if speaking on behalf of all of Ludmilla's admirers, "How can you keep up with her, this woman who is always reading another book besides the one before her eyes, a book that does not yet exist, but which, since she wants it, cannot fail to exist?" (72). Whatever the various and nefarious competing agendas of the Publisher/Editor, the Academic Reader, the Militant Reader, the Non-Reader, the Voyeur-Writer, the Censor, and the Counterfeiter-Translator, all of them defer to Ludmilla, want her, and want what she knows. All of them circulate freely in the morally charged literary universe that constitutes this Library of Babel, though each moves, as if by structuralist design, according to her/his assigned function in the macronarrative that is *If on a winter's night a traveler.*

The "mythomane" Translator, Ermes Marana, is the demonic mastermind of an industry or enigmatic sect that finishes and reproduces plagiarized (i.e., translated) and pirated incomplete editions of novels. Its aim is to flood the world with interchangeable, arcane apocrypha, false attributions, imitations, counterfeits, and pastiches, a perfectly executed literature with no discernible relation to an original language, author, or contents. Aided and abetted by a group of terrorists and computer programmers, the organization disseminates simulacra of popular as well as pseudo-esoteric novels, spanning genres as diverse as the potboiler thriller, *le journal intime*, Oriental erotica, science fiction, the nineteenth-century Russian novel, the political revolutionary novel, and the Latin American novel. Unsuspecting readers buy or find these novels only to discover that they are incomplete. These suspended, truncated narratives—"incipits"—served up to the reader outside the text in the crosscutting chapters, perform what can only be called *lectus interruptus*. Seduced and abandoned at the climax of every exciting story, readers everywhere, repeatedly (seem to want to) fall for Ermes Marana's (and Italo Calvino's) literary lure.

Using his best investigative skills, the Reader uncovers a vast conspiracy, called the OEPHLW (Organization of the Electronic Production of Homogenized Literary Works), and traces its intercontinental operations to Marana. His initial characterization of Marana as "a serpent who injects his malice into the paradise of reading . . . a trap-novel designed by the treacherous translator with beginnings of novels that remain suspended" (125) eventually yields to a more nuanced view when he learns that Marana is motivated, not by greed, but by jealously of Silas Flannery, the Author, whom Marana perceives to be his unconquerable, invisible rival for the love of Ludmilla. Marana decides that his only hope for putting himself between Ludmilla and "the silent voice that speaks to her through books," the only way to ensure his presence in her life, is through "the shadow of mystification" (159), that is, by simulating (or translating) the author she wants to be reading. Every time Ludmilla reads a book, Ermes Marana will have left his traces, will have trumped the writer, who is now especially vulnerable, because he is suffering from a metaphysical writer's block resulting from "megalomanial delusions" of the Borgesian kind (181). He cannot seem to finish any of his recent books.

The chapter devoted to the diary of Silas Flannery, in which he re- veals his innermost insecurities about his continuing ability to write, de- parts from and extends the ongoing narrative that tells the potentially limitless love story of the two Readers, by performing on a number of fronts. It enables Flannery to describe his torments in his own words, of- fering an example of yet another genre: autobiography. It also enables Calvino to pull off some light-footed philosophizing and theorizing about the inherent inadequacy of writing in relation to the divinity of speech and about the possibility of totalization (est-ce qu'il y a un hors-texte?) and revelation. Pondering such mysteries and their theological underpin- nings, Calvino speculates, could incapacitate a writer who gravitates toward "the unwritten, unwritable" (181). Flannery writes that he is crushed by the idea of having to write the book that he describes as "simply the equivalent of the unwritten world translated into writing" (171). Unable to transcend his own self-consciousness—"How well I would write if I were not here!"—and torn between conflicting notions of the Author as real person/persona and the depersonalized Author-function as mediating agent or pure medium (171), Flannery is, unwittingly, an easy target for the machinations of an unscrupulous Translator. Indeed, Flannery, not unlike Borges's Pierre Menard, has already been working as a copyist of Dostoyevsky in Constance Garnett's translation, seeking replenishment and inspiration from a related vocation, one apparently exempt from the burden of originality. However, the mystification of literature notwith- standing, "originality" is an idea in need of critical reevaluation. Homi Bhabha, invoking Benjamin and, secondarily, Baudrillard, casts Calvino's representation of translation as being at the core of literature's capacity to replenish itself.

Translation is also a way of imitating, but in a mischievous, displacing sense—imitating an original in such a way that the priority of the original is not reinforced but by the very fact that it can be simulated, copied, transferred, transformed, made into a simulacrum and so on: the "original" is never finished or complete in itself. The "originary" is always open to translation so that it can never be said to have a totalised prior moment of being or meaning—an essence.[19]

In fact, Flannery confesses in his diary that he did not feel morally outraged or commercially exploited when, in their fateful meeting, Marana "warns" Flannery (without disclosing his identity) that someone in Japan is producing "unauthorized" translations of his books. His sympathetic identification with the Translator kick-starts the critical process by which both are shown to be not adversaries, but rather each other's complicitous co-dependents, because they occupy complementary positions within the same marvelous, multifaceted enterprise that is fiction.

When Flannery momentarily envisages going into partnership with Marana, it becomes increasingly clear where Calvino, aligning himself with all of contemporary translation theory, is heading. The autonomy and privilege conventionally accorded the "original" text are subverted in favor of a model of writing and translating as collaboration, with all the connotations of that word left intact. Thus, there is no internal split between reading and translating, writing and translating, perhaps not even between "false" translations and "true" translations, between "faithful" and "unfaithful" ones. The unbounded, always incomplete text is open to interpretation—translation, a kind of filling in the blanks that, in creating new blanks, invites other translations. Calvino seems to ask, shouldn't the Translator finally benefit, especially in the age of both mechanical and technological reproduction, when subject positions are unstable, categories displaced, and hierarchies devalorized, by appropriating the artistic aura that once belonged only to the Author?

Although the "sinister" Ermes Marana appears to be parodically trading on the "bad boy" reputation of translation as embodied in the Italian catchphrase *traduttore, traditore* (translator, traitor), the theological subtext suggests that there is something potentially lethal at stake in his malevolent maneuvers. As the Reader initially asserts, the Translator represents the serpent in the Garden; he thwarts the bliss of Adam and Eve—their perfect communicability—and introduces both primal desire and transgression, facilitating the Fall (which prefigures the devastating destruction of the Tower of Babel). But this view of cosmic and artistic creation is eventually subverted in favor of one more consonant with Calvino's overarching post-modern notions of textuality as play: even as Marana remains a force to be reckoned with, that force is to be understood, not as corrupting or treacher-ous, but as vital to the expansion of the textual enterprise. Ermes Marana shares with his namesake in Greek myth a crucial role as the messenger, car-rier, or courier of messages; he can also be seen as a kind of Mediterranean adventurer, a corsair or pirate who both facilitates and interrupts the smooth transfer of currency and goods across vast spaces. As he shuttles across styles, genres, and national and linguistic borders—the creative and critical go-be-tween—he is, in Baudrillardian terms, the Figure of the Artist as Translator, the Translator as Trickster (rather than Traitor) whose special gift it is to transact and, thus, transform our relation to the world and the word.

But through this figure, as his full name suggests, Calvino proposes an even more complex, historicized approach to the question of (the mutabil-ity of) identity. If "Ermes" connotes an illicit, excessive, cavalier relation to property and propriety, the connotations of "Marana" are equally illicit, be-cause covert and pejorative. The Spanish word *marrano* or *marano,* derived from the Arabic *mahram,* means "pig" and refers to "something prohib-ited." A Marrano is defined as a "Christianized Jew or Moor of medieval Spain, especially one who accepted conversion only to escape persecu-tion."[20] By invoking the Inquisition's forced conversions, Calvino hints here at the historical link between translation and violence. The Jewish or Muslim dissembler had no choice but to practice as a Christian while re-taining an attachment to an ineffable origin that was transmuted in the process of remembering. A survivalist as well as a survivor of the Inquisi-tion, the sinister and subversive translator hoards and then smuggles the forms and content of one tradition or culture into the other. But Ermes Marana's story is, ultimately, not a tragic tale. Because in Calvino's cosmos nothing that contributes to the creating, circulating, or consuming of nar-rative and the joy of reading can be bad; what is mystified in this text is the power, not the purity, of literature: at the center of all this euphoric activ-ity is translation as endless, erotic invention.

Found in Translation: Barbara Wilson's
Gaudí Afternoon

Perfection is terrible, it cannot have children.
—Sylvia Plath, "The Munich Mannequins"

The protagonist of Barbara Wilson's comic thriller/travel mystery *Gaudí Afternoon* makes her living as a translator "chiefly of Spanish, and chiefly of South American novels" (3) and is an amateur sleuth. She introduces herself as a woman with a provocative name but no home: "My name is Cassandra Reilly and I don't live anywhere" (3).[21] This nomadic lesbian narrator sports the emblematic sensibility and idealized lifestyle of a translator; she shuttles between various remote locations and crisscrosses countless borders, nimbly maneuvering within a zone of linguistic and cultural in-betweenness. Cassandra and her narrative perfectly depict Michael Cronin's notion of the "translator agent as traveller" and translation as a nomadic practice: "A nomadic theory of translation proposes the translator-nomad as an emblematic figure of postmodernity by demonstrating what translation can tell us about nomadism and what nomadism can tell us about translation and how both impinge on contemporary concerns with identity."[22] Although Cassandra grew up in a conservative Catholic family in Kalamazoo, Michigan, she is thoroughly cosmopolitan: she carries an Irish passport and has two "permanent" addresses, one in London, the other in Oakland, California, where she returns periodically only to regroup and pick up her mail. Most often, she is traveling the globe, seeking stimulation and adventure. Her sexual identity firmly established, she wears her political convictions on her sleeve, distrustful of traditional hierarchies and gender roles and studiously avoiding secure amorous attachments. As Cassandra makes explicit, her translational and amatory practices are governed by desire, not fidelity: a purposeful and passionate commitment to the work and pleasure of the moment, which precludes forging enduring allegiances to people or places. Having effectively escaped the limitations of her origins, she is a woman with determination but no destination—a moving target for the projections of others.

Gaudí Afternoon's "light" surface belies the serious matters it addresses and the critical attention it merits. At the end of this investigation into the ever-shifting dynamics of contemporary gay, bi-, and transsexual identity politics and partnerships—in which, for the sake of family and children unlikely couples have been re-created, others reunited, and "unconventional" unions constituted—Cassandra remains resolutely autonomous, single, and child-free by design. In response to a plaintive lover who wishes she would linger in Barcelona, Cassandra explains, only half-mockingly, as if she were an international spy, guerrilla fighter, or drug smuggler: "That's what life in the translation business is all about, Carmen. Speed, violence, sex, mystery. Translators come and they go, you can't count on them. You should never count on a translator" (171).

When the mystery opens, Cassandra is temporarily quartered in London while working on her current translation project, "a lavishly written, complicated novel by the fourteenth writer to be compared to García Márquez. Actually, it was by a woman, so she was only the fifth author to be dubbed 'the new female García Márquez.' Gloria de los Angeles was her pen name, and her wildly popular novel was entitled *La Grande y su hija*—literally, *The Big One and Her Daughter*" (4). On a drab London day in April, immersed in her work, Cassandra receives a telephone call from an American woman named Frankie, who wants to hire her to travel to Barcelona to help track down Frankie's ex-husband, Ben, in order to persuade him to "sign some important papers" (9). Frankie describes the mission to locate Ben as simple and straightforward (she herself has a language problem: she is monolingual) and offers Cassandra a generous stipend for what should only be a few days' work. Despite her suspicions that there is certainly more to this story than the explanation provided, Cassandra has difficulty refusing the job; a free ticket to Barcelona makes it irresistible.

Frankie's story *is* fundamentally simple: she needs to find her free-spirited gay husband, Ben, from whom she has been amicably separated, because there are legal papers he needs to sign. His wealthy family doesn't know the true state of their marriage or his sexual orientation, and divulging such information would result in negative financial repercussions for the couple. However, Cassandra's suspicions are well placed. Bit by bit she discovers that Ben is actually Bernadette, a woman, and that Frankie is a transsexual. They were married in college and had a baby together. During the course of the marriage, Frankie decided to become a woman, Ben came out as a lesbian, and they divorced. Now, not only are their lifestyles incompatible, but they cannot reconcile their positions or roles in regard to Delilah, their six-year-old child. Ben has absconded to Barcelona with Delilah and April, her current lover, and Frankie wants to find them.

Since the first requirement of a detective story is a solitary, sure-footed gumshoe on assignment to solve an enigma, especially one that does not present itself as such, the narrative frisson generated by Cassandra's initial skepticism is familiar to readers of the genre: it propels the plot. But, in the process of solving the case, the feminist translator-detective is confronted by a larger set of self-ironic and self-protective presumptions that seriously challenge her own cognitive and visual acuity. Operating as a cultural as well as linguistic translator, Cassandra interprets current nationalist, linguistic, and, crucially, sexual-identity politics against a backdrop of international, transcultural, translingual, transgender intrigue.

Revelation(s) and Revolution(s)

A mere seven very concentrated but truly transformative days after Cassandra first meets Frankie, Barcelona becomes yet another point of departure in her endless series of comings and goings. That she will return many times is understood; a savvy sensualist, Cassandra always picks up where she last left off. But from the beginning of the story, Cassandra's intimate and informed rapport with the seductive splendors and lusty refinement of Barcelona suggests that the city and the traveler are particularly well suited for each other. Wilson maps out the monuments and parks, the plazas, cafés, and bars Cassandra frequents, the streets and boulevards she trawls, the friends she loves and leaves. As the novel's title indicates, the iconoclastic spirit of Antoni Gaudí—Barcelona's visionary, signature architect—graces all of Cassandra's and the other characters' moves. As in any excellent travelogue, context is everything: Cassandra accords the same status to search and discovery as she does to the concept of space and the urban landscape. Catalan *modernismo*'s biomorphic creations, its flora and fauna cast in stone and iron—serpentine foyers, undulating towers, and writhing columns—seem, uncannily, to resemble the overheated atmosphere and evoke the sensuous Venezuelan magical realist text she is translating. Barcelona's vitality, fluidity, and expansiveness provide the ideal locale for redefining the correlation between image(s) and identity construction(s). From the outset, *Gaudí Afternoon* illustrates that anatomy, architecture, and language are homologous systems, especially in the ways they mark and demarcate gender. In scene after scene, the reader is alerted to the idea that reading gender is an act of recognition, as the characters work to resolve, in existential terms, the conundrum of gender's culturally inscribed relation to both organic and structural form, to the decorative and the functional, style and substance, visibility and viability.

Perhaps the most obvious enactment of this theme is the scene in which the very feminine transsexual Frankie and the androgynous lesbian Cassandra meet at the entrance to the Sagrada Familia, Gaudí's monumental, unfinished cathedral dedicated to Mary, Joseph, and the baby Jesus. In this iconic space that celebrates both innovative conceptions and sacred alliances, Wilson presents the disjunctive image of Frankie standing at the Nativity façade, railing against the tyranny of the body and arbitrary gender assignments, while expressing her desperate yearning to be a "natural" mother. As Frankie speaks, it is made clear that Cassandra shares with the crowd a certain disdain for Frankie's quest for maternity, though for diametrically different reasons.

"As if it weren't completely *accidental* what sort of bodies we were born into. I mean, look at Ben. Ben has lots more male energy than I have! It's so ironic that just because she has a real uterus she was able to have our baby and not me!" Frankie's voice had risen and a small group of American tourists, who had been listening to a lecture on Gaudí's "freer approach to the design of supporting structure and consequently of the building's ultimate shape," stared at us uneasily. (84)

Frankie's desire for a family, however strange or anomalous its configuration, expressly conjoins the political and the affective. During the course of Frankie and Ben's marriage, their sexual paths diverged, stretching the boundaries of "sameness" and "difference": Ben, initially heterosexual, stayed a woman (if a masculine one) while shifting her libidinal object-choice from male to female; Frankie changed sex and is now attracted to men. Although no longer a couple, they will be forever parents, though their roles and gender positions are, to say the least, blurry. It seems inadequate or inaccurate to say, in this case, that Delilah has two mommies. Acknowledging the larger context of Catalonia's ongoing struggle for linguistic and political autonomy from Spain, Wilson stages the global struggle for gay social and sexual liberation from all kinds of constraints—some of which, as the plot unfolds, are sometimes self-imposed and, according to any radical agenda, counterproductive.[23] For the most part, however, Wilson's comic critique respects the valiant, even poignant, struggles of its gender-bending characters to pursue both personal bliss and domestic harmony.

Cassandra has brought with her *La Grande*, the story of a daughter's search for a lost mother (which is every daughter's search?), intending to complete the translation while working on the sleuthing assignment. On a stakeout, she sometimes uses the book as a cover. Immune to sentiment and sentimentalism in any manifestation, Cassandra harbors no illusions about how ideas and books are packaged in the marketplace for their niche audience. To save time, she has not read in advance the novel she is translating. Thus, her experience as a reader/translator of the lush, convoluted, and contrived narrative frames the reader's experience outside the text, as if we were reading and translating over her shoulder and identifying with her as both an innocent (she can't know what she hasn't read yet and can always be entrapped, à la Calvino) and a critically sophisticated decoder of transcultural and literary codes. This dichotomy is heightened when the manuscript she has brought to Barcelona is stolen, and, to continue the project, she is forced to purchase "the last copy of the Spanish edition" (32).[24]

As the narrative of *Gaudí Afternoon* and Cassandra's translation progress and the intersecting plots thicken, Cassandra discloses the many layers of *La Grande* and intersperses commentary on de los Angeles's style, characters, and themes, as well as on the book's catapulting success, which she disparages for both literary and political reasons. Apparently, part of what makes *La Grande* so universally successful and its author "the recipient of Venezuela's highest literary honors" (31) is its feel-good fabulist feminism, packaged with tropical flavor for easily digestible, global consumption. Its cover, displayed in bookstore windows all over Barcelona, exhibits "a black-haired, lushly naked woman with a snake wrapped around her body and behind her a jungle straight from Henri Rousseau, though heavier on the parrots, monkeys, and gardenias" (31). Hamilton, a sensitive, academically trained (i.e., politically correct) man whom Cassandra at first sight had presumed to be "Ben," earnestly sums up its highlights: "jungle, love, river, revolution, motherhood." When he learns that Cassandra is its translator, he shifts codes: "I saw *La Grande* as a political allegory as well as the riveting search for one's past. I understand that feminists have really responded to it." Cassandra responds: "'They have,' I said gloomily. 'I believe they see the obsessive search of Maria for her mother as a paradigm of the condition of contemporary woman'" (94). The shrewd critical skills and opinions that Cassandra has honed as a practicing translator, cosmopolitan traveler, and social critic have clearly informed her skills as a detective. And yet, as shrewd and enlightened as she is, this assignment has disabused her of her own received ideas, especially regarding sex, sexuality, and gender construction; she learns that retrograde and radical are not fixed points on a static grid.

Lost in the Masquerade

Thus, while *Gaudí Afternoon* propounds the idea that translation, as the paradigmatic transitive operation, challenges, indeed subverts, conventional categories of judgment, it also leaves open the possibility that the translator herself is fallible. Relatively early in Cassandra's search, not for Ben, but for the elusive Frankie, Wilson suddenly casts doubt on Cassandra's expertise as a translator. Until that point, the reader has been led to assume that her sleuthing abilities are commensurate with her progressive, super-smart, liberated, lesbian-feminist credentials and displays of aesthetic and ideological rigor. How Cassandra handles the first major reversal of her expectations, when she discovers that Frankie was not born a woman but is a femme fatale of a different order—a transsexual—twists the plot in interesting ways. That reversal enables Wilson to explore how differences in thought and behavior are parsed and boundaries drawn in even the most "open" and fluidly defined communities. Whether Cassandra and her lesbian friends are "patrolling" the streets of the *barrio* in search of Frankie or trawling Barcelona's seedy, red-hot red-light district, where female impersonators, transvestites, prostitutes and their customers, who refer interchangeably to both *amigos* and *amigas*, coexist and coalesce in the carnivalesque night, they cannot reach consensus on what makes a woman a woman. They have no doubts about the category, but they are not sure how it should be defined. Is it whom she loves, how she dresses, her primal desires? Their discussion reveals that, however reductive, certain principles of binary logic regarding nation, culture, language, sexual/gender identity and preference, and their attendant value judgments are not easily disavowed, and that some aspects of life remain irreducibly mysterious. The women's playful but soul-searching conversation concludes with Cassandra's refusal to declare "what" she is, at least in the mutually exclusive, but always relational, terms Carmen sets up for her: "'My name is Carmen,' Carmen said in English. 'I am woman. Please, what are you? Woman or man?' 'Neither,' I said in English, then in Spanish. 'I am a translator'" (74). Is Cassandra's deadpan response "I am a translator" a proclamation or a performative utterance? Are identitarianism and identity antithetical to one another? What kind of personal refuge or privileged space does "being" a translator provide Cassandra, she having for all intents and purposes forsaken all designated affiliations and forms of belonging? Is the reader to infer that the privilege of a translator operating in a foreign country is to opt out of every linguistic, cultural, and sexual category, to be a free-floating signifier? In this cheeky little scene, Wilson's linking of linguistic and sexual specificity and difference reinforces the notion that they are intertwining constructions, but this gets disturbed when Carmen speaks English or seems to be imitating, or possibly parodying, ungrammatically, an English speaker. By eliding the necessary article "a," she makes a mistake that we assume to be inadvertent but which has a meaningful turn, by which the dramatic play of the preceding discussion is extended. Cassandra's response to Carmen's assertion, "I am woman. What are you?" seems to be a deflection, if not a defection from the ranks. Cassandra has never wavered from her stance that she is a woman who loves women, regardless of the ambiguities others may enjoy or perform in regard to their own sexual identities and identifications; why she tries to wriggle out of an apparently discomfiting question becomes part of the overall mystery of the novel.

As for more immediate concerns, how does it affect Cassandra's readerly competence when, on a stakeout, the problem to be solved is not "who dun it" but "what is s/he?" In a system where the terms do not match up, Frankie is, effectively, "untranslatable." Hours later that night, the putative certainty of Cassandra's judgments about identity begins to wear down with time and alcohol, and her frustration grows. After the Castilian hairdresser Carmen recites lines from Lorca and Ana, a Catalan architect and dollhouse designer, tells about her late mother's exile, Cassandra begins to make some self-authorizing public pronouncements that are neither melancholic nor personal in nature. As she puts it, "I was holding forth on the subject of translation" (76). She explains to them: "Every author has a vocabulary and once you understand that half your job is done" (76). But she seems to violate her own precepts when she labels the style of the last writer she translated (who happens to be male) as "mechanical" and the one she is currently translating (Gloria de los Angeles) as "romantic." This sounds a strange alarm for the reader, because Cassandra is far too sharp a thinker and, it seems, too nuanced a translator to indulge in stereotypes or foreclose the interpretive possibilities of any project. Furthermore, Cassandra's most salient characteristics have been her self-confidence, self-awareness, and reliability as a narrator. The theme of the evening—appearances versus reality—finds epiphanic expression in the moment when Cassandra testifies to the reader:

I was drunker than I should have been, or more confused. For a second I had lost the sense of who I was—what sex, what gender, what age, what city, and what country. In the instant I saw the man or woman who may or may not have been Frankie I had one of those odd, powerful, and probably alcohol-induced revelations that seem to last forever and wind backwards and forwards into history and infinity. Afterwards, I could never say what it was I had experienced just then. But, it was as if I were at a masquerade ball and everyone, and at the very same moment, lifted their masks, and I saw gender for what it was, something that stood between us and our true selves. Something that we could take off and on at will. Something that was, strangely, like a game. (76)

Moments later, when Cassandra wants to reassure her friends that she is "fine," she realizes that she cannot "remember what language we'd been speaking and which one they understood" (77).

During that "second" of utter lucidity, in which Cassandra loses a sense of who she is and sees "gender for what it was"—a mask and a game—she describes herself as "confused." What is the nature of this kind of confusion, one that both confers understanding and resists communication, that denies truth as coherence while making its meaning transparent? Cast in the terms of personal revelation, Cassandra's narrative recounts an experience that is generically defined as extralinguistic and untranslatable. This paradigmatic and performative scene about the unmasking of gender has an intertext: the story of Babel, the Judeo-Christian myth that explains the human condition as the fall from the original, divine, and universal language into multiplicity and undecidability. Derrida explains that the Tower of Babel—"the origin of the irreducible multiplicity of tongues"—equals confusion.[25] Here Cassandra, the prophetess, envisions a world liberated from a singular genealogy and destiny. But this release from the constraints of linguistic sameness also condemns us to the inequality between languages, the arbitrary and contingent relation between object and referent and name and thing—cumulatively, that which necessitates interlingual, intralingual, and intersemiotic translation. And, at the very instant that Cassandra sees the "truth" about gender, she reauthorizes herself as translator, affirming the self-certainty she had professed earlier that evening when she proclaimed her transcendent, liminal status in the world.[26]

Although the narrator's frame of reference is undoubtedly feminist and "woman-centered," Wilson repeatedly questions the very idea of seamless categories and stable positions, proposing through her character's search for alternative possibilities a nonbinary, multiplicitous view of sex, gender possibilities, and arrangements.[27] In the scene in which Cassandra and Frankie meet at the Sagrada Familia Cathedral (their first encounter after Cassandra has learned that Frankie had deceived her by misrepresenting herself and her case), Cassandra rearranges all the pieces and recalibrates their correlative value in the process:

I realized that I didn't know whether to think of her as a "she" or a "he" now. She looked to me the same as the last time I saw her, but now that I "knew" that she had been born a male, I could see that she still resembled a man in slight ways. A certain boniness around the chin, larger hands and feet, perhaps the muscularity of her legs. Still I'd met plenty of women who were bigger, stronger, bonier and more muscular than Frankie. In what did her masculinity reside then? Her voice was low, but I'd thought that came from smoking. She had breasts and hips and the gestures and movements of a woman. She was more feminine than I or many of my women friends. It wasn't only surgery that had changed her sex, or hormones, it was a conscious choice to embrace femaleness, whatever femaleness is. (82)

Cassandra's careful delineation of the terms male/masculine and female/feminine reinscribes the sex/gender dyad that Wilson so adeptly links to postmodernist views of translation as a function not of equivalence or exchange but of undecidability. Still seeking Cassandra's aid, not to locate "her husband" but to mediate residual conflicts among the various parties, Frankie discloses her full story, including her overriding desire to stay close to her and Ben's daughter, Delilah. Every neat equation of sex, gender, and what used to be called sexual orientation is undone in this conversation. Ben is now a butch lesbian, currently involved with a "gorgeous" foot therapist named April. Earlier in the narrative, while trailing Frankie, Cassandra had deliberately changed course and followed April (to whom she is undeniably attracted), Ben, and Delilah to the Parc Güell, mistaking Ben for a sixteen-year-old boy and nicknaming her "High Tops." Frankie describes April as "one of those smug *spiritual* types who thinks having been born a woman means she has a direct link with the cosmos" and characterizes Ben as having "always been more a man than me" (83). In her negotiation of the theoretical and ideological line between a feminist epistemology and a gender-neutrally queer agenda, Wilson shows that essentialism in any guise is simplistic, hence uninteresting, and even oppressive.

Maternal Constructions

Gaudí Afternoon, which appeared the same year as Judith Butler's influential study *Gender Trouble*, could be considered its companion volume, inasmuch as it fleshes out Butler's conceptual abstractions and works with like-minded spirit to posit both the "troubling" and the "performing" of gender as productive principles: "Precisely because 'female' no longer appears to be a stable notion, its meaning as troubled and unfixed as 'woman,' and because both terms gain their troubled significations only as relational terms, this inquiry takes as its focus gender and the relational analysis it suggests" (xi).[28] *Gaudí Afternoon* questions the determining relation between anatomy and destiny in terms of both role and desire, playing relentlessly with the theatricality of gender. Pushed at times almost to the point of the ludicrous, gender is represented in the novel as both fluid and disruptive, never oppositional or complementary—arguably, a concrete elaboration of Butler's formulation: "Consider gender, for instance, as *a corporeal style*, an 'act,' as it were, which is both intentional and performative, where *'performative'* suggests a dramatic and contingent construction of meaning" (139). If Cassandra is both challenged and frustrated by the complexities and detours of her investigative assignment, which include a range of mistaken and transformed identities, deceptive appearances, mixed allegiances, and, ultimately, a kidnapping (merely the symptom of the virulent custody dispute over Delilah), she is also made anxious by the novel she is translating. And if her response in both instances is to be a resistant translator, what links the two projects thematically is motherhood.

As the novel progresses, Cassandra's articulated antipathy to motherhood as an institution and an ideal—like her rejection of domesticity, domiciles, and enduring commitment—begins to seem less a political principle than a psychological defense, perhaps even rooted in a painful childhood (though no explicit textual evidence supports this conjecture). Wilson acknowledges the desire for such explanations while rejecting them. Indeed, the other characters, all actively seeking alternatives to their own repressive or unhappy childhoods, construct a causal narrative to account for Cassandra's resolute autonomy (of course, her attempts to deflect their inquiries regarding her background only invite further speculation). The final word may be April's diagnosis that Cassandra's problem has no etiology, even as she nonetheless indulges in the familiar stereotype associated with heterosexual men: "You have intimacy problems, don't you, Cassandra?" (160).

In a conversation between Cassandra and Ben as they attempt to locate the missing child, Ben explores her ambivalence toward Frankie. "Maybe it's hypocritical for me to say that I like to wear jeans and a crew cut and have biceps and that being mistaken for a man and called sir doesn't bother me. I don't want to *be* a man. I'm a woman. And a mother" (104). She explains further that transsexuals "don't want the world to change, they just want to change their bodies" and that she "didn't lose a husband and a father when Frankie did what he did," she "lost a pal" (105). Although Cassandra and Ben are allied in their search for Delilah, Ben continues to regard Cassandra with suspicion, based on three factors: Frankie is Cassandra's client, Cassandra is clearly attracted to April, and Cassandra "has never been a mother" and "can't know how it feels" (105). To this last point, Cassandra responds, "And I thank god for it every day" (106). At the very end of the novel, among the dizzying array of identity twists, sexual turns, and reversals, April has left Barcelona and returned to her foot therapy practice in San Francisco. Delilah reveals, sagely and happily, that April rejected her and Ben because Delilah had discovered that, like Frankie, April "was a boy that turned into a girl." Hamilton concurs that Ben's difficulty with Frankie's transsexuality would have resulted in a repetition of the same problem with April. Moreover, April is not interested in children.[29]

Wilson's sustained critique of essentialism notwithstanding, I would argue that Cassandra's reflexive dismissal of the maternal bond may be yet another form of subjection to it. Though Wilson's parody in the novel can be seen as an amusing critique of contemporary gay social practices that serve ultimately only to replicate traditional social arrangements even as they strive to separate sex from gender once and for all, my contention is that Wilson does valorize mothering and motherhood by fracturing it from several angles, while reclaiming its power. Even as the novel reexamines the relationship among sexual subjectivity, identity, and performance and deplores the fetishization of the family and the trope of the maternal ideal, it also presents the need for kinship as an object of desire that produces its own undeniable belated, transforming effects.[30] At minimum, Wilson suggests here, the issues of bearing and raising children will be an integral part of all future queer cultural scripts, just as the traces of the archaic or the allegorical cannot entirely be evacuated from alternative or heterodox social arrangements.

If Cassandra capitalizes on her image as an erotic adventurer, she also seems compromised by her immunity to any longing that isn't sexual. Very early on in the novel, Ana, Cassandra's friend and sometime lover, proposes that Cassandra make Barcelona, rather than London, her base of operations and "settle down with someone and experience family life." She hopes she will be that someone, but she is swiftly divested of that fantasy when, among other things, Cassandra declares, "I'd be a terrible mother" (34). This is in itself no (self-)indictment, of course, but the text poses the question of whether it is necessarily an act of liberation from prescriptive norms. What is unequivocal, however, is Cassandra's view of herself as having generative powers. As she says to Ana, "Anybody can have babies . . . only some of us can create art" (109).

Wilson sidesteps any deeper character analysis in favor of formal and structural considerations. Cassandra's "maternophobia" functions as the counterplot to *La Grande y su hija,* the first-person account of a daughter's quest for her lost mother, a story of absence, nontransmission, and imaginative reconstruction:

My story is two stories, that of my own life and that of my mother, Cristobel, whom many times I am sure I have invented. I made her large because I am small, I made her Eduardo's lover because I have no lover, strong where I am weak, wise where I am foolish. She abandoned me and I could not find her, though over and over I discovered her traces. . . . There were tales of her youth, her loves, her illnesses, her triumphs. But they were told by people who also had not known her, who had, like me, only heard of her, and who had forgotten most of the story. (107–8)

Cassandra has repeatedly disdained *La Grande*'s self-indulgent, sentimental excesses and plot contrivances, but it is Maria's obsessive quest for Cristobel, as well as the overarching heterosexual politics of the novel, that most alienate her. But by the end of *Gaudí Afternoon, La Grande's* story of the daughter's quest to find a mother and the myriad possibilities of pansexuality have begun to condense in Cassandra's unconscious. The cumulative effects of Cassandra's personal and professional anxieties are manifested in a dream she has while taking siesta one afternoon toward the end of the novel. In the throes of attempting to zero in on Delilah's kidnapper, she has repeatedly been thwarted by an inability to provide straightforward gendered descriptions of the possible perpetrators—namely, any person among the cast of characters acting in concert with or as surrogates for Ben and Frankie (even Cassandra herself, in a new short haircut and bomber jacket, recounts that she has been addressed daily as "señor," which she finds mildly amusing, if disconcerting). But this dream, so steeped in ambivalence, also involves, necessarily, a dimension of wish fulfillment.

Blending the primitivist elements of *La Grande* and *National Geographic*, the dream stars Cassandra as Cristobel's "long-lost daughter," as she floats on a small raft down a river in the jungle. "Blood red parrots chattered overhead, in a language I could almost understand, Catalan perhaps" (140), she reports. This admission is a reminder that throughout the narrative Cassandra has been translating between Spanish and English— and always around the edges of Catalan. The relation between Catalan and Spanish is occasionally addressed, but, for the most part, what remains muted are the critical differences among Colombian Spanish, Castilian Spanish, and Catalan. That triangulation points to the global, imperial history of Spanish and the minority status of Catalan, the marked other.

Despite the pleasurable amniotic sensations experienced in the dream, Cassandra's anxieties surface as she realizes that she is "supposed to be looking for someone" (140). After declaring in Spanish who she is and the purpose of her journey to a group of hermaphroditic (and, she presumes, cannibalistic) villagers, she is stripped and dragged before the chief hermaphrodite. Both intrigued and threatened by these beings with both breasts and penises, Cassandra seeks recourse in self-disclosure while realizing a foundational untranslatability: "I tried to explain . . . that I was looking for my mother, I mean my daughter, but I realized that being both sexes as they were they might not understand the intensely proprietal relationship between mothers and daughters" (141). Using a torch, the huge being takes the sole of her foot in hand and begins to stroke it with fire. The fire gets hotter and hotter, and, just as the huge hermaphrodite's eyes burn into hers, Cassandra is suddenly awakened by Ana and returned to everyday life. How should the dream's rather overt symbolism be interpreted? What is its relationship, metaphorically and metonymically, to what follows?

Because of its aborted resolution, it can certainly be read as an allegory that entertains all possibilities, intertwining profound de-acculturation, queer desire, and dread at the same time that it hints momentarily at the potential for Cassandra to imagine herself a subject in a new and improved mother-daughter narrative. This psychic projection is extremely interesting, because it entails disproportionate risk, figuring both a return to origins and a leap into generativity. But it could also be argued that Cassandra has not overcome her maternophobia and that what originally motivated the journey in the dream is, ultimately, overridden by the incendiary encounter with the hermaphroditic foot therapist. Her defenses are still stronger than her occasional susceptibilities.[31]

Cassandra's uncontrollable wanderlust and her declared preferences for the transitory and the polyvalent are ultimately reinforced in the text. It is unclear, despite the rampant self-irony of Cassandra's declarations, whether the translator is implicated or why she might be exempt from the kinds of constraints to which other characters are subject. The metanarrative's privileging of undecidability over determinacy, process over product, and open-endedness over closure is dramatized in the final scene; Cassandra is the victim of theft yet again when her briefcase, containing her nearly completed translation of *La Grande y su hija,* is stolen at a café in the center of Barcelona. As Cassandra puts it, "Cristobel and her long-lost daughter had vanished" (172). Beyond the comic effects of this deus ex machina, what does the loss of this manuscript signify? In a narrative organized around numerous linguistic and textual deferrals and displacements, in which spatial symmetry, linguistic equivalence, and sexual binaries are seen as facile and reductive, Cassandra may be too quick to equate the vanishing of the translation with the permanent disappearance of the mother/daughter problem. The crack in the psychic edifice may yet show itself to be a fault line. For by now it is clear that the scene of translation in this text diverges radically from the Benjaminian vision in which translation is both genealogical and generative, and I do mean in the historical and cultural—not biological—sense. Simply, this is neither a scene of inheritance nor of transmission. My point is precisely not to claim that a rejection of maternity and a rejection of the maternal are the same. Cassandra, attached to nothing much beyond her inviolable singularity amid multiplicity and her autonomy over relationality, summarily rejects both maternity and the maternal. So threatening is the fantasy (or ideal) of plenitude to this translator that it requires renunciation rather than the risk of failure, or worse, further loss.

Thus it is imperative, in the spirit of Gaudí's Barcelona, to turn again to the primal scene of translation and Derrida's rendering of Babel as signifier: "it exhibits an incompletion, the impossibility of finishing, of totalizing, of saturating, of completing something on the order of edification, architectural construction, system and architectonics."[32] To say that translation is the paradigmatic transitive operation in this novel is only to reinforce the idea that process has crucial, performative value. Thus, Cassandra's rejection of originating concepts and final destinations seems perfectly appropriate when, at the close of the novel, the troubling translation she has been working on is stolen and her project remains unfinished—like Gaudí's monumental cathedral.[33]

Reading Himself and Others: Philip Roth's *The Professor of Desire*

Each reading is a translation.
—Octavio Paz, "Translation: Literature and Letters"

Philip Roth's *The Professor of Desire* (1977) has been largely eclipsed by his more recent writing, especially his American trilogy—*I Married a Communist, American Pastoral,* and *The Human Stain*—but it merits revisiting as a novel that argues against cultural insularity, links culture and psychoanalysis, and features a translator as a minor but crucial character. For the first time in ten years, the protagonist, David Kepesh—an American Jewish professor of comparative literature—returns to Europe. Traveling with the sane, serene, and very lovely Claire on a romantic holiday, he hopes not only to have overcome the curse of impotence but finally to have transcended tempestuousness without losing the lure of desire, the state of being where "more has no meaning" and "Claire is enough" (165). But he is not sure whether such a feat can actually be accomplished, or even that this is something devoutly to be wished. This first-person narrative is the professor's account of and reflection upon his libidinal exploits and his rhetorical efforts to overcome his longing for them.

Kepesh's complaint, or lament, embodied in the irony of the novel's title, is, in fact, the product of his erotic experience: as both a lover of women and a reader of literature, he fears that he may have prematurely come to learn the truth about the human condition by way of coupling with Claire—that passion and contentment are at cross-purposes. Kepesh, "the professor of desire," departs from Roth's prototypical alter egos in that he is defined primarily as a reader and a talker, not as a writer. Early on, Kepesh's verbal gymnastics are as important a source of gratification as his sexual performance; however betrayed he may feel by life or his own yearnings and proclivities, literature never ceases to sustain, even console him. Thus, whether imparting his wisdom about the art of fiction (somewhere along the continuum between pornography and romance) to his young, impressionable students or reporting the latest episode of his picaresque life to his analyst, Dr. Klinger, he is worrying generally about the nature of desire as it is depicted in Chekhov, Flaubert, Tolstoy, Byron, James, or any number of other writers. (Indeed, Kepesh's need to call on what he terms his "literary reserves" is a motif in his therapeutic sessions.)[34] For Kepesh, to be alive in the fullest sense is to be in perpetual thrall, yet Kepesh's desires are so heavily mediated by the literary framing to which they are made subject as to be inseparable from their cerebral constructs. Indeed, *The Professor of Desire* chronicles the ways in which, for better or for worse, Kepesh has turned eros into a field of expertise, an area of academic specialization, a thematic motif, an object of analysis. Kepesh's narrative is a melancholic celebration not only of pure sensual gratification but also of linguistic prowess.

That reading fiction can be a dominant mode of experience in itself, what Roth described in an interview with *Paris Review* as "a deep and singular pleasure, a gripping and mysterious human activity that does not require any more moral or political justification than sex," is a driving assumption of this narrative.[35] Thus, reading is neither derivative nor parasitic, and not necessarily self-referential; it is always primal. Moreover, it is nothing less than a species of translation, as Wolfgang Iser observes: "The concept of the implied reader thus describes a translation process whereby textual structures translate themselves through ideational acts into the reader's existing stock of experience."[36] Indeed, that the tension between literature and life is both problematic and generative (one might say generative *because* problematic) is one of the conceits of the novel. Kepesh's readerly sensibility places him in a long line of literary heroes and heroines, such as Paolo and Francesca, Don Quixote, Catherine Morland, Werther, and Emma Bovary, to name just a few, each of whom reads and misreads the world of lived experience through the prism of the book, usually with devastating consequences.

If there is a distinctive pattern to these characters' formal and thematic misreadings (mimetic and conflating), it is not only, as might seem on the surface, the gross matter of textualizing experience, adopting a model of behavior derived from the norms of a literary text, or imposing on life the plot of a novel with its dramatic intrigues and happy or tragic ending. There is also, as we shall see in greater depth in the next chapter, the genre-specific nature of these constructions and their implications. The phenomenon of readers reading in texts extends beyond characters patterning their behavior on or forming their judgments in life from fiction, of viewing life through the lens of imaginative literature (and, therefore, of always finding life lacking by comparison). It entails the more fine-tuned issue of the genre or mode that frames the literary perspective they use, a frame usually out of joint with their historical moment, as Cervantes, Austen, and Flaubert demonstrate with both terrible and comic acuity in *Don Quixote*, *Northanger Abbey*, and *Madame Bovary*, respectively. What is often being thematized in the tension between romantic and realist fiction (chivalric, gothic, etc.) is the romance of reading as a distorted and distorting ideal: reading itself as a romance that not only gives desire a certain shape but also is produced and reproduced through romance's specific allegorical rerepresentations and rearticulations of loss. This is not to say that David Kepesh shares fundamental similarities with any of the displaced reader heroes/heroines I refer to above. On the contrary—and this is crucial—Kepesh is, above all, not a naive reader, any less than is Roland Barthes, for example, in *The Pleasure of the Text*. The intertextual affinities are exceedingly fraught in *The Professor of Desire*, in which Roth explores the problem of desire as refracted through a lifetime of reading (if not living) well.

In the most general sense, putting a reader at the center of a text enables an author to wrestle with the implications of a character's literary interpretations for his/her textual life. To read (with) *The Professor of Desire* is to read not only intertextually and metacritically but also complicitly, in a way that can work to mitigate and diffuse the effects of Kepesh's own narcissistic obsessions, since over the course of the novel, these obsessions take on larger political and cultural concerns. One could say that in this novel "the personal (or the psychological) becomes political" in response to history; we read Kepesh reading his postwar, post-1960s American Jewish identity and consciousness through an Other: Europe. (As a comparatist, Kepesh is primarily a reader of foreign texts, but we are never made aware of his proficiency in languages other than English.) Kepesh's orientation at this stage in his life conforms to Lawrence Venuti's characterization of the "foreignizing method" as one that "send[s] the reader abroad," in search, not of an essence, but of a strategic construction "whose value is contingent on the current target-language situation."[37]

Although Kepesh has long been obsessed by the theme of romantic disillusionment in Chekhov's stories, it is Kafka's "preoccupation with spiritual starvation" that resonates with his most pressing concerns. Perhaps, among other factors, Kafka's enigmatic, ascetic angst makes Kepesh feel guilty about his own insatiable lust and seemingly incurable, if transparent, unhappiness. Kepesh—for whom enough is never enough—is fundamentally mystified by Kafka's professional hunger artist, for whom life offers barely any temptations at all. After visiting Mann's Venice and Freud's Vienna, Kepesh and Claire arrive in Kafka's Prague, where Kepesh makes his pilgrimage in pursuit of Kafka's legacy, which he finds, for better and for worse, everywhere.

Roth's own developing personal and professional interest in eastern Europe and eastern European writers is first made manifest in *The Professor of Desire*, where Roth seems impelled to look outside gentile America for versions of alterity and difference that will complicate the psychoanalytic model that provided him with so much material for so long. From 1974 to 1989, Roth served as the general editor of the Penguin series Writers from the Other Europe, introducing in their cultural and historical context the writings of postwar eastern European authors who, as Roth says in the preface published with the series, "though recognized as powerful forces in their own cultures, are virtually unknown in the West."[38] Whatever the particularities of Roth's attraction to Kafka, the more pertinent questions to explore are: how does Roth, that self-congratulatory, maligned scribe of American Jewish intellectual life, assume the role of intercultural translator, and what are the extratextual implications of that activity for the novel? To what call is he responding? At a crucial post-Watergate moment in American history and in Roth's own career, a destructive inertia, insularity, and monolingualism characterize the cultural landscape. For Kepesh, impotence and complacency are disabling; thus, he needs to put his situational impotence in perspective, to understand its causes and find a means to overcome it.

How intercultural translation figures in this process is critical to Kepesh's overcoming the stagnancy he suffers from. The parallel between Roth's work as editor of a series dedicated to facilitating literary exchange across problematic borders and Kepesh's odd encounters with a translator of Melville and "Kafka's whore" in Old Prague represents a belief in the power of translation to produce cultural and political change. No doubt the encounter with Professor Soska—a former professor of literature who, having been fired from his university post after "the Soviets invaded Czechoslovakia and put an end to the Prague Spring reform movement" (168), is now a tour guide—had its origins in a meeting Roth had on one of his trips to Prague. And yet, if this man didn't exist, Roth would have had to invent him: he is none other than Kepesh's counterreader. Kepesh asks the thirty-nine-year-old, prematurely retired academic how he maintains his morale under such debilitating circumstances. His immediate answer, not surprisingly, is "Kafka," which is code for "that's the way it goes here now." But, as survival strategies go, "Kafka" has limited usefulness and Professor Soska has also abandoned political activism. Instead, he translates *Moby-Dick* into Czech, even though a very fine translation already exists and "there is absolutely no need for another." Kepesh asks him, "Why that book? Why Melville?" Soska responds:

In the fifties I spent a year on an exchange program, living in New York City. Walking the streets, it looked to me as if the place was aswarm with the crew of Ahab's ship. And at the helm of everything, big or small, I saw yet another roaring Ahab. The appetite to set things right, to emerge at the top, to be declared a "champ." And by dint, not just of energy and will, but of enormous rage. And *that*, the rage, that is what I should like to translate into Czech . . . if—smiling— that can be translated into Czech. (170)

The question of the translatability of rage into Czech aside, not only does a distinguished translation of *Moby-Dick* already exist, but no translation of Soska's could even be published in Czechoslovakia at that time.[39]

Thus, "political hopelessness" is underwritten by a valiant act of futility, which becomes Soska's "deepest source of satisfaction." When he asks

Kepesh about his attraction to Kafka, Kepesh explains that it has to do "in large part, with sexual despair." Their conversation centers on the subject of authoritarian regimes, with Kepesh positing an analogy between their respective situations, between the repression perpetrated by a government against its people and the repression perpetrated by the body/mind against itself. The academics' rather poignant exchange ends with an elegy to the subjective nature of reading and reader response: "to each obstructed citizen his own Kafka"/"and to each angry man his own Melville." Readers do, sometimes desperately, project their own unfulfilled desires onto literature, finding in novels what they were looking for all along, and the reader outside this text is reminded that one reads not only according to one's ability but also, to a great extent, according to one's needs. When Soska, in conversation with Claire later in the day, refers to Kafka as "*the* outlawed writer," the reader might infer that Roth, attempting to get some distance on his own "obsessional themes," is conceding that political repression trumps sexual repression, at least regarding its effects on artistic creativity. Or he might merely be saying that personal paralysis and cultural constraints are opposite sides of the same coin, though it seems that Roth is contextualizing Kepesh's self-analysis in precisely the critical terms of an assimilated American Jew in the second half of the twentieth century. Such insights he can learn only from Europe. He is having his Freud and his Foucault, too.

Are we to offset this view of the task of translation as a mode of renewal, a catalyst for social change—and hence of survival—against the American pragmatist's perspective, one that would regard Soska's enterprise as a symbolic act of folly, like Captain Ahab's own wild quest for the Great White Whale? There is no clear answer to this question, for it is the gift of translation to always offer a double vision, neither domesticating *nor* foreignizing, but doing both. Roth simultaneously makes explicit here that the task of translation is to articulate cultural differences in specific cultural and political contexts; but translation is also more than simply a medium for unilateral or even bilateral transactions. Soska's translation is a profound act of resistance that will subvert the regime's norms and values, Roth seems to suggest, however delayed the reaction: Roth is deeply moved by eastern European views of the Great American Novel. Kepesh is invigorated by his conversation with Soska; the Czech professor's defamiliarizing perspective has redirected his energies and compelled him to read even more comparatively and dialectically, even if the result is to encourage his habit of finding psychosexual patterns in all figuration. It is no coincidence that Soska's vision of America was crystallized in his personal experience as a European student on a yearlong exchange program in the postwar boom of the 1950s. Kepesh's intercultural encounter with Soska moves him to foreground his teaching of Kafka in a new way. Kepesh had taught a seminar on Kafka the previous semester and was pleased with his students' understanding of the writer's "moral isolation" and "those imaginative processes by which a fantasist as entangled as Kafka was in daily existence transforms into fable his everyday struggles" (166).

It is fitting that on his last night in Prague he returns alone to the Old Town Square and, seated on a bench under a streetlamp, spontaneously begins composing the first three lines of his introductory lecture for the following year's comparative literature seminar. His model is Kafka's story "Report to an Academy," beginning with the satirical address: "Honored Members of Literature 341." Later, in a café deserted but for two young prostitutes offering their wares at nearby tables, he begins in earnest to write his heartfelt lecture. Both the setting of the scene and Kepesh's tone suggest that we have been made witnesses to what may be Kepesh's most private act of testimony, of confession: the professor's desire to be teaching, and "not in September but at this very moment!" (181). The rhetorical thrust of this entire episode pivots on the students' transformation from penitents into voyeurs, jurors, and confidants, and the professor's transformation into a text (an erotic history) they will read (his transformation into a breast had occurred in another novel). What seems particularly crucial here, though, is that, for once, the scene is performative and not constative; we are already reading his story.

His pilgrimage with Claire to Kafka's grave at the Jewish cemetery, which precedes his imaginary lecture and his dream of visiting Kafka's whore, invokes the death of Kepesh's mother (he acknowledges that he hasn't visited the graves of either his grandparents or his mother since the unveiling of her stone) and symbolically prefigures the death of his father. Kepesh declares silently that he has exorcised the ghost, has been "deKafkafied," meaning that both his "obstructed" and his "*un*obstructed days" are over: "no more more, and no more nothing either!" (178). But the reader is suspicious of his overly simple resolution to what is understood to be an interminably complex problem. His dream later that night in which he meets

Kafka's whore suggests that, despite his earlier feelings that day of having "overcome," he has not yet mastered his trauma of impotence, so thinly disguised in intellectual garb. In his translated interview with the now old woman, who ostensibly knew an aspect of Kafka otherwise hidden from public view, he seeks an answer to the mystery of "The Hunger Artist." Indeed, although Kepesh claims to be interested in Kafka's "spiritual starvation," he seems capable of communing with him only through the silences and recesses of Kafka's life and text. Kepesh emerges from this dream revulsed and somewhat chastened, but it is precisely what remains unresolved that propels him to undertake two writing projects simultaneously upon the couple's return to the United States: a scholarly study of Kafka entitled *Hunger Art* and this chronicle that we are reading, the expanded version of the lecture whose prologue he composed in Prague. The reader knows that the academic book on Kafka will not get written, that all Kepesh's psychic, intellectual, and erotic energy will be channeled into his personal story, since, in a sense, to write both books would be redundant.

The Cold War is over. There is no longer a Soviet Union or a Czechoslovakia, and Prague is once again a lively place, overrun by expatriate Americans, many of whom are there, presumably, for the Kafka theme park that characterizes the present-day city. The "Writers from the Other Europe" series was discontinued in 1989, having served its very useful cultural purpose. Indeed, Czech literature, along with other minor literatures, circulates more freely now across the globe by way of translation (though the famous—and self-exiled—Czech novelist Milan Kundera now writes in French). The ever-changing politics and economics of translation still regulate the literary marketplace, if along new lines. But what remains is Roth's reinforcement of the notion that translation is the most intimate act of reading possible. Through that act, involving translator, author, and reader as well, ever new interpretations of texts are produced, affirming and inspiring; one struggles with the text as with one's personal and political life. The endless vitality of the process—in both reading and living— is valorized here. Translation is called upon to provide the shot in the arm, the boost, the infusion of otherness that will save the stagnating cultural, textual/sexual body. Translation is aligned with the volatility of ideas and affects, with the bringing of unconscious material into individual and collective consciousness.

Morbidity and Mortality

Of the two visits to the country cottage that punctuate the summer idyll of Kepesh and Claire and bring *The Professor of Desire* so painfully and poignantly to its close, the second one concerns us here. It is the point of intersection for all of Roth's preoccupations. Kepesh's father's visit takes place on Labor Day weekend, marking the end of summer and the onset of an autumnal denouement signaling both rupture and continuity. The Chekhovian weekend is suffused with bittersweet tenderness, longing, and the fear of death. There is a fateful symmetry to the two couples and the foursome they compose: on the one side, Kepesh and Claire (whom he adores calling "Clarissa"), the young lovers who exhibit all the trappings of domestic contentment, but whose bliss carries within it the seeds of its inevitable dissolution (at least for Kepesh). And on the other side, the elderly father and his widowed friend and Holocaust survivor Mr. Barbatnik, both of whom have struggled, loved, and lost their spouses and who are now approaching the end of their lives. Kepesh reads the situation as if it were a scene from Chekhov's "The Lady with a Lapdog" and refers to himself as "the lover." Kepesh lives in dread of the death of his vivacious, nonstop-talking father. Through Mr. Barbatnick's appearance, the Holocaust, the absent signifier in Roth's rendering of Kafka's Prague, makes its appearance in America.[40] Death casts its very long shadow in the form of a reminder, a metonym, a link to that other lost world; and it is precisely the interpenetration of the tragic and the bucolic, of death in life, that lends gravitas and the burden of history to this apparently conventional American get-together.

Asked by Kepesh to tell his "survivor's story"—a testimonial genre quite familiar now but less so when this novel was published—Mr. Barbatnik, standing in as witness for those who cannot speak, recounts in very few words what happened to him in the war, while not actually attempting to explain the mystery of his survival. Stacked against cataclysmic history is Kepesh as another kind of survivor, of "a vicious, ridiculous, inexplicable joke" (262). Scrutinizing the past, looking ahead, he has already begun to mourn his many, undifferentiated losses. He sees himself as condemned: "Never to know anything durable. Nothing except my unrelinquishable memories of the discontinuous and the provisional . . . within a year my passion will be dead" (251–52, 261). Kepesh is nothing if not self-aware: having successfully terminated his analysis halfway through the novel, he knows full well what his problem is—that he suffers in true literary fashion from "the libidinous fallacy," and he knows, true to the pattern, that he will be crossing Dr. Klinger's threshold once again. Recognizing that he might not be able to "survive" the state of almost insufferable plenitude that Claire has created for them, he predicts the inevitable loss of his desire for her and the impossibility of a cure: "And feed me not the consolations of the reality principle!" (262).

The novel's final, cinematically constructed scene invites a range of psychoanalytic interpretations, all framed by Freud's *Beyond the Pleasure Principle*.[41] In the style of a split screen, Roth's ambivalent, irreconcilable conclusion could serve as a metapsychological illustration of Freud's theory of the instincts (as well as of Kepesh's psyche). In *The Language of Psychoanalysis*, Jean Laplanche and J.-B. Pontalis define the competing instincts in the following way:

The death instincts tend towards the destruction of vital unities, absolute equalization of tensions and a return to the hypothesised inorganic state of complete repose. The life instincts, also called Eros, embrace not only the sexual instincts but also the instincts of self-preservation. The life instincts tend not only to preserve existing life unities but also to constitute, on the basis of these, new and more inclusive ones. (241)[42]

On one half of the "screen" is projected the room of Kepesh, just awakened from a night of bad dreams, and Claire, the loving woman with whom he shares a bed and a life. On the other half of the screen is projected the room where the two elderly, monastic guests are sleeping. Kepesh narrates:

My willing Clarissa is with me still! I raise her nightgown up along the length of her unconscious body, and with my lips begin to press and tug her nipples until the pale, velvety, childlike aerole erupt in tiny granules and her moan begins. But even while I suck in a desperate frenzy at the choicest morsel of her flesh, even as I pit all my accumulated happiness, and all my hope, against my fear of transformations yet to come, I wait to hear the most dreadful sound imaginable emerge from the room where Mr. Barbatnik and my father lie alone and insensate, each in his freshly made bed. (263)

Kepesh is, arguably, a caricature of the Freudian libidinal personality in which the lack of libido is tantamount to death. Kepesh is reassured upon waking that Claire, aroused from her own sleep by his erotic ministrations, is still a "willing" object of his libidinal desires (a sign, clearly, that *he* is still alive). In "desperate frenzy," Kepesh sucks at her breast.[43] Her pleasurable moans are opposed to the sounds that he so strangely "waits" to hear: the dreaded death rattle from the other room. He sucks for his life, so to speak, engaging in a form of repetitive compulsive behavior that would seem to erect itself as a barrier against what he appears to fear even more than the actual death of his father: that he will be, like the two elderly men in the other room, "alone and insensate . . . in his freshly made bed."

However, Roth's moving description of Kepesh's expression of the life force is not, of course, life-affirming in the least. Laplanche and Pontalis elucidate: "The aim of [Eros] is to establish even greater unities and to preserve them thus—in short, to bind together; the aim of the destructive instinct is, on the contrary, to undo connections and so to destroy things."[44] Kepesh may consciously believe that in seeking stimulation (tension), he is avoiding stasis, that the inherent conflictual nature of life ensures he will maintain a state of perpetual desire. However, the pull toward destruction against which he seems quite helpless—to end his relationship with Claire, despite its obvious life-preserving qualities—signifies, inexorably, a death wish. "The fundamental aspect of instinctual life: the return to an earlier state and a return to the absolute repose of the inorganic."[45] What Roth has so vividly portrayed throughout *The Professor of Desire* is not the opposition between the two instincts, but their inseparability. So the question remains: with exquisite precision and passion, Kepesh may profess desire, but what does he want? "The death wish is furthermore the chosen expression of the most fundamental principle of psychical functioning; and lastly, in so far as it is 'the essence of the instinctual', it binds every wish, whether aggressive or sexual, to the wish for death."[46] The translator's intervention provides insight into this phenomenon. Even though Soska makes a fleeting and, it would seem, tangential appearance in the narrative, his encounter with Kepesh has a positive, catalytic effect upon the events that follow. In this text in which impotence is a form of death, the translator's admittedly futile practice is nonetheless instrumental, illustrating that, especially in a depressed or insular cultural/psychic economy, translation as a repressed or censored term becomes a lifeline to the outside, pointing a way out of solipsism and stagnation. In *The Professor of Desire*, reading and living, and reading and loving, are fatally intertwined, with translation serving as the cultural elixir that invigorates art when the sexual/political body is moribund.

*

What do these texts reveal in their representations of translators about translation? Conversely, how does the conscious foregrounding of "the task of the translator" alter the reading of these texts, or of any literary texts, for that matter? As I have argued, these texts work figuratively to show that translation is not only a procedure applied *to* a text or a language, or even simply a decoding or co-implicating process that occurs *among* texts, languages, and cultures. Fundamentally, what the reader comes to appreciate is that because there is language, there *is* translation. All of these texts, read together and alongside others I have mentioned, also further the notion that where there is literature there is translation, that culture requires mediation, that transitivity is the great cultural constant. Both rapture and rupture involve translation. By making central the proclivities, activities, and interventions of translators, these texts show that there is no sexual, aesthetic, economic, or political endeavor that escapes the circuit of translation.

Might there be a correlation between the heightened visibility of the translator figure in fiction and the parallel rise of translation theory in the latter part of the twentieth century? An author who uses a translator is deliberately choosing to highlight metalinguistic issues, however obliquely. The translator acts as stand-in for the reader's—and the author's—increased semiotic awareness that language systems are models revealing the interplay of underlying structures of human culture. These characters—eroticized mediators, objects of suspicion and desire, and repositories of knowledge—act as links between high theory and popular culture, presenting the translator as a corporeal being who embodies all of the disjunctiveness and drama of a fragmented, multilingual world. By unleashing the unknown potential of language, translation gives us access to other dimensions and interpenetrates the stories and histories of others with our own. The charge of translation, as performed on every conceivable level, is not to maintain equivalence, level differences, or smooth over what is missing or flawed. Rather, its task is to alter linguistic and textual frameworks by disrupting sameness and injecting otherness. In doing so, translation graces the intimate and the ultimate, defying oblivion, stasis, and death.

2

Genre and Genealogy

THE SLAVE NARRATIVE TRANSLATED
OTHERWISE AND ELSEWHERE

> Genres are not to be mixed.
> —Jacques Derrida, "The Law of Genre," in *Acts of Literature*

When we speak of translation as performing the vital function of a language or culture by extending and renewing generic definitions, we are also remarking on the fact that when meanings migrate—constantly, though not always voluntarily—some aspects are shed as others are assumed. Whatever the combination of desire, design, improvisation, or imposition, a translated text or narrative is one that has been so moved (and if it hasn't, there is a good chance that we aren't reading it). In this chapter, I concentrate on the ways in which literary and historical narratives of and about slavery are displaced, transferred, and transported from one cultural/geographical site or framework (a source context) to another (target context) as well as how our understanding of the experience of slavery as a global, though not singular, catastrophic event is revised, challenged and subsequently enriched as a result of this process. This examination of transcultural literary engagements with the question of slavery as historical memory considers three novels written within a ten-year period as exemplary instances of generic translation: Charles Johnson's *Oxherding Tale* (1982), Buchi Emecheta's *The Slave Girl* (1977), and André Schwarz-Bart's *La mulâtresse Solitude* (1972).[1] To conceive of these late-twentieth-century novels as translations of the American narrative of slavery means not thinking or reading unidirectionally: the scene of translation necessarily involves referral and deferral, for even as a translation harks (back or across) to an original or source text, the original also "anticipates" its futural reinscription(s).

Johnson's postmodern novel is narrated by an erudite antebellum "mulatto" ex-slave; its pastiche of literary techniques and modes violates almost every assumption about the slave narrative, its origins, and the tradition it has spawned. After one reads *Oxherding Tale*, it is impossible ever to understand Frederick Douglass in the same way again. Emecheta's postcolonial text about indigenous slavery in Nigeria invites comparison to the classical slave narrative of Harriet Jacobs and to the sentimental novel, but it sensitizes the reader to the problem of universalizing forms of bondage according to Western literary and social models. Schwarz-Bart's transatlantic text about a doomed eighteenth-century Guadeloupean slave revolt is, from the beginning, implicated in a double reading with the Holocaust as historical paradigm, but through imaginative recovery it resists any privileging of one collective catastrophe over another. Read translatively, the three texts expose "resistance," "liberation," and "redemption" as paradoxes that haunt the rhetorical discourse about slavery.[2]

The history of this discourse is so bound up with a struggle for determinacy that even a twentieth-century slave narrative is met with a set of ethical, cultural, and literary expectations or assumptions from readers about how slavery should be represented, or what constitute the "normative" experiences of slaves. These assumptions derive from slave narratives, as distinctive forms of testimonial expression, being inextricably identified with the historical experience of transplanted, enslaved Africans in America—confirming their canonical status in American discourse and letters. So strong is this literary legacy that the American image of how black slaves endured bondage and achieved freedom has been "embodied" by the dominant modes of its textual representation. So strong is this legacy that although slave narratives were produced in a specific historical context, their imprint is detected in *all* subsequent African American writing, not only those engaged in rewriting or translating slave narratives per se. But what is this struggle for determinacy I refer to above? Generic conventions and constraints regarding the treatment of grave subject matter exert a certain force upon readers and dictate protocols, creating what Hans Robert Jauss calls "horizons of expectations" or "the rules of the game." Jauss presents a phenomenological and "objective" schema of what constitutes "a literary event," whose reception and influence are "mediated in the horizon of expectations . . . that arises for each work in the historical moment of its appearance, from a pre-understanding of the genre, from the form and theme of already familiar works, and from the opposition of poetic and practical language."[3] Arguably, that opposition still holds readers in its sway.

Slavery as an institution has persisted, indeed flourished, since ancient times across continents and empires, exceeding even those boundaries from the fifteenth to the nineteenth century, when an international slave trade made human bondage virtually a universal practice.[4] In turn, the discourse on slavery has itself become a kind of master narrative in which reductive and restrictive categories both co-opt and occult critical racial and gender differences in the name of a universalist paradigm. Slavery as idea has been distinguished from slavery as social system. Comparative historians and theorists recognize a continuity and contiguity between older and more modern forms of slavery, while differentiating between abstract legal status and an actual set of institutions involving economic functions and interpersonal relationships. Although the ambiguous status of the slave as both property and person had been interrogated from Aristotle to Locke, it was in eighteenth-century debates over natural law that slavery assumed a central position among American and European moral philosophers, theologians, and political theorists, such as Montesquieu and Jefferson. In the nineteenth century, the great slave controversy between abolitionists and advocates for slavery pivoted on whether American slavery, based on the total subjugation of one race by another, was essentially different from historical varieties of bondage and serfdom.[5]

Late in the twentieth century, literary critics began wrestling with the discourse of American slavery as much as with the institution itself, if indeed they are separable. The debates have centered to a great extent on the discursive construction of slavery as a key to national identity. For Deborah McDowell and Arnold Rampersad, "slavery is perhaps the central intellectual challenge, other than the Constitution itself, to those who would understand the meaning of America."[6] As David Brion Davis has brilliantly shown, an irreconcilable moral contradiction underlies America's mission and meaning: America—the idealized projection of European hopes for a new beginning—did not flourish by liberating itself from previous structures and practices, but rather by extending and perfecting the institution of slavery. The transatlantic slave trade, which was an essential aspect of colonization and, eventually, an integral part of the economic and social development of the nation, predated Columbus. Missing in all the earlier debates was the perspective of the enslaved subject, because, as Davis puts it, until modern times, "few slaves recorded their thoughts and . . . scholars did not think the subject worthy of study."[7] But, as we well know, this voice is not difficult to locate: one need but turn to slave narratives.

The rich generative potential of the slave narrative, its formative influence on narrative structures and strategies of subsequent African American literature, makes it possible to argue that "after 1865 the generic expectations of these autobiographies altered drastically."[8] That alteration parallels a striking rhetorical shift in slave narratives, from the antebellum comparison of slavery to a tomb to the postbellum comparison to a school of life. Linking this change in representational strategy to the development of African American literary realism, William Andrews characterizes these different portrayals of the experience of having endured and survived slavery as a movement from "existential" (antebellum) to "pragmatic" (postbellum) paradigms. Elsewhere, Andrews contends that the valorization of the romantic, rebellious antebellum fugitive slave narrator has skewed our notions of the history of the genre, prescriptively limiting a necessarily dynamic signifying process for ideological reasons. Contrary to orthodox critical opinion, which has fixated on one model, Andrews argues, "the image of slavery, along with the metaphor of black selfhood, undergoes revision as the nineteenth century evolves."[9]

Beyond the debate over nineteenth-century texts, slave narratives are widely regarded as the pretext and/or master paradigm for all African American autobiography and fiction. These first-person accounts of human bondage are necessarily generic hybrids, ingeniously combining elements of autobiographical, fictional, and historical discourse; as reflexive and symbolic performances, they enact modes and forge models of black subjectivity and identity in the most challenging of contexts. Testimonials to the transplantation, brutalization, and enslavement of black people by those who endured, survived, and, not incidentally, managed to gain access to crucial networks of publication, they are predicated on an individual narrator's capacity to represent, stand for, and stand *in* for those whose voices have been silenced, but whose stories are interwoven with the narratives of others.

Thus, as foundational American texts whose parameters have been variously contested, slave narratives are figurative cultural documents that

reveal the discursive complexity of slavery as a rhetorical construct at particular moments in American history. In italicizing the word "slavery,"
Hortense Spillers offers a provocative reminder that (even) the notion of
slavery belongs to a discursive field and therefore is not exempt from the
play of radical textuality:

It seems to me that every generation of systematic readers is compelled to "reinvent" slavery in its elaborate and peculiar institutional ways and means. . . . In a
very real sense, a full century or so "after the fact," "slavery" is *primarily* discursive,
as we search vainly for a point of absolute and indisputable origin, for a moment
of plenitude that would restore us to the real, rich "thing" itself before discourse
touched it. In that regard, "slavery" becomes the great "test case" around which,
for its Afro-American readers, the circle of mystery is recircumscribed time and
again. . . . It becomes increasingly clear that the cultural synthesis we call "slavery"
was never homogeneous in its practices and conception, not unitary in the faces it
has yielded. . . . To rob the subject of its dynamic character, to captivate it in a fictionalized scheme whose outcome is already inscribed by a higher, different, *other*
power, freezes it in the ahistorical.[10]

As Spillers asserts, the dynamic literary legacy of slavery embeds multiple
historical and cultural discourses. Residual tendencies toward reifying or
"captivating" the "cultural synthesis we call 'slavery'" continue to be contested and challenged, not only by scholars but also by the steady flow of
novels that insistently revise and reconfigure slavery as historical event and
literary legacy.[11]

The first slave narrative was published in 1703. Through the first
forty years of the twentieth century, though slavery had been abolished in
the United States, the writing of slave narratives continued, when former
slaves interviewed for the Federal Writers Project provided volumes of oral
testimony about their childhood experiences under slavery. However, according to the definition of Charles Davis and Henry Louis Gates, slave
narratives are only those "written works published before 1865, after which
time slavery *de jure* ceased to exist." By "slave narrative," Davis and Gates
mean contemporary "written and dictated testimonies of the enslavement
of black human beings." They argue that "the very structure of the narratives, their rhetorical strategies as a genre, altered drastically once the mi-
lieu in which they were written and read altered drastically. Once slavery
was abolished, no need existed for the slave to *write* himself into the human community through the action of first-person narration."[12] Allowing

for no space between the moment of origin and the moment of production, Davis and Gates's rather juridical definition stakes a claim for generic authenticity using both formalist and historical, rather than merely thematic, criteria: just as an original "slave's narrative" was once formerly authorized by supporting documents attesting to its veracity or authenticity, so now is it legitimized—at least rhetorically—by having preceded the American Civil War and black emancipation.

And yet defensive efforts such as those of Davis and Gates do not really change the terms of the debate about origins: the original already contains aspects of otherness within itself, what Derrida calls "an internal division of the trait": a structural fault that engenders repetition. That repetition produces not identity, but difference through translation, and translation ensures the survival of a work of art, enabling a genre to live on beyond its historical limitations. This is a variant of what Maria Tomyczko calls "translation as a speech act . . . translational engagement . . . on a meta-level."[13] Put less abstractly, slave narratives were in their historical moment an oxymoronic response to the fact that slaves, members of the "inferior" black race, were legally forbidden to learn to read and supposedly could not write. The slave narrative, the United States' great story of both liberation and redemption, testified to the "ascent to literacy" and for some offered the strongest argument of the basic injustice of the institution. As the theme of literacy as performance helps us appreciate the slave narratives' original programmatic thrust, it may also account for the engendering of the slave narrative in ever new contexts and frameworks.

By rehearsing the history of the discourse of slavery here, I have insinuated slavery as a silent term into the space between translation and genre, thus producing the intersection of translation with race/genre that frames this set of interrelated readings.[14] Even a translational poetics of the most formalist persuasion has an undeclared politics and will be reflexively pressed into service when pressure is brought to bear. Genres, too, as we now recognize, are no less political—but especially so when they are race-inflected, or categorically racialized, as slave narratives are.[15] And yet, or rather, precisely because each of the texts I analyze is a slave narrative in translation, none of these texts—one African American, one Anglo African, and one Franco Caribbean—is, by normative criteria, a slave narrative "proper." As each site of translation indicates a different aspect of the problematic of genre and genealogy, questions regarding their relation to an

original text come to the fore: what if the origin(al) is always already heterogeneous? What is the status then of its translations? When is a narrative
of/about slavery *not* a slave narrative? How does it matter, and to whom,
and is this slippage of dire political or critical consequence?

Perhaps it is not by chance that slavery and translation, along with
metaphor, share a certain tropic quality: both are schematized and put into
operation through similar means. They necessarily involve passage, movement, displacement, the transfer of bodies, languages, and texts. However,
it must be reiterated that in the process of carrying over or carrying across,
something happens: the meanings attached to the source or original
change. Translation is the stage on which language in its widest (and sometimes wildest) sense is called upon to perform, project, and disperse the
very meaning of "original," elsewhere and otherwise. In the event of translation, the original is also understood as being derivative and incomplete,
and language, though never totalizable, as always supplementing and sup-
plementable, sharing, overlapping, and recovering meaning even as it loses
what it never fully possessed in the first place.

Like the concept of race, the concept of genre is not self-evident.
Both signify comprehensive codification schemas that distinguish and determine one kind from another, according to a set of explicitly established
structural, thematic, or functional criteria. Throughout history, these criteria, as well as the foundational premises that justify them, have varied
and been contested, so much so that each term has a theory attached to it:
to wit, "genre theory" and "race theory." Whether we are referring to the
laws that govern nature/biology or the values attached to artistic or poetic
expression, the very idea of genre seems "natural." Of course, this is far
from the case. Precisely because typologies produce the sets as well as what
belongs in them and are thereby excluded from them, genre and race posit
fundamental ways by which we mark and re-mark (the politics of) identity and difference. Indeed, it would appear, that in one inevitable, slippery
move, description then leads to proscription—and the rest, as we say, is
history.

To suggest, as I am about to do, that genre and race constitute parallel kinds of conceptual structures and social formation—and, moreover,
that they have entire discourses in common—is not to argue that "race"
and "genre" are interchangeable terms. Rather, it is my aim here to show
how and why it matters critically for any structural or thematic analysis of

the slave narrative and its African American literary progeny that race and genre are so mutually implicating. I am interested in how generic and racial boundaries are defended and maintained, as well as in how they are challenged and subverted in literary critical terms—by whom, and under what conditions. Precisely because generic and racial taxonomies have been pressed into service by oppressive, reductive, and reifying regimes, it is in our best critical interests not to reflexively conflate aesthetic and political criteria, but to delineate their differences as well as their generative, unifying possibilities. This chapter is decidedly not a reception study. Nonetheless, a main concern is how "unfaithful" generic translations, especially in relation to fraught subject matter, can call into question unspoken allegiances, sharpen differences, divide and disarm, producing mutually exclusive constituencies and interpretive communities.

Race, Genre, and Identity Politics in Charles Johnson's *Oxherding Tale*

What is Africa to me?
—Countee Cullen, "Heritage"

My understanding of Charles Johnson's extravagantly intertextual *Oxherding Tale*'s translation of the slave narrative hinges on an implied comparison of race and genre as similar regimes. To read it is thus to entertain the assertion of Jacques Derrida's essay "The Law of Genre" that "genres are not to be mixed." Twin prohibitions frame this narrative: that which forbids the mixing of the genres and that which forbids the crossing of racial boundaries. Or, put another way, that which forbids racial mixing and that which forbids the boundary-crossing that separates the genres. Genre and race are taxonomies; de facto, they create borders and establish limits that are both enabling and disabling, meaningful and senseless, empowering and destructive. Whether the object is kinds of literature (the realm of art) or kinds of human beings (found in nature), Derrida asserts in "The Law of Genre" that

as soon as the word genre is sounded, as soon as it is heard, as soon as one attempts to conceive it, a limit is drawn. And when a limit is established, norms and interdictions are not far behind. . . . One must not cross a line of demarcation, one must not risk impurity, anomaly or monstrosity. . . . If a genre is what it is or if it is supposed to be what it is destined to be by virtue of its Telos, "then genres are not to be mixed." Or, more rigorously, genres should not intermix. And if it should happen that they do intermix, by accident or through transgression, by mistake or through a lapse, then this should confirm . . . the essential purity of their identity. (224–25)

Suggesting that more than genre is at stake in this interdiction, Derrida is making a larger claim, one both ethical and ideological, about the nature of classificatory logic and identitarian thinking. Derrida exhorts us to consider how cognitive, formal, and conceptual distinctions are drawn, how descriptive terms become prescriptive ones, how these differences are exercised depending on the context, and to what uses they are put in the service of which ends. Why "must" these divisions and separations be enforced? For the simple reason that it is "impossible *not* to mix genres." What, Derrida queries, if there were "lodged within the heart of the law of the law itself a law of impurity or a principle of contamination. . . . The a priori of a counter-law, an axiom of impossibility that would confound its sense, order and reason"? Is "the law of genre" actually "the law of the law of genre," and thus a law that seeks enforcement precisely because it is always already broken—because it is impurity, and not purity, that is irreducible?

Perhaps the ultimate threats to generic or racial purity come, not from the outside, but from the inside, for genres necessarily exceed the boundaries that bring the law of genre into being. Clearly, thinking about genre in critical and pragmatic terms involves more than either contesting or ignoring both the fact and principle that typologies and taxonomies exist—or striving, as some critics have done, to move beyond them altogether. It also involves more than celebrating genre-crossing for its own sake, but rather necessitates considering how each text negotiates its generic identity in terms of what Derrida, in a move strangely reminiscent of racial terminology, calls "participating but not belonging." Derrida's formulation of "the law of the law of genre" as "a principle of contamination, a law of impurity, a parasitical economy" resonates boldly in a study of slavery and the slave narrative.[16]

Two short chapters in *Oxherding Tale*—didactic and performative "intermissions," the author calls them—disrupt the narrator's already digressive tale to engage the reader in metacommentary on literary form and technique.[17] The first intermission "worries" the formal conventions of the Slave Narrative (Johnson's capitalization) and its genealogical relation to

St. Augustine's *Confessions* and its descendant the Puritan conversion narrative, from which the slave narrative directly draws its arclike movement. This digging into the "archival tomb of literary history" reveals three kinds of slave narratives, including but not limited to "the Slave Narrative proper" exemplified by Frederick Douglass, but inflected as well by both the nineteenth-century picaresque novel and the novel of manners (here Harriet Jacobs is implicitly cited). So essential for Johnson's project, it would seem, is this information, both pedagogically and rhetorically, that the narrator has to interrupt the suspenseful account of his first encounter with the Soulcatcher to provide it. The perverse pleasures of Johnson's quasi-eighteenth-century storytelling aside, it is precisely his point that because of its "long pedigree," which should be no less valorized for being mixed, engaging in "philosophical play" with this testimonial form is entirely justified. "No form . . . *loses* its ancestry," Johnson announces, alerting the reader to *Oxherding Tale*'s dialogue with those who seek to protect the boundaries of a genre that has, in fact, been impure since its conception; "rather, these meanings accumulate in layers of tissue as the form evolves."[18]

The second intermission, reflecting on the conventions of the slave narrative, focuses on its "only invariant feature," which is the technique of first-person viewpoint; it "liberates" the technique, as well as the subject of "the Negro Slave Narrative," from its own "limitations." Johnson's text liberates the slave narrative, not only by signaling its own status as belonging to a specific genre and de-essentializing those very features that mark it as such, but by insisting precisely on a notion of generic and racial identity that is both contingent and indeterminate. Indeed, Johnson's interrogation of the subject of "the Slave Narrative" transcends constructs and constraints, especially the notion of the first-person narrator-perceiver who is condemned to literary realism's single consciousness. As Johnson puts it, Andrew Hawkins, the slave-protagonist, is a "palimpsest, interwoven with everything—literally everything—that can be thought or felt" (152). What we would call a contradiction in terms, perhaps—an omniscient first-person narrator—Johnson here calls "first-person universal" (153). That is to say, though *Oxherding Tale* is predicated, like other kinds of autobiographical narratives—fictionalized or not—on a principle of the "I" as a repeatable singularity across time and space, it also seeks to diffuse and displace that singularity by re-marking it as heterogeneous and performative. In so doing, it repeatedly, joyfully, and strategically challenges readerly expectations and inherited assumptions not only about race and genre but also about the dominant representation of slavery as it has been passed down to us in African American literature. Because plantation slavery in the Americas was, of course, an economic and political system based on a ruthless racial classification that admitted neither compromise nor contradiction, Johnson's notion of philosophical play disrupts and contaminates the categories it invokes, as realized through the imagined experience of a consummately wry and erudite biracial slave in the antebellum South.

All of *Oxherding Tale*'s metatextual gestures point to the often vexed relation between genealogy and genericity, inheritance and performance. From the novel's opening pages on, Johnson sets into motion a story of survival that can be called unorthodox only when judged by the normative criteria of slave narratives. The exquisitely self-conscious slave narrator's comical account of the strange and absurd circumstances contributing to his conception (à la *Tristram Shandy*) at a plantation called Cripplegate turns many of the models and conventions established by Frederick Douglass's exemplary 1845 narrative upside down and inside out, beginning with the situating of his paternal as well as maternal origins. Unlike the paradigmatic slave narrator, who, lacking the legitimizing accoutrements of personhood, is de facto relegated to the sphere of nature, Andrew Hawkins's patrimony is not only knowable, but documentable. Moving stealthily between parable and history, Andrew's rich, novelistic account of his coming into being provides the reader with an account of his own genealogy and of its cross-fertilizing implications. Andrew's in-betweenness as a racialized/enslaved subject is analogous with this text's (as well as this genre's) perturbing indeterminacy and mixed parentage: "When I look back on my life, it seems that I belonged by error or accident—call it what you will—to both house and field, but I was popular in neither, because the war between the two families focused, as it were, on me, and I found myself caught from my fifth year forward in their crossfire" (8).

Where does he belong and how to identify this text? How does a translation problematize, in terms of both race and genre, an inherent incongruity that the original narrative might suppress? Andrew is the biological result of an unintended interracial union between a male slave and his white mistress and a manifestation of the legal, physical, and material inequality under slavery of "the two families." Yet from Andrew's perspective, "the war" was fought between two parties equal in every other way. In this profoundly patriarchal text, Mother Nature is effaced in favor of Culture, and it is the Law of the Fathers that determines Andrew's destiny. But, to be more precise, it is his status as the beneficiary of "a perfect moral education" (12) that sharpens all the contradictions and ambiguities and structures his perceptions of who he is and what he knows. In an economy in which the market value of black flesh is not ambiguous, however, Andrew's identity is clear. He is indubitably "property," as his deceptively affable stepfather Master Polkinghorne characterizes him, but he has both real and symbolic capital. Notwithstanding his metaphysical view of the world, Andrew learns that economic relations structure everything, so that in another Johnsonian reversal of slave-narrative conventions, it is not only Andrew's esoteric education that will prove to be oddly commodifiable within the slave economy, but his sexuality as well. In a provocative gender reversal, the very cerebral and sensual Andrew is subjugated to the exorbitant demands of a sexually obsessed, hysterical mistress named Flo Hatfield (her plantation is called Leviathan); his servitude in the Big House is described in salacious, parodic detail as being as arduous and arbitrary as that of any "field nigger." As Andrew puts it, fully aware of how this will play in certain quarters, "It would have been easier to pick cotton" (61). In a crucial moment of misreading, however, in which he physically expresses rage and frustration at his condition and oversteps a boundary with Flo, he is brought up short and relegated to his proper position in the master-slave dialectic.

Such episodes propel the plot forward and broaden Andrew's subjective and cultural formation, reinforcing the blending of genres that constitutes the slave narrative's patrimony. According to the norms of the bildungsroman, Andrew must leave home (even if that home is a slave plantation), go out into the world, have experiences, and achieve social integration, physical liberation, and spiritual enlightenment. Indeed, in a variety of generic contexts, as Johnson interrogates the problem of interchangeability as well as reproducibility, the "original" is counterposed with its translation, producing a double reading, and the differences are always both provocative and instructive. As the narrative progresses, structure and event are incongruously juxtaposed and often at odds with each other; toward the end of the narrative, nearly dulled by having finally achieved the pleasures of conventional (i.e., white) domestic bliss without being either identified or caught, Andrew addresses the reader: "But what came to pass, as you've probably guessed, was quite another story" (147). Although Andrew does make the passage from bondage to freedom, he does so by transgressing the laws of both racial and generic purity: by only somewhat ambivalently passing as a white man and by traversing genres and modes as diverse as comedy, romance, melodrama, satire, picaresque, allegory, bildungsroman, and the Zen parable.[19] The novel draws on references to authors and texts as far-reaching as Melville's *Pierre, The Odyssey, Oedipus Rex*, Hobbes's *Leviathan*, Franklin's *Autobiography*, Hegel, Schopenhauer, Thoreau, John Stuart Mill, Sir Walter Scott, Harriet Beecher Stowe, William Wells Brown, and Kafka, and it even includes an anachronistic encounter between Andrew's Transcendentalist tutor Ezekiel Sykes-Withers and Karl Marx.

Throughout the narrative, Andrew is haunted by his ancestral past: he struggles to expiate the guilt he feels for having betrayed both his father and his Afrocentric values by passing over into the "White World" (Johnson's capitalization), and for his inability to save his first love, Minty, from slavery and then from an excruciating death from its effects. Ironically, his father's last words to him—that he *could* pass if he wanted to, in an act of voluntary, if passive, identification with his white side—might actually have given Andrew the idea of passing in the first place. But that testament is not intended to be a recommendation. In this scene of inheritance, the legacy is tribal, and it carries with it an unequivocal obligation to his people; turning his back on the Race would set the "world-historical mission of Africa" back (21), instead of helping to push it forward. When his father says, "Be y'self" and Andrew swears he will, the problematic nature of that seemingly simple promise has only begun to be explored. For, of course, the question for Andrew is and will always be: what *is* that self to whom he is supposed to be true? And is it black or white? As for Minty, the slave girl he sought to marry, it is Andrew's desire to see her free that ignites his "urgency for freedom" (101), and sends him out from Cripplegate and on his picaresque journey.[20] When the paths of Andrew and Minty cross again, Minty is on the auction block, a used, abused, and diseased piece of property whose fortunes have severely declined since their separation, whereas Andrew is now in the position to buy her, though under totally fraudulent pretenses.

His father and Minty, both figures of blackness ineluctably associated with slavery and suffering, die so that he can live. Andrew faces in gruesome form what he has abandoned in order to be free (Minty decomposes before his eyes) and acknowledges that, though he has been spared the horror and violence that pervade the lives of most slaves and that things have turned out well for him, he has debts to the past, "duties I must discharge, if I am ever to be free" (161).

Existence Precedes Essence

Johnson is, above all, preoccupied with the existential aspects of slavery, with slavery as a fatal modality of consciousness, as allegorized in the figure of the Soulcatcher, Horace Bannon. When Andrew meets Bannon for the first time as the slave lover of Flo Hatfield, he is in the process of seeking to buy his freedom. Bannon identifies him as a runaway slave he is looking for and already designated as his prey by virtue of a racial syllogism. "These things interest me, you see," Bannon explains, "because one drop of black blood makes a Negro, and Negroes are mah trade" (68). By intricately examining the metaphysical condition of what it means to be enslaved and resisting the comforting resolutions of such staple oppositions as ignorance and knowledge, bondage and freedom, and black and white, the novel consistently questions the transcendental signifier of racial subjectivity that underwrites the slave narrative and posits instead a notion of identity and genre that is fluid, polymorphic, and truly transcultural. Later, in one of the most moving, unsavory, and harrowingly comic scenes in contemporary American literature, the bounty hunter describes his modus operandi for capturing a runaway Negro slave—especially one who is passing.

Indeed, Andrew's moves across and between racial and generic boundaries are nothing if not fluid. (It is worth noting that in all his peregrinations, Andrew never crosses what is considered to be every slave narrative's most crucial boundary: the Mason-Dixon line. The radical message is that he doesn't have to: his true freedom doesn't depend on it.) And yet, while endless self-invention and renewal are an integral part of the pragmatic and romantic ethos of American individualism, and even of slave narratives— as the ending of Douglass's *Narrative* demonstrates so dramatically—there are racial lines that are not to be crossed. When Andrew, the product of what he calls a "pansophical education" (128), reflects with bemused distance on his newfound situation as an overqualified white English composition teacher in Spartanburg, South Carolina, he confesses to being "pleased to be employed. . . . I was no less pleased that my passage into the White World went unmarked. The ease with which I buried Andrew Hawkins forever and built a new life as William Harris was not peculiar" (128). Having perfected what can only be called the art of accommodation, Andrew's outwitting of the "peculiar institution" is impressive, though, ironically, premature. Part of the ruse includes having his less sanguine friend Reb the Coffinmaker pass as his slave. The ease and sense of well-being Andrew associates with his slipping into whiteness is explained by the laws of minoritarian logic, of double consciousness: there isn't anything about being white that he hasn't always known.

In Andrew's case, "love conquered the illusion of race" (170) through Peggy, an iconoclastic white woman with an insatiable intellectual curiosity, incisive wit, and profound decency, who domesticates most of life's external dangers for him. In return, Andrew enhances what had undoubtedly been her unbearably prosaic life before he arrived on the scene. Peggy's capaciousness and her strange willingness to suspend all inquiry concerning Andrew's past are linked to her own misfit status and her otherness as a reader of books and writer of stories, and to her almost palpable desire for the kind of radical, racial alterity that only one genre—romance—can provide. Here, Johnson explicitly presents race and genre as analogous and interrelated, as enabling and disabling devices for negotiating the world, as well as this very text. One could say that this portrait of a marriage is a model of racial and generic intersubjectivity; what constitutes romance for her is realism for him.[21] Indeed, it may explain the structure of their mutual attraction. In a conversation in which someone tells Andrew that Peggy is not living "entirely in the real world" (cannily characterized by Andrew as "the White World"), in a somewhat sentimentalized white projection of lost ideals and utopian fulfillment, it is also parenthetically proposed that "the Negro *is* a creature of romance" (127). So closely does Andrew, passing as William Harris, fulfill Peggy's literary fantasies that she might actually believe that she has created him and single-handedly abolished the evils of slavery through their happy home.

With all the pieces of the plot now in place, what remains for the conjugal scenario to be fully realized and Andrew's freedom to be achieved is a final confrontation with Bannon the Soulcatcher. That inevitable, eerie encounter with his destiny that I referred to earlier has cast a nearly gothic pall over all Andrew's actions. If the Agent of Death's complex characterization and performance brilliantly illustrate Johnson's view of racial subjectivity as being to a critical degree a matter of address and attribution, it nonetheless demonstrates that identity/identification, while inseparable from language, is anything but a surface act:

From the get-go, hours before Ah spot him, there's this thing Ah do, like throwin' mah voice. Ah calls his name. The name his Master used. . . . Mah feelin's, and my voice, fly out to fasten onto that Negro. . . . You *become* a Negro by lettin' yoself see what he sees, feel what he feels, want what he wants. . . . You nail his soul so he can't slip away. Even 'fore he knows you been watchin' him, he's already in leg irons. When you really onto him . . . you tap him gently on his shoulder, and he knows; it's the Call he's waited for his whole life. His capture happens like a wish, somethin' he wants, a destiny that comes from inside him, not outside. . . . Ah never finish the kill 'til the prey desires hit. (115)

This thick translation of the terrifying landscape of the slave hunt—with its dogs, swamps, chains, and whips—concentrates instead on the far more insidious psychic legacy of slavery as internalized assent.[22] "The Call" is represented as if it were indeed a spiritual vocation, a performative utterance requiring a response in kind to be realized. The meanings exchanged between the Soulcatcher and his prey do not promise initiation but fateful resolution, prepared through a carefully choreographed dance of death, in which the Negro body is merely an occasion for an event ultimately enacted in language, most precisely and individually in the vocative: "There's this thing Ah do, like throwin' mah voice. Ah calls his name. The name his Master used . . . and he knows; it's the Call he's waited for his whole life" (115).

Johnson is also signifying on the slave narrative's commonly obscured affiliations with other literary genres and identity models. *Oxherding Tale*, as the narrator explains in his first "intermission," is certainly related both formally and genealogically to the conversion narrative. But in this generic translation, the story of the sinner's/slave's conversion from one state or condition to another, the ascent from ignorance to knowledge, from bondage to freedom, is pushed to the extreme. Here the very boundary of identity itself—defined as the possibility of being freed from one's previous state so as to pass over into another—is conceived of as an act of individual agency grounded in a transaction with the Other, who is, of course, an aspect of one's Self. In conventional slave narratives, the slave must escape pursuit and capture by the slave catcher, who stands in for the master, to cross the line into freedom. But the point in *Oxherding Tale* is that the Soulcatcher cannot be eluded, because he is, for all intents and purposes, fundamentally *metaphysical.* Both the master and the slave live within each of us until our role in the "cosmic drama" (173) has been fully played out, when the dialectic of identification and alterity comes to its proper end—total intersubjectivity—by absorbing everything.

Thus, in their final confrontation, the Soulcatcher responds to Andrew's question, "You *are* Death?" by saying, "The promised death, yes, sweetah even than the poetry of liberation" (170). If slavery—or death—is the path of least resistance in a world obsessed with race, an even more cynical reading of Johnson's view is that to submit is merely a failure of imagination and a fundamental act of complicity with what is most base and inert in human thought (although this may be true of both masters and slaves, it has disturbing implications for its real historical victims). Johnson refuses to conceive reflexively of slavery in exclusively racial or even corporeal terms; this is made most strikingly clear in the ultimate showdown with the Soulcatcher, where chattel slavery is understood to be a metaphor for the affinity among all types of bondage and emancipation its mode of release. It turns out that the Soulcatcher had met his match and been "bested," not by Andrew, but by Reb the Coffinmaker, who has safely reached Chicago and is now legally free. Reb eludes the Soulcatcher precisely because he is a Negro who had no wants, no desires, and who therefore cannot be destroyed. As Bannon puts it, "Ah couldn't entirely become the nigguh because you got to have . . . —an image of yoself—fo' a real slave catcher to latch onto" (174). There was nothing to nail, he says with anachronistic panache: "[He] was like smoke. . . . He wasn't *positioned* nowhere" (173–74).

What saves Reb and makes him the hero of this postmodern tale—his inessentialism—is what kills George, Andrew's father, who is the perfect prey for Bannon. Categorically different from George's oedipal legacy to his biological son, Reb's legacy to Andrew is accepted as a claim that is not attached to guilt and, hence, carries no debt. In addition to the road he paves for Andrew's freedom by besting Bannon, this is a form of liberation in itself. Having found a slave he couldn't catch, the Soulcatcher formally retires from his chosen profession, but there is still unfinished business. "Rupture" and "betrayal" are terms waiting to be redefined. Andrew needs to confront his past and mourn the death of his father before he can be released from his bonds; he needs to know whether his father hated him for passing. Bannon shows Andrew his chest, a "flesh tapestry" in which, grotesquely and beautifully, every image of life and death is inscribed, including the images of both Andrew and his father, who, in the process of having doubled and exchanged places, have been reincarnated. "[N]othing was lost in the masquerade" (175), "all is conserved; all" (176), Andrew says of this vast, ever dynamic, transfigurative view of history and memory, which for Johnson *is* the principle of life. Bringing "all" the cosmic strands together in their irreducible multiplicity, Andrew closes his remarkable story of survival simply and irrefutably, having put his ultimate faith in the telling: "This is my tale" (176).

Gender, Genre, and the Discourses of Slavery in Buchi Emecheta's *The Slave Girl*

> The way back is lost, the one obsession.
> The worst is over.
> The worst is yet to come.
> —Carolyn Forché, "The Testimony of Light"

Generic translations remind us that we cannot witness slavery through a unitary prism—historical, national, cultural, ideological, racial, or sexual. The dangers of doing so are glaringly apparent in David Brion Davis's classic account of the historical problems of defining slavery "in Western culture." As he puts it, certain "nagging contradictions . . . originate in the simple fact that the slave is a *man*" (*PSWC*, 31). Davis's point is designed to highlight the paradox of the dignity of "man" and his commodification; and "man" means *not* an animal or a thing but a universalized rather than gendered human being.

In the lines that follow the emblematic formulation, however, "man" takes on more specific gendered connotations and the slippage between the universal and the gendered meaning of the terms is crucial:

In general it has been said that the slave has three defining characteristics: his person is the property of another man, his will is subject to his owner's authority, and his labor or services are obtained through coercion. Since this description could sometimes be applied to wives and children in a patriarchal family, various writers have added that slavery must be "beyond the limits of family relations." (*PSWC*, 31–32)

Davis's formulation writes off one form of enslavement against another, privileges one version of experience over another. A reader sensitive to a more diffuse collection of "nagging contradictions" notices that effacing gender as a category of analysis here has enormous, long-range implications. A logical sleight of hand makes it possible to acknowledge that the practice of slavery crosses structural boundaries and intersects with other forms of patriarchal domination—while dismissing the real and theoretical consequences of that realization. It has obviously been easier to preserve the abstract universalist pretensions of the concept of slavery as extrafamilial, nondomestic oppression than to question the epistemological (in this case, Eurocentric *and* gender) bias underlying the notion of what constitutes "family relations" in a particular society. (Oh, that's not slavery, that's family!) Despite or perhaps because of the rich and textured exchange that surrounds slavery as an originating cultural narrative, it remains a point of convergence for exclusionary, insular, and arbitrary readings.

Thus the counterintuitive question is: what is gained by reading contemporary literary texts about slavery through the lens of translation, by reading them as examples of intercultural exchange? All critical coordinates shift dramatically when the context is African slavery in the early years of the twentieth century and the text is *The Slave Girl*.[23] The shift first reveals that the intertextual markers of the slave narrative novel are not only linguistic and national, as Gates suggests—"a sub-genre of American, English, French, and Spanish fiction"—but diasporic. These diasporic intertextual relations redraw the map, crucially, encompassing colonial and postcolonial Caribbean and Latin American writing. An anglophone, postcolonial text, *The Slave Girl* perturbs the relations between nation and race, gender and genre, that figure so strongly in African American slave narratives, including those by women: it subverts any totalizable discourse on slavery. Even as it participates in the premise that all slave narratives are narratives of liberation, *The Slave Girl*'s colonial context fractures many of the thematic, tropic, and structural affinities among nineteenth-century slave narratives and the novel's translation.

For Emecheta, slavery—a fundamental feature of African social and political economy—is inextricably tied to sexual oppression, a specific and traditional form of oppression that was reinforced and extended through the more generalized subjugation of African peoples by Europeans; but the terms of this oppression must be relativized, localized, historicized. Unlike the occidental export slave trade, which valued men for their productive capacities, the great majority of slaves within the internal African market were women and children; women were in higher demand and generally more valued, less because of their reproductive capacities than because they performed a high amount of productive labor in African society. Of course, the importance of women's roles within the system did not preclude devaluation of gender and marginality of status. Women's submissive socialization and the outsiderness that always characterizes the slave point to the crucial and diverse function of women in real as well as symbolic slave economies. My purpose here is not to compare slavery in the Americas to the complex variety of African slavery; to do so would only implicitly reinforce the idea that African slavery was a particularly "benign" (read, deviant) version, since it did not correspond to the Western model. Rather, I prefer to redirect attention to the uses to which such monological discourses on slavery can be put, namely, the Eurocentric stereotypes and images of slavery, struggle, and freedom that until recently were for Western anthropologists and historians (and even literary critics) the norm against which non-Western institutions and practices were identified, named, measured.[24]

By comparison, a postcolonial novel about indigenous slavery in colonial Nigeria by an African woman writer further complicates the Western contemporary discourse on slavery, precisely because Emecheta's enslaved heroine would seem to fulfill the requirements of what Cynthia Ward calls "a unified representation of the perfectly other 'Other'—black, female, colonized." Yet how this "authentic" African female subject is "othered" depends, as it always does, on who is doing the "othering" and from which theoretical position. When Emecheta—who has played a major role in the global marketplace of women's literature in English—translates a set of intelligible African cultural terms for consumption by Western readers, they become utilized by criticism "available in the United States" differently. According to Ward, the West interprets Emecheta's novels as "feminist parables," while "appropriating the 'African woman's experience' as part of a universal liberatory discourse" without "regard for issues that concern African literary critics." By contrast, "'African' readings of Emecheta seek to situate her work within the African literary canon . . . rejecting the imposition of neocolonial—European and North American—values and imperatives, including feminism" (that is, critical of individualist-inflected imperial feminism).[25]

Such divergent attempts to press Emecheta's writing into essentialist service of one kind or another make clear that her representation of African women is neither unequivocal nor reducible to a singular perspective; indeed, her fiction is saturated with such sharp irony that it challenges any particular ideological agenda. Emecheta is credited, quite appropriately, with "bringing the Nigerian novel by women onto the stage of world literature."[26] Her texts insist on the global implications of how women's roles are to be interpreted.

Domesticating Slavery

Beginning with the prologue's function—the panoramic unfolding of a physical landscape—the third-person narrator of Emecheta's *The Slave Girl* insists rather didactically (as if translating a set of cultural terms for a foreign audience unfamiliar with the lexical territory) on specificity of place, history, subject, and the forces that connect them. Although Emecheta certainly does not mitigate the devastating effects of foreign intrusion into native traditions or the horrors of colonial domination, her novel offers an ironic warning to those who choose to forget that "slavery begins at home." The double entendre of the word "home" figures powerfully in a narrative set against the backdrop of colonial rule, in which an African child is sold into slavery by her older brother in her own land after the premature death of her parents. The novel's title, resonating with the titles of the many African American slave narratives that precede it, suggests the divestment of individual identity by the overarching category of "slave girl," but the far-reaching implications of the protagonist's enslaved condition are not grasped by the reader until the final paragraph, when Emecheta's narrator directs her attack on the patriarchal institution of marriage and the status of women in Igbo society.

Emecheta's novel portrays "naive" Igbo tribal life in Ibuza at the dawn of the twentieth century, some time after the abolition of the Euro-American slave trade. The narrator maintains a consistently ironic tone; her epic perspective situates the narrative at the privileged point of intersection of history and myth, both temporally and spatially inside and outside the system.

[T]he people of Ibuza—at a time when it was glorious to be an Englishman, when the reign of the great Queen Victoria's son was coming to its close, when the red

of the British Empire covered almost half the map of the world, when colonisa-
tion was at its height, and Nigeria was being taken over by Great Britain—did not
know that they were not still being ruled by the Portuguese. The people of Ibuza
did not realize that their country, to the last village, was being amalgamated and
partitioned by the British. They knew nothing of what was happening; they did
not know that there were other ways of robbing people of their birthright than by
war. The African of those days was very trusting. (15)

This is a classic description of what Abdul JanMohamed has delineated as
the "dominant," as distinguished from the "hegemonic," phase of colonialism; the dominant phase "spans the period from the earliest European
conquest to the moment at which a colony is granted 'independence.' . . .
During this phase the 'consent' of the natives is primarily passive and indirect." It is precisely the "colonizer's ability to exploit preexisting power
relations of hierarchy, subordination, and subjugation" within the indigenous society that makes his domination of the native so insidious. As economic and social practices, slave trafficking and female subjugation were
superimposed on African structures that were already in place. By contrast,
JanMohamed argues, "in the hegemonic phase (or neocolonialism) the natives accept a version of the colonizers' entire system of values, attitudes,
institutions, and modes of production. . . . The natives' internalization of
Western cultures begins before the end of the dominant phase." Emecheta
here provides many examples of the "contradictions between the covert
and the overt aspects of colonialism."[27]

Ojebeta, the first daughter in her family to have survived beyond the
first few minutes of life, is born into this political context. Although girls
were not "normally particularly prized creatures," Ojebeta is especially
cherished by her parents; her singularity is a sign of her preciousness. To
ensure that "she remains in the land of the living," her father journeys to
Idu, the mythological name for the old Benin empire, "said to be situated
at that point where the blue sky touched the earth, [where] the people of
Idu were the last humans you would see before you came to the end of the
world" (20). He returns with special charms and rattles designed for the
baby girl to wear to frighten away her friends from the land of the dead,
who will want to spirit her back to the other world.[28] At a time when, as the
narrator says, "there was little division between myth and reality," between
the microcosmic world of the village and the mysterious realms that extend
beyond it, Ojebeta's father's arduous but successful journey takes on fatally
symbolic overtones. While the mystical powers of the charms suggest that

Ojebeta's life is symbolically overdetermined, their range of influence is limited; they will not protect her from the threats of the material world. The degree to which she is loved by her father represents the monetary value placed on her by her brother in the absence of protective parents.

The 1918 influenza epidemic kills her parents as well as many others in the village. At first ascribed to "natural" causes, the narrator soon makes it clear that "Felenza" is "white man's death": "they shoot it into the air, and we breathe it in and die" (25). Moving in and out of this self-contained conceptual world into the larger geopolitical sphere of events, the narrator attempts to make sense of this strange and violent incursion. Finally, she provides a concrete but no more assimilable account of chemical warfare waged by the superpowers of World War I:

Most people living in the interior of Nigeria did not know that the whole country now belonged to the British who were ruling them indirectly through the local chiefs and elders. Now, in the year of 1916, the rumors said that the new colonial masters were at war with their neighbours the "Germanis"; and the latter fought the British by blowing poisonous gas into the air. . . . Many inside Ibuza were asking themselves what they had to do with the Germanis, and the Germanis with them. There was no one to answer their questions. (27)

When Ojebeta's father is stricken, her mother is "confined to her hut like a prisoner until her months of mourning were over" (29); although exempt from death herself, the child is surrounded by it. Indeed, in the scene in which her mother has died in the night, she literally sleeps in its arms. Snuggling close to her mother's breast in the early morning hours, seeking "warmth, reassurance, and protection" (28), Ojebeta lies unaware that now only a spirit occupies the maternal space.

While taking care not to attribute the child's subsequent enslavement to any one cause, the narrator establishes a connection between the devaluation of subjectivity within colonialism's extensive representational network and the domestic devaluation of females within the patriarchal family and Igbo society generally. If not for the attention paid to historical context and concrete detail, this narrative might begin to resemble a folk- or fairy tale in which just the right confluence of circumstances creates a vacuum that only evil can fill. In Emecheta's hands, the slave-narrative trope of the journey is ultimately subverted and used for different ends; it also prefigures Ojebeta's passage from childhood to womanhood. For Florence Stratton, who reads *The Slave Girl* as a female bildungsroman, an archetypal story of entrapment, the sexual suggestiveness of this particular journey marks a crucial inversion of human development. Tragically, the contours of Ojebeta's life shrink as she moves "from autonomy and self-assertion to dependency and abnegation, from the freedom and fullness of girlhood into the slavery and self-denial of womanhood."[29] Whereas her father's arduous quest involves risking his life to save Ojebeta, her brother Okolie, at first opportunity, sacrifices her for his own gain. At seven years of age, Ojebeta is deceived into believing that she and her brother are taking a day trip to Onitsha, one of Africa's central markets, to visit a relative who has married out of her tribe. Instead, after hiking for miles, "through various kinds of forests, wading streams, and being ferried in a canoe" (46), they reach clusters of brightly colored stalls. In a painfully protracted scene in which the "small, helpless, and terrified child" is treated as a commodity in the human bazaar—sold for the few pounds her brother needs for his coming-of-age celebration—Emecheta plays the pathos of the child's situation against her older brother's despicable weakness.

Throughout the transaction, Okolie is coolly observed through the eyes of the cosmopolitan female merchant who understands the "true" value of things and people. He is depicted as a greedy and foolish village farmer whose social pretensions and crude manners merit ridicule; his behavior there provides an afternoon's entertainment for all. That his personality defects transcend the limitations of his rural background and are not circumstantial but essential is later borne out, when neither his marriage nor his business dealings prove fruitful. It seems important that his moral failure be contrasted with the strength of Ojebeta's character and intelligence, so that even as a slave she surpasses him. The irony has a double twist, however, because although Okolie never achieves anything, his failures could only be realized at Ojebeta's expense, so to speak; in the end and regardless of everything, gender overwrites subjective possibility. When Ojebeta's charms are cut off, signifying to her and the outside world that she has lost her connection to her dead parents and her previous identity, the reader knows that her brother's betrayal is complete. His characterization as a pathetic but not malicious human being is tied to Emecheta's general portrayal of colonized men as self-centered, vain, and childish, sometimes even well-intentioned, but crucially susceptible to delusions of power and the lures of immediate gratification, be they sensual or material. Ultimately, men are weak, propped up by a system that reinforces their self-delusions. Only Ojebeta's father is exempt from such categorical derision.

Using the technique of free and indirect speech—"He had never sold anyone before and now he persuaded himself that what he was about to do was not selling in its actual sense" (37)—the narrator outlines the differences between the buying and selling of human beings for foreign white markets, an internal commercial system that depended on thriving labor, and a class system based on acquired wealth, but not without reminding the reader of the links between them. Hours after he sells his sister into slavery, Okolie in his attitude and bearing recalls "those days when it was easy for the European to urge the chief of a powerful village to wage war on a weaker one in order to obtain slaves for the New World" (73). One wealthy female trader justifies domestic slavery as a social service as well as an economic necessity: "Where would we be without slave labour, and where would some of these unwanted children be without us?" The narrator's response is short, its tone sharp: "It might be evil, but it was a necessary evil" (64). Hence the reader is apprised that it was within the brother's power and right to sell his younger sister into slavery, that it was neither illegal nor culturally unsanctioned, but that the act was to be understood, nonetheless, as an emotional betrayal or a familial transgression. Indeed, it appears that when certain kinds of kinship relations are overdetermined, kinlessness and exploitation go hand in hand; Emecheta indicates that it is precisely the slippage between kinship and abuse that enabled indigenous slavery to exist.

What is "selling in its actual sense"? A young African man about to exchange his seven-year-old sister for money measures his action against a fixed standard, and, moved by his own rhetorical argument, concludes that his (trans)action can be distinguished from "selling in its actual sense." Especially ironic because structured as a negative assertion—"He had never sold anyone before and . . . he . . . was not selling . . ."—the older brother's exercise in critical self-deception is an exemplary moment in *The Slave Girl* that must be read in a broader, comparative context. Is the crime here, as well as the motivation, economic? Is slavery an affliction with multiple varieties? How do different cultural narratives about national, social, and individual identity, sameness, and difference frame our "sense" of slavery? And how does a gendered approach to issues of subjective agency and possibility, economics and social structure, power, property, and propriety ("le sens propre du terme") change the character of such an inquiry, especially in the twentieth century (by North American criteria, a postemancipation era)?

For Ojebeta, the transition from security to slavery is psychologically wrenching. Unlike African American narratives in which slavery fuels a rural agricultural economy and emancipation means escaping the terrors of the southern plantation for the perils of the northern city, an immediate opposition is established here between the poor tribal ways to which Ojebeta was accustomed and the busy, sophisticated urban life to which she must adapt. As a slave, Ojebeta sleeps in special quarters and works with other slave girls as a seamstress. Her wealthy black mistress is represented as cunning and complicitous with the powers that be and have been; formerly the concubine of a Portuguese man, she owns one of the largest textile stalls at the Onitsha market, which serves as the commercial center for the entire region. She traffics in human labor but is portrayed as a kind of benign despot: she cares about her slaves. The cruelties of slavery are not mitigated in this portrait of an African slave girl's existence, but they have a human face—that of the harsh but caring surrogate mother, Ma Palagada, who strives to create a version of an extended family, supported somewhat by her husband, Pa Palagada.

Emecheta's detailed and carefully drawn depiction discloses slavery's structural and functional aspects, but she seems concerned ultimately with the ways in which women have internalized their sexual subjugation. She represents slavery not only as a signifier of social status or position, or even a particular historical destiny, but as a psychic condition, a way of being. Thus there are no rhetorical indications here that the narrator knows more than she chooses to tell, that she is censoring, protecting the reader from worse revelations, or that she is negotiating the limits or boundaries of what can be represented, as is often the case in African American slave narratives, most notably in Harriet Jacobs's *Incidents in the Life of a Slave Girl.* It is surely a fundamental aspect of Emecheta's agenda in this third-person narration to show that there is no gap between the slave's lack of subjective agency and her capacity to express. Under this system, the limitations of female experience and slave consciousness are synonymous.

The "Civilizing" Mission

Ojebeta's initial sense of estrangement gives way to a sense of belonging to a community; the sororal relations she enjoys with the other slave girls help to compensate for the childhood she has lost. During her years of servitude, Ojebeta is exposed to the "civilizing" effects of education, etiquette, and Christianity. In contrast to the paradigmatic scene of instruction in African American slave narratives, in which the slave is both symbolically and actually empowered by her ascent to literacy, in *The Slave Girl* literacy is not seen as dangerous knowledge; in fact, its effects benefit all the participants in the system. The fact that Ma Palagada's slaves know how to read enables her to charge more for the dresses they make; her profits and prestige increase; not only do her slave seamstresses copy European fashions for the wealthy women in the region, but they themselves also wear silk to church on Sundays for all to see. The irony is that, instead of providing the slave girl with the means to conceptualize and, one would assume, seek her own freedom, education here signals socialization into a colonially inflected system of cultural values. By highlighting the development of her slave heroine's social and intellectual abilities, Emecheta introduces new variants into what seemed to be a closed system, including the exercise of relative choice in a world where none would seem possible. When Ma Palagada dies, chaos ensues, and Ojebeta has the chance to run away and return to her people.[30] Ojebeta suffers the death of her mistress "as if she had been her real mother," weighs alternatives, and decides that "she would rather go back to Ibuza and eat the mushrooms of freedom than stay in this house and eat meat in slavery" (146–47). Deviating sharply from African American slave narratives and defying the expectations of readers familiar with them, the escape itself is described in a few lines and with no special significance accorded this symbolic passage beyond the expected emotional stress Ojebeta experiences.

Ojebeta is welcomed warmly when she returns to her village and is celebrated for the polish and sophistication she has acquired; she carries herself differently from Ibuza women and speaks like a girl born in Onitsha, "with rounded 'Rs' and a slowness of delivery, each word drawn out" (107). Others refer to her nine years of slavery as if she had spent them at finishing school—an attitude that recalls Andrew's characterization of the accommodation strategies of the postbellum African American slave narrator. Although her brother is severely criticized by the people in the village for his greedy act, they regard this malevolent act as having produced a positive outcome. However, as Ojebeta's practices and beliefs begin to diverge sharply from those of the community, she feels a strange ambivalence: great affection slightly undermined by a sense of her own cultural superiority. As Emecheta notes, "So afraid was Ojebeta that all she had learned at Ma Palagada's would be wasted that she prayed to God to send her an Ibuza man who had experience of the white man's work and would know the value of what she had learned" (154). Now an enthusiastic member of the Church of England, she finds a group of friends who deem it stylish to take European names; soon Ogbanje Ojebeta becomes Ogbanje Alice, an ironic invocation of the act of renaming so central to African American slave narratives. Emecheta suggests that Ogbanje Alice is too naive to understand how deeply susceptible she is to competing and contradictory ideologies of power.

The narrative moves rather abruptly to its next stage. When Ogbanje Alice meets Jacob—a gentle, educated man who lives and works in Lagos (that is to say, does white man's work) and has returned to his village to look for a girl to marry—the reader knows that a match is imminent. For them to marry, however, Ojebeta's two older brothers must give their permission. More crucially, they must determine Ojebeta's bride price. After some negotiations, the marriage takes place and the couple's conjugal life begins happily enough. The narrator's well-placed comments about "the eternal bond between husband and wife being produced by centuries of traditions, taboos, and latterly Christian dogma" (173), however, cause the reader to suspect that this is not a marriage of equals, in spite of their mutual intelligence and cultivation. And Ojebeta has other problems, one outstanding: she begins to lose her babies, a sign that she has not escaped the destiny of an unredeemed slave. She must be bought back from Ma Palagada's son, who after the death of his mother became Ojebeta's legal owner.

In the penultimate scene in which Jacob pays Clifford, Ma Palagada's son, the eight pounds—the exact sum paid for the child Ojebeta twenty-eight years earlier—Emecheta moves sharply between the characters' thoughts and the words they actually say to each other. Handsome, uniformed Clifford (serving in the British Army in the Great War being fought in Europe) is astonished by the sight of Ojebeta, now "the ghost of the girl he had known so many years ago" (176). No longer the energetic, laughing girl with the straight carriage and jet-black skin, she looks thinner and incomparably older than he could ever have imagined: "Momentarily he wondered what had happened to change her so much?" (176). The implicit response is that she had been eating "the mushroom of freedom." She passes these same moments engaged in self-justification: looking around her one-room home and at her untidy, well-intentioned husband with the red eyes, she confirms that "she would rather have this than be a slave in a big house in Onitsha" (176). After an exchange of superficial niceties, Jacob sends Ojebeta back to the kitchen to finish her cooking so that the men can "finalize the arrangements for her permanent ownership" (177). The transaction completed, Ojebeta's two brothers, husband, and former owner sit down to a meal of steaming rice and hot chicken stew. Since Ojebeta's own position seems to preclude the possibility of self-irony, Emecheta leaves the final commentary on slavery to the narrator: "So as Britain was emerging from war once more victorious, and claiming to have stopped the slavery which she had helped to spread in all her black colonies, Ojebeta, now a woman of thirty-five, was changing masters" (179).

These scathing words indissolubly inscribe Ojebeta's status as a female subject into the larger colonialist narrative, a narrative in which the structure of patriarchy subsumes all others. Using the fictional conventions of slave narratives as well as the autobiographical interventions of slave novels, this postcolonial African author, whose mother's name was Alice Ogbanje Ojebeta, reads the politics of domination from the position of the (daughter of the) twice-mastered native woman. Ojebeta figures metonymically in this narrative *as* the colonized nation, whose status and destiny are ultimately determined by the precolonial meanings attributed to class and gender differences, rather than by any specific colonialist configuration of exploitation or opening up of those differences.[31] When Ojebeta is enslaved, her special charms are cut off, breaking the links to her past identity and enabling her master to constitute a new one for her: slave girl. When Ojebeta becomes a married woman, the sign that she is still a slave and not quite a wife—the link to her previous identity—is her childlessness. Her debased status is therefore unrelated to her actual enslavement, but only to the unfulfilled terms of its contract. Once the exchange value of her body as the site of both productive and reproductive labor is recontextualized, though never questioned, she can assume her social identity as wife, properly understood. So much, says Emecheta's narrative, for liberation.

The Slave Girl's acerbic ending provides yet another twist on the oft-cited line from the conclusion of Harriet Jacobs's *Incidents in the Life of a Slave Girl*: "Reader, my story ends with freedom, not in the usual way, with marriage." For as Jacobs apologizes for not having met the traditional requirements of the domestic novel by "only" achieving freedom and not romance (i.e., marriage), she subverts her readers' expectations of how the plots of both domestic fiction and slave narratives are resolved. By recalling Jacobs's claim that different conditions produce different conventions, Emecheta makes her point all the more painful to consider. What if the story ends with marriage, but not with freedom? What might link the destinies of a nineteenth-century independent and romantic heroine such as Jane Eyre ("Reader, I married him") and Ojebeta, the twentieth-century slave girl? Reading *The Slave Girl* as a text that translates the slave narrative across time and space means reworking an extensive play of textual relations and intersections: between African and New World women's writing, between nineteenth- and twentieth-century postbellum and postcolonial slave narratives, between texts by men and those by women. Attentiveness to the processes of intercultural translation reconfigures a traditional question such as "How might a modern Nigerian novel about slavery have been influenced by North American slave narratives?" into "How might a modern Nigerian novel about slavery affect a contemporary reading of slave narratives?" When the discourses of slavery that are constructed and reflected in nationalist mythologies of literary history are opened up to more diverse interpretations, the limitations of national readings stand out in stark relief. To set up an equation between sexual subjugation and slavery, as Emecheta has done in all her novels, perforce modifies the terms of what constitutes slavery, just as it modifies "patriarchy" in its global as well as local manifestations. Emecheta's poignant and sobering text militates against the reflex toward totalization by rendering in assimilable terms the insidiousness of all systems of bondage and the recuperation, indeed the domestication, of history.

The Textualization of Memory in André Schwarz-Bart's *La mulâtresse Solitude*

> Passive: the un-story, that which escapes quotation and which memory does not recall—forgetfulness as thought. That which, in other words, cannot be forgotten because it has always already fallen outside memory.
> —Maurice Blanchot, *The Writing of the Disaster*

The relationship between the Holocaust and André Schwarz-Bart's *La mulâtresse Solitude*—a novel about exile, slavery, and revolt in the Antilles at the end of the eighteenth century—may appear to be gratuitous, at best oblique.[32] What are the moral and political implications of displacing one narrative into the terms of another, as the author himself has done? What is the nature of this connection and how is it constructed beyond the level of thematization? What kinds of metaphorical equivalences, intersections, and gaps are generated by this extraordinary act of translation? Which interpretive constraints are operative or set into motion, which protective defenses are erected by invoking the Holocaust as a referent or symbol of absolute horror in the context of imaging another people's "singular" catastrophe, especially one that preceded it historically? Might we envision "source" and "target" differently, or has the Holocaust remained a privileged term—rhetorically as well as otherwise incomparable—not applicable, transferable, or iterable?[33] To pursue this line of inquiry is also to weigh in on some of the most enduring and impassioned debates in contemporary theory surrounding the issues of universalism versus particularism and essentialism versus positionality. In exemplary fashion, *La mulâtresse Solitude* presents what has been most crucially at stake in these debates about identity and representation: that which at every moment exceeds the theoretical, yet goes to the heart of the symbolic. By suggesting that singularity can be shared, Schwarz-Bart enters that space of contamination and compromise about which Derrida has theorized in relation to the law of genre: "An absolute, absolutely pure singularity, if there were one, would not even show up, or at least would not be available for reading. To become readable, it has to be *divided*, to *participate* and *belong*. Thus it is divided, and takes *its part* in the genre, the type, context, meaning."[34]

As evidenced by the minimal critical attention given to *La mulâtresse Solitude* since its publication in 1972, finding a place for this estranged, nomadic text—not quite a Holocaust novel, not quite a Caribbean slave narrative—has been remarkably difficult. The problem might not appear to be "merely" a matter of generic classification, but it is my view that, in fact, it is. Schwartz-Bart's amazing extension of boundaries, however ambiguous and ultimately unachieved, raises deeper, thornier questions about racial identity and identification: where does it belong and whose history is it, anyway? For the problem of identity/identification carries with it the interrelated problems of sexual as well as racial political representation and appropriation. Is this account of a central event in Caribbean history (and a peripheral one in the history of metropolitan France) a repetition of French colonialism and black bondage, a cultural and sexual appropriation, as well as a book *about* it? How to read a modern, European white male's efforts to translate into prose the disordered consciousness, the abject victimization of a deeply distressed black woman slave who lived in the Caribbean two hundred years ago? If powerful historical, ideological, and literary-critical constraints have made it impossible to receive this text in more enabling terms, perhaps we can now reexamine the issues it raises and enacts by confronting what is most elusive and discomfiting about it. By offering a revisionary reading of *La mulâtresse Solitude*, my aim here is not to attempt to "resolve" or even defuse the difficulties in the text. Rather, it is to trace its recuperative and exclusionary, disfigurative and transfigurative discursive effects against competing critical notions about subjectivity and identity as they have developed since the end of World War II.

      La mulâtresse Solitude is not the first venture in which Schwarz-Bart, the French-born son of a Yiddish-speaking Polish family exterminated at Auschwitz, has textually or historically linked the victims of the Holocaust and those of the Atlantic slave trade. The novel *Un plat de porc aux bananes vertes* (1967), the dually inscribed, fictionalized life history of a half-blind Martinican servant in a Paris old-age home, was co-authored with his Guadeloupean wife, Simone Schwarz-Bart, and dedicated, emblematically, to Aimé Césaire and Elie Wiesel. The novel was conceived as the first in a cycle about the blacks of Martinique and Guadeloupe from 1760 to the present, of which Solitude was to be the central figure. When *La mulâtresse Solitude* appeared in print, it was designated the inaugural volume, whereas *Un plat de porc aux bananes vertes*, the story of a woman who might have been one of Solitude's descendants, was identified retrospectively as its prelude. Although the collaborative project as a whole was subsequently abandoned, Simone Schwarz-Bart published *Pluie et vent sur Telumée miracle* in 1972, the same year as *La mulâtresse Solitude* appeared. It is perhaps because of all this cross-fertilizing that a sense of authorial indeterminacy hovers over the latter text, at least in the minds of certain bibliographers and critics. However, the means by which scholars have arrived at their different "resolutions" of the "problem of authorship" appear to be symptomatic of something larger.[35] The ongoing critical history of this novel suggests that the set of readers of "Holocaust" literature and the set of readers of "Caribbean" literature define themselves in mutually exclusive terms, and the problem posed by *La mulâtresse Solitude* is that its modes of identification are not reducible to either/or binary terms. A text like *Solitude* demonstrates that the only way out of such a reductive politics of genre is to think translationally and transnationally.

Nonetheless, it is tempting to attribute this "confusion" over joint or single authorship to André Schwarz-Bart's article in *Le Figaro littéraire* (1967) entitled "Pourquoi j'ai écrit *La mulâtresse Solitude*" ("Why I Wrote *La mulâtresse Solitude*"), in which he retraces the path from *Le dernier des Justes* to *Un plat de porc aux bananes vertes* (whose overarching title is *La mulâtresse Solitude*).[36] The referential ambiguity stems, not only from the novels' overlapping titles, but also from the impression given by the use of the past tense that *La mulâtresse Solitude* had been completed; this rich autobiographical meditation reveals instead the unfolding of a process of coming-to-writing-again, the emergence of a work in progress that five years later will become the novel *La mulâtresse Solitude*. It is not merely on the level of an expressed poetics of intentionality that this essay touches and fascinates the reader of *La mulâtresse Solitude*, but as an example of the move toward "diversity" that Édouard Glissant calls "the human spirit's striving for a cross-cultural relationship, without universal transcendence."[37] What is especially striking in Schwarz-Bart's assertion of a principle of interconnectedness between two histories of exile, oppression, and resistance is that it actively seeks to escape the totalizing and essentialist approach to Jewish identity and experience that Holocaust survivors and their texts characteristically—and understandably—embrace.

The *Figaro* article begins in 1955 with Schwarz-Bart's reflection on the nature of his affinity with the émigré Caribbean community in Paris, an affinity originating in a sense of existential identification with a displaced population whose history is haunted by slavery and whose daily lives are plagued by racism and the marginalizing, debilitating effects of colonialism. (Since Martinique and Guadeloupe's "accession" to departmental status in 1946, massive migration to the metropole has produced a phenomenon Glissant calls "genocide by substitution.") It closes with a celebration of collaborative work and the signaling of Aimé Césaire's final approval of *Un plat de porc aux bananes vertes*. Thus, *how* rather than *why* Schwarz-Bart's identification with the African diaspora was translated into literary production—within the context of his intimate relationship with a Guadeloupean woman—serves as the real narrative here.[38]

Supremely conscientious and fearful of violating the integrity of the Other, of appropriating difference for one's own ends, but fully committed to "the possibilities inherent in all communication" (my translation), Schwarz-Bart wrestles with the rhetoric of traditional humanism and is reassured when his undertaking is sanctioned by Alioune Diop, Jacques Rabemananjara, and ultimately Aimé Césaire. His own life and writing steeped in the Jewish tradition of responses to catastrophe, he recounts the immense technical challenge of now combining "vérité historique" and "vérité romanesque," using wholly different coordinates. From both oral and written histories of Guadeloupe, notably those of Oruna Lara and Henri Bangou, he recounts that he found in the mythical-historical *mulâtresse* Solitude a figure capable of carrying the symbolic weight of a narrative devoted to the reconstitution of African Caribbean collective memory.

Schwarz-Bart's commemorative project is, by necessity and design, a form of counterdiscourse. Propelled by the desire to challenge the received or interpretive model—in this case, official French history, which treats Caribbean history as merely a reflection or refraction of its own—it takes as its point of departure the notion that writing is an invocation and that its task is to recover and reclaim that which has been lost, taken away by force, or has yet to be inscribed. In Glissant's account, reminiscent of Foucault's archaeologies, the primal psychohistorical trauma that continues to plague the Antillean imagination is emblematic of an entire cultural condition:

The French Caribbean is the site of a history characterized by ruptures and that began with a brutal dislocation, the slave trade. Our historical consciousness could not be deposited gradually and continuously like sediment, as it were, as happened with those peoples who have frequently produced a totalitarian philosophy of history, for instance European peoples, but came together in the context of shock, contradiction, painful negation, and explosive forces. This dislocation of the continuum, and the inability of the collective consciousness to absorb it all, characterize what I call a nonhistory. The negative effect of this nonhistory is therefore the erasing of the collective memory.[39]

The "ruptures" referred to here are not the result of the experience of slavery as such, but of the "brutal dislocation" that was the transatlantic slave trade, initiated by the Portuguese in the fifteenth century and lasting until the middle of the nineteenth, when slavery was finally abolished in Brazil and the United States. (Actual slavery in the New World continued, however, for another twenty or so years, and in some parts of Africa, forms of slavery still exist.) The prime mover of colonialism, the international slave trade, was "one of the most significant population displacements in the history of humanity, the deportation of somewhere between twelve and fifteen million men and women," of whom a million and a half died in transport.[40] In the collective Caribbean imagination, this original commercial triangle—Europe-Africa-America—functions as a symbolic, if not actual, web of interrelations, signifying multiple origins and affinities based on a shared, tragic discontinuous past.

On the level of metanarrative, Glissant's charge against a "totalitarian philosophy of history" implicitly opposes concomitant assumptions about the writing and reading of history as neutral, objective, comprehensive, and exempt from the conditions that govern other kinds of narrativizing. Of course, whether such histories are seen as "universalist" or "particularist" is a matter of one's position. As marginalized and oppressed groups increasingly view history as the ground on which competing versions of history are fought and relativized, the power that accrues to certain complicit interpretations and investments in those interpretations is contested correlatively. And as C. L. R. James has demonstrated in *The Black Jacobins*, such rewriting can become the script for social change.[41] To press the case further, it may even be a requisite for cultural survival. As postcolonial literatures and theory testify, cultural identity or its extinction may ultimately depend on understanding history and memory, not as static repositories of archival content or unmediated experience, but rather as complex, often conflictual, symbolic, interactional processes.

In the spirit of Nietzsche, who seized so well the idea that competing interpretations can be put to a variety of ideological uses, we note the "life-providing, life-preserving, and perhaps even species-cultivating"[42] potential of current metahistorical narratives that have moved away from equating oppression with passive victimization. Africanist and feminist historians, respectively, have increasingly stressed the role and symbolism of resistance in slave culture, thus challenging racial and sexual stereotypes and showing how subjugated groups exercise subjective agency and resourceful survival strategies even in the most repressive and dehumanizing of systems.[43] In her introduction to a volume of *Nouvelles questions féministes* devoted to the condition of women in the Antilles, Arlette Gautier reaffirms this point in fine: "Did women consent to the horror of slavery or colonial oppression? Although most historians or novelists silently overlook examples of female resistance, others invoke legendary figures such as the famous *mulâtresse* Solitude, Guadeloupean rebel against the reestablishment of slavery in 1804" (my translation).[44] Figured along a continuum spanning imaginative inter-vention and overt revolt, resistance signifies—in its elaboration of appro-priative and subversive emancipatory strategies—changing configurations in identity politics.

History and Memory

In all its variety, literature in the late twentieth century reflects an al-most global obsession with the transmission, preservation, repression, and potential effacement of memory as an instrument of historical conscious-ness. Contemporary theorists and philosophers of history, most notably Pierre Nora, have analyzed, in Nora's words, the "reflexive turning of history upon itself" in a "historical age that calls out for memory because it has abandoned it,"[45] recognizing the marked response of those who have expe-rienced, personally and collectively, the worst horrors of our age and who dread history's tendency to consign to oblivion what Blanchot calls "the un-story, that which escapes quotation and which memory does not recall."

If all writing is a form of memorializing, and contemporary writing especially so, none may be as determined (in every sense of the word) as that which remembers the Holocaust. Beginning with Lamentations, which mourned the Destruction of the First Temple in 586 B.C.E., "the writing of the disaster" has functioned as a collective performative utterance within the Jewish textual tradition, predicated on a fear of remaining unwritten or being written out of history—human or divine—and perceived as an act of group survival. However, when exile—understood theologically to be the transcendent category and historically to be the normative condition of Jewish experience—became genocide in the Final Solution, paradigmatic or archetypal representations were radically challenged. Among Jewish theolo-gians and philosophers debates rage: Is the Holocaust an apocalyptic event, without precedent or analogy in history, a catastrophe unique in nature and degree? Or is it another episode to be absorbed in a long cyclical history re-lentlessly punctuated by suffering and necessarily subject to the same criti-cal models of remythification and ritualization?[46]

This problem, posed in a variety of ways, constitutes one of the prin-cipal themes in Holocaust writing. Schwarz-Bart's *Le dernier des Justes*, which won the Prix Goncourt in 1959 and attracted a wide audience, uses a medieval paradigm to wrestle with the fact that Jews were singled out by racial criteria for extermination by the Nazis.[47] His semi-fictional chronicle of the Levy family of Just Men traces a genealogy based on self-sacrifice and suffering that originates with the suicide of Yom Tov Levy in York in 1185 and ends with the martyrdom of Ernie Levy in the gas chambers at Auschwitz. Sidra DeKoven explains that "[i]n its focus on persecution as the organizing principle of communal memory, *The Last of the Just* is a fictional derivative of the medieval lamentation literature," but that it goes beyond that interpretive tradition by seeking redemption or consolation in human compassion.[48] For Lawrence Langer, the text's desperate effort to situate the crematoria within a design of universal signification is best understood in Ernie Levy's "last instinctive gesture" inside the gas chamber, in which he embraces his friend's body, when he attempts "to vindicate the terror of the present by somehow uniting it with the past." However, parallels and precedents are lacking here; the text signals "the end . . . of a redemptive tradition of suffering," and "the meaning of [Ernie's] death, and that of six million others, is transferred to the imagination of the survivors . . . the only living memorial to Ernie Levy is *The Last of the Just* itself."[49]

Thus, the text's challenge to a tradition steeped in martyrology is precisely its ambivalence; as the narrator declares, "I shall not translate. So this story will not finish with some tomb to be visited in memoriam." Both faith and futility underwrite a prayer for the dead that mourns, blasphemes, and praises divine will all at once. For even as the litany of names of concentration camps recited by the narrator, Ernie's "friend," constitutes a defamation of God's creation and a deformation of his discourse, it is nonetheless a reclamation:

And praised. Auschwitz. So be it. Maidanek. The Eternal. Treblinka. And praised. Buchenwald. So be it. Mauthausen. The Eternal. Belzec. And praised. Sobibor. So be it. . . . (*LJ*, 408)

In an extraordinary final gesture that crosses historical, spatial, and racial boundaries, Schwarz-Bart's *La mulâtresse Solitude* joins the tragic destinies of Caribbean blacks and European Jews by linking two heroic events, one from the French Revolution and the other from the Holocaust: first, a suicidal black slave insurrection against Republican and Bonapartist efforts to reinstate slavery after the Jacobin abolition of slavery in 1794, and second, the suicidal Jewish resistance to the Nazis in the Warsaw Ghetto in 1943. Recounted in the penultimate and final chapters is the celebrated last stand at Fort Matouba, Guadeloupe, of the leader of the insurrection, Louis Delgrés, his three hundred rebels, and the countless women and children who preferred to die rather than surrender to the six thousand French soldiers surrounding them. Recounted also is the butchery that followed this doomed revolt.

The appropriation of this significant event by official French historians and its erasure in Caribbean collective memory are dramatically illustrated in Schwarz-Bart's reconstructed life story of one of the survivors of the resistance, the legendary slave heroine Solitude. Her ultimate fate is already inscribed in the novel's epigraph, a one-sentence entry in Oruno Lara's *Histoire de la Guadeloupe*, the first national history written by a Guadeloupean: "The mulatto woman Solitude was with child at the time of her arrest; she was executed on 29 November 1802, immediately after the delivery of her child."[50] Solitude's legacy is both singular and emblematic: although she did not survive slavery or resistance, her child was "spared" death so as to be preserved for life as a slave.[51]

Solitude's public execution closes Schwarz-Bart's narrative proper, which, reinforced by the logic of analogy and continuity, is sublated in the explicit leap that constitutes the novel's epilogue: here the Matouba slave revolt and the Warsaw ghetto uprising converge symbolically in the imagination of a predisposed contemporary "traveler." Visiting the "remains of the old Danglemont plantation," the site of the battle on the heights of Matouba at the edge of the Soufrière volcano, the traveler comes upon a "remnant of a knee-high wall and a mound of earth intermingled with bone splinters." Because of the teleological terms of the narrative, "traveler" here seems oddly casual and deliberately understated, evoking the archetypal image of the Jewish wanderer, the figure of the nomad who, having no place, finds himself momentarily in this one. But it calls up as well the image of the pilgrim who has come to this site in search of something particular, although everything points to a collective memory "concealed" and "dispersed"; at best, it is randomly buried and dug up again by "the innocent hoes of the field workers." Against this leveling, his meditation attempts a purposeful, meaningful restoration: "If he is in the mood to salute a memory, his imagination will people the environing space, and human figures will rise up around him, just as the phantoms that wander about the humiliated ruins of the Warsaw ghetto are said to rise up before the eyes of other travelers" (178–79). In this tortured landscape of martyrdom and extinction, Schwarz-Bart's vision is a testimony to the sheer will to remember, or the inability to forget, what has happened there. Through a kind of "commemorative vigilance," his transfiguration of the monumental ruins of wall, bone, and ashes makes possible—indeed, creates—what Pierre Nora has called *les lieux de mémoire*. Nora's elaboration of the difference between memory and history depends on the notion that "there are *lieux de mémoire*, sites of memory, because there are no longer *milieux de mémoire*, real environments of memory."[52]

If, as Clarisse Zimra has noted, "in the Caribbean, topography is destiny,"[53] and the volcano is a dominant Caribbean metaphor for both the "explosive" and the "blanked past" of African Caribbean collective experience, then perhaps the Matouba landscape is a text resistant to certain kinds of interpretation. The presence of ashes psychically links two highly dissimilar landscapes (without eliding the distinction between volcanic ashes and those produced by gassed bodies subsequently burnt in crematoria), because what truly connects them is a likeness of effect. "The traveler" invokes that place definitively named by David Rousset in one of the first Holocaust narratives to emerge following the war: a universe in which total, self-contained horror and merciless human devastation have occurred, all the while coextensive with the familiar, quotidian world: "*L'univers concentrationnaire* shrivels away within itself. It still lives on in the world like a dead planet laden with corpses."[54] But, in uniting the image of the phantoms haunting the site of the Matouba slave revolt with the image of the spirits moving about the "humiliated ruins" of the Warsaw ghetto, Schwarz-Bart is memorializing not only persecution, terror, and suffering, as he did in *Le dernier des Justes*, but defiance in the face of certain disaster as well.

The symbolic significance of the Warsaw ghetto uprising insists upon a double legacy: of destruction, certainly, but, more important, of heroic resistance against the final roundup and liquidation of Warsaw's Jewry. Lasting over six weeks and involving more than 50,000 ghetto Jews, only a handful of whom survived, the Warsaw Ghetto Uprising was, "outside of Yugoslavia's national uprising . . . the largest and longest armed resistance in Nazi-occupied Europe during World War II."[55] A monument marks both the place and the event of the uprising. The site has changed drastically over the years, as recounted by James Young:

Dynamited, torched, and then bulldozed by the Germans, the Warsaw Ghetto had been demolished one block at a time. In 1948 all that remained was a moonscape of rubble, piled sixteen feet high, covering hundreds of acres. Anchored in this landscape of debris, the granite blocks in the monument appeared on its unveiling to rise out of the broken stones, emerging from them almost as congealed fragments of the destruction itself. As a singular tombstone rooted in this great burial mound, it seemed initially to draw its strength, massiveness, and authority from its relatively solitary placement amid the very destruction it commemorated. Location would reinforce here the sense of this memorial's link to events as a metonymical fragment of the event it commemorates, not just its displacement. Today the monument still stands alone in a large, well-kept square, but it is now surrounded by block-style apartment buildings, which diminish its earlier monolithic impact. Instead of seeming to pull order together out of the mounds of rubble around it, even being vivified by these ruins, from a distance it is now one rectangular block among many others. The trees, green lawns, and sunbathers during the summer combine to domesticate this memorial a little.[56]

By so strongly identifying with the events and symbolism of the Matouba slave revolt as a place of memory, Schwarz-Bart is drawing upon more than merely a private network of memorial associations. As Sander Gilman has pointed out in his study of "culturally determined patterns of Otherness," Jews and blacks are often seen as analogues of each other. Incorporated into the modern rhetoric of race, the "blackness of the Jew" can be understood as "the synthesis of two projections of Otherness within the same code." The black and the Jew were associated, argues Gilman, "not merely because both were outsiders but because qualities ascribed to one became the means of defining the difference of the other."[57] Such an analysis helps advance the present inquiry because it focuses, not only on the construction of stereotypes by privileged groups, but also on the ways in which the qualities projected are internalized by those so objectified.

The Legacy of Solitude

Schwarz-Bart's indictment of colonialism and slavery is a decidedly genealogical project, in which the history of Guadeloupe is mapped onto Solitude's reconstructed life story. Her story of slavery is a legacy from her mother, one that she passes down to her daughter even in death. But, unlike most narratives about slavery, this text seeks to restore collective memory and dignity by beginning, not with "the one-way passage of the deportation of Africans to the Americas," but with the portrayal of life in precolonial West Africa.[58] Thus, the first of the novel's two sections is entitled "Bayangumay" and is devoted to the childhood and youth of Solitude's mother, Bayangumay; the second, entitled "Solitude," continues in Guadeloupe and treats the two stages of Solitude's life, slavery and *marronnage*. The African point of the triangle figures here, as it does in many French Caribbean texts, as the lost mother from whom Bayangumay will be brutally separated; for her *métisse* daughter Solitude, conceived in violence and confusion, symbol herself of absolute estrangement in the New World, mother Africa remains an abstract object of desire, the unknown continent.

Solitude's own child, fathered by the Mozambican "wandering soul" Maimouni, symbolizes the tragic irony of her sweet but ill-fated momentary reunion with Africa. Not only is Solitude condemned to death, and her execution delayed until she can deliver her child into slavery, but the imprint of exile already marks her unborn offspring. Maimouni "was never able to say what sort of heart he wanted for the child. He could not wish it an African heart, which would be useless in a foreign country, and still less could he resign himself to a white, black, or mulatto heart beating to the obscure rhythm of Guadeloupe" (152–53). Read allegorically, the violation of Bayangumay's body and psyche, her *refoulement* and renunciation of the product of her pain, and Solitude's anomalous beauty and madness—that is, the deformation of the maternal legacy—recounts the narrative of colonial penetration of Africa, the deportation and enslavement of its people in the West Indies, and the overall disorientation of subsequent generations of Antilleans, who continue to struggle to constitute a nonderivative, nonmimetic cultural identity.[59]

Despite the polymorphism and polyvalence woven into the very texture of this quintessentially nomadic narrative, *La mulâtresse Solitude*'s precise blending of discursive elements, practices of myth, folktale, proverb, documentary, and psychological realism, its restrained, detached classical style and its deeply ironic tone produce an effect quite dissimilar from "un style antillais." Put another way, what is absent in its expressive mode is both the tension between and fusion of the written and the oral, French and Creole. Assuming an audience of non-Creole speakers/readers, Schwartz-

Bart presents Creole words or phrases either parenthetically or in translation, as if to stress the problem of cultural transmission. But, whether or not this entails a deliberate strategy, the narrative relies most heavily on formal description and allusion rather than linguistic interpellation: the reader must infer what Maryse Condé has identified as "the civilization of the bossale," the oral heritage of slaves in the Caribbean.[60]

This is evident in Schwarz-Bart's reconstruction of Diola culture in the mid-eighteenth century, opening in the valley of the Casamance River in Senegal, southwest of the Gambia River in Gambia, with a fairy-tale description of cyclical rhythms, oral traditions, and serene beauty: "Once upon a time, on a strange planet, there was a little black girl by the name of Bayangumay. She had made her appearance on earth about 1755 in a calm and intricate estuary landscape, where the clear water of a river, the green water of an ocean, and the black water of a channel mingled—and where, so it is said, the soul was still immortal" (3). Already suggested here is a gently insistent rhetoric of myth in which the tragically ironic perspectives of the fabulist and historian are purposefully interfused. A pervasively lyrical tone, dependence on condensation of image, and frequent ellipses impress a sense of elemental harmony, a density of congruence, spiritual calm, and immanence. This impression is only heightened by the intrusion of Bayangumay's approximate date of birth in the second line, which jars stylistically and functions more as sign than as mere "information." Reference to the Western timeline suggests the imminent, cataclysmic incursion of history. Alerted, the reader learns that in this actual and symbolic geography where water is the generative source, the natural setting for rice-growing, shell-fishing, "shade and quiet luxury," water is also the gateway through which, unbeknown to the spirited young woman coming of age in this chapter, this world is being infiltrated by "the sellers of men" (32), ultimately to be consumed by "the evil that had been instilled in its blood" (31).

The center of the French slave trade in this region was Gorée, a small island sixty days' march northward from their village, a site symbolically charged as the grotesque gateway to transatlantic slavery—"the first step toward madness."[61] Schwarz-Bart, invoking Lamentations, recounts the transformation of the name of Bayangumay's birthplace, "the big city on the river" Sigi, meaning "sit down," into its slave port designation, Sigi-Thyor, meaning "Sit down and weep." The blending of aestheticism and atrocity is also characteristic of certain strains of Holocaust writing. As the slave hunters extend their network and penetrate deeper and deeper into the interior, "the Elders likened the new body of Africa to an impaled octopus losing its substance drop by drop while its tentacles squeeze and rend each other without mercy, as though to punish each other for the stake that traverses them all" (31). For Schwarz-Bart, it is imperative that this absolute *déchirement* be conveyed from its first ravages of consciousness to final dissolution. Thus, he does not gloss over the raid of Bayangumay's village, the fires, the roundup, the massacres, the march "shackled and collared" (36) to the coast, or the captivity in slave pens on Gorée, but attempts to painstakingly render the horror and utter incomprehensibility of these events as perceived by the young woman.

What begins as Bayangumay's dream of death ends with her desperate effort to convince herself that she is human. The narrator's depiction of the grotesque and agonizing experience of the slave transport renders the sense of linguistic, psychic, and physical dislocation from everything familiar; the terror of loss, of sensibility and of identity; the loss of bodily control, the shame and pain. Her rape during the collective bestial ritual of the "Pariade" when the female prisoners, newly washed in seawater but still chained, were given over to the drunken crew, is depicted as a series of disconnected sensations and animist images, for she is haunted by spirits she cannot understand: "Diolas, Diolas, isn't there a single Diola in this fish?" (42). What she does understand, however, in this horrific Babel of languages that was the Middle Passage, in which communication with others was virtually impossible and translation nonexistent, is the process of dehumanization upon which the system of slavery depends. The acuity of her response is rendered in this attempt at simultaneous self-redemption and suicide: "trembling as though with fever, she awoke to her miseries—hunger, thirst, vermin, the lack of air, the smell of others, and the smell of her own feces that had escaped during the night. Yes, she was wholly human and alive again. Inspired by this marvelous thought, she tried to swallow her tongue" (45). Despite three months of sustained practice, she doesn't succeed. Part I of the book closes with Bayangumay composing a dirge "for the absent" in her head and singing out, "Oh give me a message to take to the ancestors" (46)—her last attempt, it would seem, to use her own tongue to express herself with a past she will never recover.

If Bayangumay signifies the intentionality, self-possession, and empowerment drawn from her identity as a Diola, the daughter born to her on the du Parc plantation signifies total divestment, both of tribal identity and subjectivity. As the product of that infelicitous union of the races, Rosalie (whose name, through the mere act of substitution, is taken from the "Permanent Register") has eyes of two different colors: "one dark, and one light-green, as though belonging to two different persons" (50). Indeed, the irreparable split between body and consciousness, history and identity that is reflected in Rosalie's eyes is inscribed in the slaves' own classification system of "saltwater" blacks and "freshwater" blacks. For Bayangumay, renamed "Man Bobette" by her white owners, and the other "saltwater" African-born slaves, the loss of the African homeland is absolute; for the "freshwater" slaves like Rosalie, who are born in captivity, the sense of loss is somehow more destructive because impossible to localize. Thus, in this context, to be *métisse* is to be doubly cursed; scorned by the blacks and rejected by her mother, for whom the child embodies the whites' appropriation of her shame, Rosalie is a more highly valued commodity and thus susceptible to greater exploitation by her masters. The other slaves have another name for her, "Two-Souls," in reference to her differently colored eyes, mixed-race body, and disintegrated psyche. Eventually, after a succession of degenerative metamorphoses, the *mulâtresse*, object of derision and desire, renames herself "Solitude." Ultimately, she triumphs over abjection through an act of solidarity with the rebels of Matouba, by linking her destiny with that of others.

The history of Guadeloupe's collective trauma is represented in the harrowing and heroic story of the *mulâtresse* Solitude. Hovering between schizophrenia and catatonia in an unrelentingly bleak universe, Solitude's range of possibilities is severely limited. Thus, although there is something fundamentally awful about portraying her "militancy" as the expression of an almost vacated subjectivity rather than of agency, to dwell on the implications of such symbolism is to forget that there are many different kinds of revolt. Solitude is the daughter of a woman who, in response to having survived unspeakable horror, tried to swallow her tongue. As a testimony to the struggle for historical memory, this text so obsessed with dispossession is also its own commentary on the disfigurative and mutative effects of exile and cultural nomadism.[62]

*

The traumatic collective experience of slavery has enduring, even inescapable power, which novels that address the most grievous and shameful aspects of that experience, such as Toni Morrison's *Beloved*, explore so pointedly.[63] That a text as tortured and oracular as *Beloved* closes with the thrice-repeated disclosure/injunction "This is not a story to pass on" suggests that this historical burden is fundamentally unutterable, perhaps untranslatable. However, the text's technical exploits attest to the affirmative value of that negative assertion. The story of this burden, and others both like and unlike it, can be assumed and discharged differently with each generation, because the terms of our symbolic contract with the past change with the passage of time. However, as passengers are reminded in air travel, the contents of our cultural baggage may have shifted in flight; although the total weight of the burden may stay the same, we surely do not control how such discontinuous shifts in stress and balance affect the overall diffusion of effects.

By reading translated narratives of slavery comparatively (and hence relatively) against the singular grain, we see how an "original" experience or paradigmatic generic form exceeds its temporal and spatial limits. Such disruptions and displacements are themselves liberating, because they complicate received notions about race, gender, subjectivity, and identity politics in relation to genre and to slavery as a culturally specific or historically defined/conditioned phenomenon. They compel us to examine more closely the presumed congruence between aesthetic form and historical, as well as symbolic, content and the nature of our investment in that congruence. Each of these provocative and perturbing texts implicitly and explicitly pushes from a different vantage point, in a different direction, repositioning the limits of genre. Read through the lens of generic translation, they keep in suspense and in suspension the very issues of similarity and difference, inclusion and exclusion, universalism and particularism that intercultural translation inevitably brings to the fore.

3

Scenes of Inheritance

INTERGENERATIONAL TRANSMISSION
AND IMPERILED NARRATIVES

> Here is a story my mother told me, not when I was young,
> but recently, when I told her I also talk story. The beginning
> is hers, the ending, mine.
> —Maxine Hong Kingston, *The Woman Warrior:*
>   *Memoir of a Girlhood Among Ghosts*

Walter Benjamin's essay "The Task of the Translator" (1926) asserts that translation marks a stage of continued life, of a literary work's potentially limitless afterlife in succeeding generations. Yet, in a dramatic departure from conventional views of translation, Benjamin emphasizes that "no translation would be possible if in its ultimate essence it strove for likeness to the original. For in its afterlife—which could not be called that if it were not a transformation and a renewal of something living—*the original undergoes a change*" (73; emphasis added).[1] In this chapter Benjamin's theory of translation encounters two texts, a French Holocaust survivor memoir by Claude Morhange-Bégué, *Chamberet: Recollections from an Ordinary Childhood* (1987), and a contemporary Nigerian diasporic novel written in English, T. Obinkaram Echewa's *I Saw the Sky Catch Fire* (1992). My reading of that conjunction, as in the previous chapters, is another example of translation, whose sources are Western theoretical frameworks and contexts and whose target is a highly mediated literary construction, Western or not. Here I direct my attention to processes of intergenerational and intercultural transmission, conceived as acts of translation, to how the value of memory or remembrance as an instrument of historical consciousness is inscribed in a culture as conditions and modes of transmission are—in-evitably—altered. What, if not communicable content, what Benjamin calls "information," gets passed on, passed down, or passed across? What connects and divides two generations and their respective cultural narratives, where are the borderlines of a life and a text, what are the ways in which processes of translation perform as well as disrupt the work of cultural memory?

Two aspects of the Benjaminian and Derridean link between translation and survival figure centrally in Morhange-Bégué's memoir and Echewa's novel, and in the following discussion: that the original lives on or after through its translation, and that the bond between the original and its translation is one of reciprocal claim and debt. "The Task of the Translator" proposes a genealogical approach to the bond or relatedness between the original and its translation. Benjamin suggests that this bond is based on the kinship, though not on the resemblances, between (the two) languages: "Translation thus ultimately serves the purpose of expressing the central reciprocal relationship between languages. . . . As for the posited central kinship of languages, it is marked by a distinctive convergence. Languages are not strangers to one another, but are, a priori and apart from all historical relationships, interrelated in what they want to express" (72). What is it in the nature of languages that they want to express, and how is the specificity of their interrelatedness perhaps manifested or demonstrated only by way of translation(s)? Why is translation a privileged—indeed, an exemplary—linguistic procedure? In a celebrated essay on the role of difference in Benjamin's theory of language, Rodolphe Gasché points to the incompleteness of the original:

[T]ranslatability indicates the work of art's search for a fulfillment in something other than the original itself. Translatability . . . calls for a liberation of the work of art from itself . . . a translation implies a displacement, even a disregard of the original's sense. . . . The objective possibility of translation, a possibility that is also a call for it, can thus best be described . . . as a structural feature that, within the work itself, points beyond it.[2]

Thus, says Benjamin, the traditional aims of the translator—to achieve adequation, literalness, and likeness between two languages—are displaced by a more intimate and elusive notion of intention, "which no single language can attain by itself but which is realized only by the totality of their intentions supplementing each other: pure language."[3] Benjamin's concept of "pure language" seems not to refer to a distilled form or ideal or transcendent realm of undifferentiated, unmediated speech that exists beyond translation, but to "languageness" *tout court*. Languages share a mode of being—a striving to mean in language—over and across their semantic, syntactic, and structural differences. In the act of translation, each language is denaturalized, and as each retains its distinction from the other and its internal difference from itself, it recalls the bonds it shares with every other language as language and within language: its communicability and its incommunicability. In Benjamin's early theologically inflected work, language as act is the site of revelation but not necessarily of communication—or at least, not of communication in any instrumental or utilitarian sense. Derrida says that in not seeking to say this or that, translation re-marks its alliances, exhibits its own possibility: "In a mode that is solely anticipatory, annunciatory, almost prophetic, translation renders *present* an affinity that is never present in this presentation."[4]

Trauma Inherited, Trauma Reclaimed in Claude Morhange-Bégué's *Chamberet: Recollections from an Ordinary Childhood*

Don't get me wrong. I wasn't obsessed with this stuff. . . .
It's just that sometimes I'd fantasize Zyklon B coming out
of our shower instead of water.
—Art Spiegelman, *Maus: A Survivor's Tale*

At the end of *Totem and Taboo*, Freud poses the question, "What are the ways and means employed by one generation in order to hand on its mental states to the next one?"[5] By drawing on Freud's inquiry into the nature of intergenerational transmission—conscious, unconscious, telepathic—I am suggesting that culture's necessarily overarching orientation toward the future only obtains by sharing its past. Thinking both psychoanalytically and historically also means that while we harbor the dream of plenitude, we always begin with a gap. How are psychic legacies or testaments—and more pointedly, the traumatic or traumatized kind—constituted and communicated? And, correlatively, in what manner are they received by their designated recipients? In what forms do they then (re)appear?

Since the 1970s, numerous theoretical and clinical studies have appeared that strive to track the effects upon Holocaust survivors' children of the European Jews' massive traumatization resulting from Nazi persecution and extermination. A growing corpus of autobiographical narratives by these children of survivors has emerged as this second generation moves toward middle age and addresses the complex relation between traumatic history and personal identity from its vantage point.[6] What are the modes of transmission of what may be unbound, unintegrated, unshared trauma? How central is spoken and/or written language to such communication? As this chapter aims to demonstrate, a culturally inflected analytical or interpretive model for the transmission of trauma finds its structural parallel in translation.

Consistent with Freud's notion of psychohistory, in which human behavior is seen to be predetermined by the historical past, one foundational psychoanalytic study describes children of survivors as showing symptoms that

would be expected if they [had] actually lived through the Holocaust. They have to deal with the conflictual issue of intrusive images of their parents' suffering and the association between these images and ideas about their own vulnerability to death. They seem to share an anguished collective memory of the Holocaust in both their dreams and fantasies reflective of recurrent references to their parents' traumatic experiences. . . . The children come to feel that the Holocaust is the single most critical event that has affected their lives although it occurred before they were born.[7]

The pathological patterns at work, according to another psychoanalytic study of intergenerational transmission of destructive persecution, are "contagion, imitation, and identification,"[8] metaphorical terms often used to describe some of the less salutary aspects of translation. What features do they share and how do they potentially intersect? It is precisely in the transferential process, in the projection and displacement of identity and meaning, in the mixing of signals and messages, as well as the crossing of boundaries, that the convergence can be seen. And yet, however stark the symptoms of the second generation's syndrome may be, trauma inherited and processed as if it were one's own lived experience is not—all susceptibilities, predispositions, and echoes accounted for—the same as that originating from an actual universe in which fear, suffering, and death were

pervasive. The difference, in fact, seems to produce another kind of survival complex.[9] To complicate and compound the problem of identity and
identification even further, the children of Holocaust survivors are, in
some cases, also child survivors themselves.[10]

Child survivor narratives, most of which have been published in the
past twenty-five years, recount how their authors, children often separated
from their parents, managed to stay alive. They reveal the long-term effects
of such traumatic losses so early in life. One and a half million Jewish children died in the Holocaust; put another way, only 11 percent of the 1.7 million Jewish children under the age of 16 alive in 1939 survived. With the exception of the few who miraculously survived concentration camps, those
were children hidden in convents, orphanages, barns, forests, caves, attics,
cellars, and sewers for months, even years.

The tension between these two positions or typologies is enacted in
Claude Morhange-Bégué's elliptical French Holocaust memoir *Chamberet:
Recollections from an Ordinary Childhood*, which unites the characteristics
of child survivor narratives with those of children of survivors born after
the war.[11] Carefully delineating the identity of each, it speaks from more
than one space of remembrance, from more than one experiential position.
As the title mordantly suggests, firsthand witnessing and recollection of the
Holocaust appear to be its governing intention and dominant perspective,
yet it ultimately seeks to assume the burden of memory for the previous
generation of survivors, and in particular for the narrator's mother, whose
story of heroism and victimization would otherwise be lost were her
daughter not to transmit it through her own story of terror and loss. If this
mode of secondary witnessing compels an exploration of the intricate and
intimate processes of rememoration, it also leaves intact the mysteries of
the imagination.[12]

The primacy of the mother-daughter bond frames this memoir of
traumatic separation—the mother's abrupt departure and long absence,
while the child, Claude, waits for her return. Its paradigmatic connotations
of loss for an understanding of trauma's pivotal role in human experience
immediately suggests Freud's famous example in "Beyond the Pleasure Principle": his grandson Hans's *Fort/Da* game is the means by which the young
child masters the anxiety produced by his mother's departure. The game
consists of endlessly repeating her absence and desired return in the form
of a disappearing and reappearing toy; the child gains a sense, retroactively,

of mastery of the situation, which otherwise would be overwhelming, impossible to bear—an experience whose traumatic character is based on the loss of the sense of control over one's life. As Freud puts it, the child playing the *Fort/Da* game "at the outset . . . was in a passive situation—he was overpowered by the experience; but, by repeating it, unpleasurable though it was, as a game, he took on an active part."[13]

The "child" narrator's account begins in April 1944: "When I was not quite eight years old they came and took my mother away from me." Claude's mother is a Jew and a member of the Resistance who has been interrogated and arrested by the Gestapo after her denunciation by the only other doctor in the Vichy-governed village of Chamberet in central France. Only a rescue organized by two schoolteachers, the town clerk, and a dressmaker spares her from deportation along with her mother to the French transit camp Drancy and then to Auschwitz. Had it not been for their rescue, she says, "chances were that I would be turning into a little pile of ashes in a partially drained swamp on the confines of Germany and Poland." Morhange-Bégué attempts to reconstruct a scene of mystifying terror, "to put into words something that there is no name for but which lies within human grasp all the same."[14]

Morhange-Bégué's rendering of the unassimilability and displacement that characterize traumatic experience resonates exactly with Cathy Caruth's formulation: "Trauma is not locatable in the simple violent or original event, in an individual's past, but rather in the way that its very unassimilated nature—the way it was precisely *not known* in the first instance—returns to haunt the survivor later on."[15] Or, as Caruth puts it elsewhere, "The trauma is a repeated suffering of the event, but it is also a continual leaving of its site."[16] In Morhange-Bégué's narrative, the site of original traumatization—her mother's arrest, with all of its reverberations—is revisited again and again in traumatic flashbacks. Indeed, Morhange-Bégué's representation of the constellation of events surrounding Claude's mother's disappearance and her own "escape" into hiding exhibits the same "strange connection between the *elision* of memory and the *precision* of recall" that Caruth claims in a later discussion to be intrinsic to the phenomenon of unintegrated trauma. To paraphrase Caruth, Claude's past was never fully experienced as it occurred: "what returns is not simply an overwhelming experience by a later repression or amnesia, but an event that is itself constituted, in part, by its lack of integration into consciousness."[17]

In the scene in which the original disappearance is first described and in its subsequent, increasingly detailed reconstructions and retellings, what is most striking is the disjunctive relation of image and language to memory. Image belongs to the realm of imputed certitude, language to that of shadowy indeterminacy. Claude can recall—can visualize with perfect clarity (for eternity, it would seem)—"the black and white checkerboard" design of her savior Marie's back and chignon as Claude follows her across the deserted village square to safety. Similarly, Claude seems to see a clock on the wall of a bedroom, whose pendulum strikes every fifteen minutes. But, despite the clarity of these images, she laments:

I do not remember any words being addressed to me; I can't say now whether anything was said at all, whether they explained that my mother had been taken away and that I wasn't likely to see her for a while or even ever again. From within the great emptiness that filled me there does indeed arise one sentence, be it actually memory or phantasm: *Your mother has been arrested.*[18]

Soon afterward, a quest for concrete images to which she can attach the meaning of words brings her to the dreaded word *deported*, which she has heard, and about which she claims to "truly know nothing," except, oddly enough, that "it rhymes with arrested" (a francophone reader hears the rhyme of *déporté/arrêté*). Her frustration with the vagaries of adult speech, which would provide the only means for conceptualizing the extreme gravity of her situation, is demonstrated in the way that she accounts for the discrepancy between words that are said and words that might have been said, should have been said, were implied if not uttered, uttered but forgotten: "Your mother has been arrested, *but* . . . appears an implicit negative structure which contradicts what I am being told." The "*but*" is the compensatory conjunction that she dares not accept, suspicious that either it elides the real truth or is too insubstantial to merit her investment. Sometimes she prefaces her attempts to recall specific incidents with qualifications such as, "I remember or I imagine and this hesitation irritates me." Clearly, memory and imagination are mutually reinforcing, if self-critical, modes of accommodating an unbearable situation.[19]

As language fails to provide access to knowledge of her mother's whereabouts and return in a world so destabilized and deferred, linguistic agency becomes an obsession. The child begins to harbor a reserve lexicon of words and phrases that she hopes will serve her later. She describes herself as a child who, in her excruciating loneliness and fear, projects a "someday" when she may "tell what these events left behind in me and what fantasy has woven itself around them." Some of these have the status of "speech acts"—they are reported speech, marked with italics in the text. In one such passage, Morhange-Bégué recalls the seemingly ordinary beginning of the day their lives changed forever, rehearsing the words her loving, "omniscient" mother had spoken to her while dressing: "*Your name is Jeanne Duval, your name is Jeanne Duval* followed by *We are going to go over to the Balards . . . there is nothing to worry about.*" This memory cedes to her own internal response: "I perceive the inconsistency without telling myself so, without even knowing that I perceive it and that I am burying it away inside me [so] that it revive[s] there more than thirty years afterward, revive[s] now, as I write."[20]

Although these strategies of self-containment and preservation—(*I must remember these events so I can tell about them/I must bury these events so I can resurrect them*)—seem bounded by the desire to bear witness, they are in fact conceived within different temporal frameworks and have different trajectories. The first passage takes the perspective of the vigilant and silenced child narrator who projects an abstract "someday," whether imminent or infinitely deferred, when she can tell what happened to her and measure the effects of those experiences. The second passage assumes the vantage point of the adult autobiographer who, "thirty years afterward," is writing this memoir—presumably, about those very events—and thus is bringing to consciousness and textually representing what had been retained but so long suppressed. Just as each act of testimony is marked by a different modality, speech or writing, so each is/was destined for a different audience. The projected audience of the child's perspective, its designated recipient, is, I would argue, a very intimate one: the absent mother, the significant Other for whom she waits. Dori Laub and Marjorie Allard describe the need for survivors to inscribe the other in the restorative act of testimony: "The listener embodies the return of the other. Thus the latent meaning of the desire to bear witness is reparation of the impaired dyad in the imagined or attempted act of communicating. The wish is to reinvent the responsive other through testimony so as to reconstitute the self as *one who is heard.*"[21] This insight privileges oral testimony, as do many theoretical accounts of the act of bearing witness. But, in fact, all testimonial narratives—regardless of their temporal and spatial proximity to events—being in language, are always already mediated, and subject to subsequent revision. Of course, different language events create and insist upon their own interpretive contexts and narrative constraints. Each requires or merits different kinds of critical sensitivity. Morhange-Bégué signals this difference within the text itself. Thus, the adult voice projects a different audience, an undifferentiated "world," comprising future generations—but including her own daughter, who is exactly the age that she was when her mother was taken away.

Trauma's Afterlife

At the opening of her chapter 3, a third of the way into what is a very concentrated narrative (115 pages), Morhange-Bégué reveals what underwrites this memoir:

And when I come to this point in what I have been saying I am at an end, having reached the bottom of myself. Still wishing to go on, I manage it by doing so outside of myself, that is, by relating what I have experienced through another person rather than directly, by relating things she told of when later on she returned, told over the course of days and over the course of years, things which I grew up on for a long time, as a child, as an adolescent, and that I listened to without a word, evening after evening, then one evening out of two, then one out of three, then one evening a week, one a month, and finally no longer, but which remain inside me, buried in my depths, something hardened, some stone-like cyst, some node, undetermined in character but persisting, malignant.[22]

The autobiographical "I" of this narrative has thus buried within her, like a malignant tumor that can't be excised, not only her own trauma of maternal loss, but her mother's trauma as well. Fourteen months after her departure ("one day, one fine day"), the child gets her mother back, but in an utterly changed form. Her mother has come "back" from the dead—from Auschwitz-Birkenau. She is tattooed and skeleton-thin, faded, shorn, broken, and driven to unburden herself "with repetitive, obsessive talk, a litany that would graft itself upon all other speech and associate itself with any other image, liberating but also evidence of the hurt sustained . . . in her customary voice and without any perceptible feeling, as if horror were to be taken for granted."[23]

So the two survivors—mother and child—each seeking "reparation of the impaired dyad" in the act of communicating, occupy their respective positions, though surely not according to the desires of the child. Yet it cannot fall to Claude to dictate the terms of their co-testimonial space. Reunited with her most beloved mother, Claude hopes to finally tell and to be heard, in a mode of reciprocal exchange; nevertheless, Claude's narrative is overwhelmed and overcome by the grief and catastrophe of her mother's story. Claude's mother finds the necessary empathic and receptive listener invoked by Laub and Allard in her daughter, whose extraordinary capacity to absorb—perhaps at her own expense—functions in inverse relation to the mother's infinite need to talk. However, although this psychic economy is marked by the unassimilated, boundless, traumatic speech of the mother, it is still the daughter's belated narrative—her imaginative reconstruction in writing of her mother's experience, her translation—that re-marks the dynamic as a recuperative response to a designated demand or appeal as part of an already mutually implicating process. When describing the terms of this legacy, the daughter writes not in the narrative past but in the present tense; she assumes the burden of memory and the burden of intergenerational transmission as they were implicitly passed on to her, as an ongoing, enduring imperative:

Later on in the course of her talking during that unending series of evenings, sometimes her voice breaks, a lone tear wells up in each of her eyes, and I, ten years old, eleven, twelve, I do not stir, I listen, I am initiated into the secrets of modern times and of History, and I wait in the expectation that she will write, that she will bear witness and make her protest known. But she does not, and so it is I who out of the stories she told me am weaving her protest, in her behalf and in her name . . . a generation later.[24]

By doing so, the daughter not only makes possible the mother's story, but through the redemptive pretext of telling her mother's story, she can, of course, also tell her own: "Our paths diverged, the paths of a child and its mother suddenly, forcibly separated, and yet we underwent a simultaneous experience, our experience of the war." The daughter's insistence on relationality in spite of separation, on "simultaneous experience" despite divergent paths, reveals the doubleness of her position. Even as she declares herself to be the repository of her mother's story, she stakes her claim as a survivor in her own right. Indeed, her use of "our" indicates both a mark-

ing of difference and a recognition of shared trauma. So great is her identification with her mother's experience that, while recounting her mother's
transport's arrival in the death camp, an indeterminate or vicarious "I" slips
in: "Have I seen, have I read of, have I dreamt of those naked bodies clam-
bering up pipes toward the ceiling." That there is a near conflation of the
mother's experience with the daughter's account of it is also evident, in her
descriptions of the destinies of other victims, destinies that might have
been her mother's or her own, had they been together: "Straight to the gas
chamber they go . . . more fortunate, those victims, than an entire trainful
of living children that are burned without first being gassed when toward
the end they run out of gas."[25]

Only retrospectively, belatedly, then, does the daughter come to realize that her traumatic experience of the war consisted of more than a child's
suffering and desperate longing for a mother she feared dead. Her traumatic
experience entailed as well the return of a mother who did not resemble
either physically or psychologically the mother who had departed, who had
become a vaguely familiar stranger. The impossibility of dissolving that difference, even in reunion with the mother, produces many more traumatic
dislocations for the child. Not unlike other Holocaust narratives, *Chamberet*
is riddled with tragic irony and enigmas. Most strikingly, Claude's insistent
identification with her mother's experience speaks to her realization that the
enforced separation from her mother—her mother's departure—probably
ensured her own survival:

[T]he trauma consists not only in having confronted death, but in *having survived, precisely, without knowing it.* What one returns to in the flashback is not the
incomprehensibility of one's near death, but the very incomprehensibility of one's
own survival. Repetition, in other words, is not simply the attempt to grasp that
one has almost died but, more fundamentally and enigmatically, the very attempt
to claim one's own survival. If history is to be understood as the history of a trauma,
it is a history that is experienced as the endless attempt to assume one's survival as
one's own.[26]

Moreover, the reader strongly suspects what the narrator perhaps cannot
say: that the experience of having been a helpless witness to her mother's
suffering—of having been so long subjected to those relentless verbal accounts of starvation, degradation, and terror in the death camp—must
have produced something akin to a secondary trauma. She survives trauma

a second time, but its impact continues to reverberate throughout her life. As Caruth explains, the survivor of trauma "requires integration both for the sake of testimony and for the sake of cure . . . the transformation of the trauma into a narrative memory that allows the story to be verbalized and communicated, to be integrated into one's own, and others' knowledge of the past."[27] Caruth's description, I would argue, applies to both mother and daughter. However disparate their experiences, the unassailability of their psychic and linguistic bond ineluctably enabled a convergence of the two. Lest this convergence sound too idealistic, however, Morhange-Bégué ends her narrative with this final meditation:

Henceforth it would be mine to listen in order to become imbued with her stories, without yet knowing that this ingestion preluded another task: that of speaking for her and in her name about the unspeakable that she had the strength both to live through and to vanquish but which she would not be able to bring herself to consign to words intended to remain, relying instead on oral tradition and for its preservation upon this link to the future sprung from her, who has now assumed her mission.[28]

Morhange-Bégué's reference to herself in the third person provides a strange and poignant shading to this description of intergenerational transmission. As inheritor of her mother's stories and the "link" to her Holocaust past and to its afterlife, she invokes a process ("ingestion") that is at once organic and abstract, biological and historical, repetitive and cumulative. This testimony externalizes what has been most profoundly internalized, incorporated; like Benjamin's notion of translation, it is driven by an imperative. It answers an appeal or a demand.

Testimony and the "Drive to Translate"

In Jean Laplanche's formulation, the framing concept of psychoanalysis (and existence) is translation. Translation is so critical and intrinsic to psychic functioning (though never completed) that it is a "categorical imperative":

The unconscious, as I envision it, is the result of repressions bearing on fragments of communications, which it, by so doing, makes foreign to the context which is their origin. . . . It is the inexhaustible sources of material that each human being in the course of his existence strives as a last resort to translate into his acts, his speech and the manner in which he represents himself to himself. . . . The obligation to translate, its inevitable *Trieb* (drive), doesn't come from meaning; the drive to translate—and here I use my own terms—comes more from the untranslatable.[29]

And, conversely, thinking psychoanalytically informs our understanding of the translation process as being fundamentally rooted in a temporal dialectic. Claude's literary response to her mother's traumatic legacy, *Chamberet*, is an act of intralingual translation, a highly mediated movement or displacement from the language of the mother's "unspeakable" experience—her unbounded oral narrative—into writing. The difference that elicits the translation, and that which it strives to overcome, serves to memorialize their mutual loss. The original lives on, indeed surpasses itself, because in being remembered, its content is not replicated but becomes part of an ongoing process of transmutation. Thus, translation affirms intimacy—but not fusion—through difference.

The thematic and structural convergence of traumatic memory and translation in *Chamberet* is perhaps best illustrated through Benjamin's image of the shattered vessel. Benjamin presents this kinship between the original and the translation as expressing the fragmentary nature of languages:

Fragments of a vessel which are to be glued together must match one another in the smallest details, although they need not be like one another. In the same way a translation, instead of reassembling the meaning of the original, must lovingly and in detail incorporate the original's mode of signification, thus making both the original and the translation recognizable as fragments of a greater language, just as fragments are part of a vessel.

The allegory of the shattered vessel also helps us to conceptualize the relationship between translation and trauma: the shattered vessel is the post-Babelian, post-traumatic condition—as theologically and psychoanalytically defined—that presupposes an underlying prior unity before the break. The fragments relate to each other by contiguity; "*articulated* together," they may evoke a lost totality or their prior unity, but they cannot be reconstituted, instead remaining forever essentially fragmented and fragmentary.[30]

More specifically, the relationship between the original and its translation is analogous to the relational dynamic between mother and daughter in *Chamberet*, whose idealized union is elegized and whose rupture is mourned in the daughter's (translator's) narrative. Because of their forced separation and the gap caused by such a rupture, a bond of mutual claim and debt obtains between the original and its translation. Although the translation owes its existence to the original, it also gains something, becomes more than itself by virtue of its being translated; both need each other to fill in spaces that would otherwise remain in the realm of images, unarticulated and unsignified.

Paul de Man stresses the perverse over the redemptive aspects of Benjamin's theory of translation, attacking the symptomatic failures of Benjamin's own translators (Jacobs excluded), who privilege in their reading of Benjamin the purposefulness of life and nature, rather than the melancholic and mortifying tendencies of history. De Man also stresses the instability and nondefinitive nature of the original (otherwise, it wouldn't require translation), and the distinctly nonorganic character of the critical relationship between the original and its translation. Translations, he reiterates, "disarticulate, they undo the original, they reveal that the original was always already disarticulated. . . . The translation reveals that [this] alienation is at its strongest in our relation to our own original language, that the original language within which we are engaged is disarticulated in a way which imposes upon us a particular alienation, a particular suffering."[31] For de Man, this suffering is a specific function of language, whereas I am insisting here on the crucial link between language and trauma and the psychoanalytic attributes of that relation, as well as the one between mother and daughter in this text. Of course, the daughter will never know the suffering her mother experienced, just as what was lost can never be restored. However, translation challenges silence and oblivion; it makes what would have been effaced into a textual event. It signals both translatability and untranslatability. As Benjamin puts it, "Translatability is an essential quality of certain works, which is not to say that it is essential that they be translated; it means rather that a specific significance inherent in the original manifests itself in its translatability."[32]

In *Chamberet*, translation points unequivocally to the incompleteness or constitutive uncontainability of the original, which may otherwise be called its "specific significance": in this case, the specific significance of one woman's experience in the Holocaust and its traumatizing effects upon her child. The call for translation would appear to be unequivocal. The enterprise is shot through with anguish; the mother's overwhelming need to talk paired with her refusal to write produces, as it were, a structural fault in the narrative that can be completed only through, and by way of, the daughter's translation. What is crucial here is that without the translation, neither story would have survived. As the story of the transmission and translation of this narrative demonstrates, when "survivorship" itself is at stake, the "task of the translator" is overdetermined, serving as a figure for processes of intergenerational transmission, as well as of intercultural transmission across temporal and spatial boundaries.

Since this intergenerational translation is intralingual—the language of both the source (the mother) and the target (the daughter) is French—its intercultural aspects are recessed, if not invisible. Furthermore, the translation history of this narrative—apparently, a translation of a translation—has political implications. I first discovered this French Holocaust mother-daughter survivor narrative in a used bookstore in Saint Paul, Minnesota, and was drawn to the story as it was described in the blurb on the back cover. I was especially intrigued by a seemingly irreconcilable contradiction: the front cover of Marlboro Press's English edition of *Chamberet* says, "translated from French by Austryn Wainhouse," while the inside cover says "original edition." How could the English translation be an original? Where was the "original" original? Later, reading Wainhouse's translation, I was moved by its elegant and evocative precision and sensibility. I spent months pursuing every means possible to locate the original French text, including trying to track down the author and her work through the Centre de documentation juive contemporaine in Paris. Her memoir was unknown to them as well; there were no traces of *Chamberet* in French. I reached an impasse.

There was only one stone left unturned in my investigation of the mystery of the missing original. *Cherchez le traducteur.*[33] Austryn Wainhouse confirmed my suspicions, which were exciting in theory but disappointing in reality. If the mother's oral testimony in French is an unrecoverable original that made both necessary and possible a call for translation, the daughter's written text in French, it turns out, is an unrecoverable original that does not exist, and never has, in any published form. (Wainhouse received the French manuscript in typescript.) The question that persists is, why wasn't Morhange-Bégué's book published in France in the first place? Why did the book skip that step in the process of transmission and go straight to a translation for an American audience? Why was it "untranslatable" in Benjaminian terms? Clearly, either the author did not seek

to have her memoir published in French (for a host of personal and political reasons that one can easily imagine) or—and the two are probably related—she could not find a receptive audience in France in the late 1970s–
early 1980s.[34] There is little doubt that she would find it now.

History, Cultural Memory, and the Tasks
of Translation in T. Obinkaram Echewa's
I Saw the Sky Catch Fire

> If you think you can grasp me, think again:
> my story flows in more than one direction
> a delta springing from the riverbed
> With its five fingers spread
> —Adrienne Rich, "Delta"

Within a framework of transmission more extensive than that of
Chamberet, T. Obinkaram Echewa's *I Saw the Sky Catch Fire* (1992) presents the construction of identity and difference as a problem of translation: not only temporal—between generations—but also spatial—across
cultures. This fictional text, by performing the processes of history and cultural memory it thematizes, also signals an imperative: the value and vitality of intergenerational transmission as a crucial form of cultural survival
in a postcolonial context. Told in the first person, the narrative moves between two distinct orders and realms of action and experience, one male-
identified and the other female-identified. Echewa's insider/outsider protagonist, Ajuzia, is an African male intellectual torn between competing
gendered claims of familial responsibility and self-interest. Cast in the terms
of the novel, his personal predicament takes shape as a stark dilemma:
should he pursue his doctorate in America, or should he stay in Africa and
ensure the preservation of the family compound? The nativist rhetoric of
"the politics of return" would cast his situation this way: should he continue his errant, diasporic existence in the West, or should he return and
live a reclaimed life, near his heritage and history? Ajuzia himself puts it
another way: "The simple fact was that I was abandoning *our* collective
past for what I thought was *my* inevitable personal future."[35]

What Ajuzia calls "our collective past" crosses gender here and is represented emblematically in this text by the 1929 "Women's War," the tax

revolt organized by a group of women of his grandmother's generation against the British colonial administration and its warrant chiefs. Ajuzia interweaves his grandmother's story, first performed to/for him, into his own, creating a densely textured, multifaceted, heteroglossic feminist manifesto. By embedding and implicating one generation's story in the folds of another's, the text invites the reader to think in terms of modes, as well as levels, of translation, and to ask: What are the enabling and disabling narrative conditions upon which this contemporary African novel in English depends? Is there a mother tongue in this text? How to identify the tensions, the stress points, the violence incurred when the colonial language and its literary conventions and cultural assumptions encounter the indigenous, oral Igbo modes and the values they convey? In this exemplary instance of a type of postcolonial textuality, how is each language altered, transformed by its encounter with the other?[36] The novel ends on an ambiguous note with Ajuzia's concession "America can wait," suggesting a spatial and temporal suspension of the resolution of his personal predicament. As R. Radhakrishnan asserts in another context, the choice is not between two pure identities or modes of existence, Western and indigenous, but between two different narratives and their intended teleologies.[37]

Clearly, Ajuzia's predicament is not only a personal one. As K. Anthony Appiah puts it, "[M]ost African writers have received a Western-style education; their ambiguous relations to the world of their foremothers and forefathers and to the world of the industrialized countries are part of their distinctive cultural (dis)location."[38] *I Saw the Sky Catch Fire* presents and pursues the extensive implications of this legacy of dislocation for the postcolonial europhone generation of African writers. Preoccupied with the familial experience of migration or nomadism, the indigenous "language" has been further decontextualized through exile, displacement, or suppression, and the heritage is in crisis or in peril of extinction. The burden of the legacy or task of cultural translation borne by the second generation thus becomes acute, because the survival of the original depends on it. Yet the novel shows that the inheritor's survival is also at stake, though in a way different from the previous generation's. Using precolonial, colonial, and postcolonial formal and cultural resources, Echewa has created a text that incorporates an original narrative but also revises it on its own differential terms, demonstrating Homi Bhabha's rendering of "the postcolonial perspective" as one speaking "from this hybrid location of cultural value—the transnational and the translational."³⁹

I Saw the Sky Catch Fire begins on the eve of Ajuzia's journey to America, where he has won a university scholarship. Ajuzia tells his story in a retrospective, nonlinear rendering of the events that led up to his departure and to his protracted return to the ancestral compound when, five years later, his grandmother is on her deathbed and Stella, his wife and mother of the daughter he has left behind, is pregnant by another man. Ajuzia's account of his romance with, marriage to, and abandonment of Stella is characterized by poignant, incisive self-reflection and ambivalent self-justification. Ajuzia has felt both compelled and entitled to pursue advanced studies abroad, while the women in his life have been expected to conform to his timetable: to stay home and wait. Although Ajuzia assumes masculine privilege to be normative, the novel itself repeatedly and emphatically decenters notions of male authority. Indeed, the text's graphic representation of gender relations, which are characterized by a kind of defiant pragmatism, disrupts every conceivable hierarchy, save the grounding of female power in women's capacity to bear children. An irreconcilable tension between constantly contested notions of privilege (ascribed) and power (endowed) animates the narrative.

Because Ajuzia is his grandmother Nne-nne's only descendant, and male, his position in the family is unique. His grandmother insists on passing on her story to him before he leaves the world they have shared. Her personal and communal oral history is framed by the wars women seem eternally to wage against male treachery, truancy, inadequacy, and injustice: some illustrative chapters are entitled "Women's Wars," "Why Women Go to War," "At War!" "Stella's Wars," "Civil and Domestic Wars," and "Modern Women and Modern Wars." As he listens to his grandmother, he acknowledges that this "eerily fateful nocturnal memoir" fills him with dread and sadness. An inextricable link is being established among the grandson's imminent departure, the grandmother's sense of her impending death, and this occasion. If he were not leaving, she would not need to bind him to her with the threads of her narrative; if he were not leaving, she would not feel the same imperative to tell her story now, and there would be no imperative for him to receive it and undertake its translation, as a way to ensure its living on. But the occasion is overdetermined for another reason: Ajuzia can leave the ancestral home only because Nne-nne is there to maintain it. If Nne-nne fears that she will lose her hold on Ajuzia, he fears that she will die and he will lose the right to leave. The fear on both sides of impending loss is part of a larger master narrative that compels revision. In the moral and material economy of reciprocal claim and debt—the transaction that underwrites this redemptive act of intergenerational transmission and eventually produces the intercultural translation that is *I Saw the Sky Catch Fire*—redemption may come at the other's expense or at the expense of the Other. Saving or securing someone or something for a life beyond life (sur-vival) sometimes involves paying back, buying back, buying out, buying off, or making amends for a life already lived, for a life not yet lived.

Female ingenuity, courage, autonomy, and survival in the face of male impotence and unreliability are the dominant strands of this particular discourse. By recounting her story to Ajuzia at this moment, Nne-nne, who had always tended to be silent and fierce, is speaking on behalf of herself, her gender, and her culture. Her embattled stance is an urgent condemnation of male privilege and pride, serving at the same time as an overture to her only heir to take his proper place in line after her. In a spirit that recalls Benjamin's sense of translation, Ajuzia translates Nne-nne's Igbo story into English and interweaves it with his own; his highly mediated response to her call, a text produced in response to her original narrative, ensures that she and the other women of whom she speaks will live on.[40] Nne-nne's oral history challenges any suggestion of female subordination; indeed, the organizing principle of her testimony is *Ndom*, translated from Igbo in the text as "the universal autonomy and solidarity of women." *Ndom* is a form of what Randolph Starn, echoing Michel Foucault, calls counter-memory: "the residual or resistant strains that withstand official versions of historical continuity."[41] It is *Ndom*, the grandmother tells her grandson, that sustains and empowers Igbo women, and it was solidarity that made it possible for the women of southeastern and coastal Nigeria to make war against the British tax offensive in 1929, at great risk to their lives.

Translation and Cultural Memory

Nne-nne's testimony consists of fine-tuned descriptions of extraordinary women, bawdy songs, birth and mourning chants, proverbs, invocations, and exhortations, many marked in the text by italics or other graphic indications, and some untranslated from Igbo. This feature of Echewa's text is particularly intriguing for a reader attuned to the problematic of "untranslatability." Clearly, this novel is intended for those Igbo speakers whom Chantal Zabus refers to as "deracinated contemporaries," as well as non-Igbo-speaking anglophones—those who find themselves "reading" transcribed Igbo without having at their command the exchange value of many of these expressions. The glossary at the back of the book is incomplete. Echewa's decision to retain Igbo strangeness and foreignness in the text, so as to call attention to the act as well as the effects of defamiliarizing Igbo language and culture, requires readers to sharpen their intuitive responses to the unassimilable. Nonetheless, it is possible to surmise contextually, through some sustained effort, as well as an imaginative, sympathetic leap, encouraged by the text, what many of the Igbo terms and expressions mean. Echewa's effort to textualize linguistic differentiation and convey African concepts is an example of "indigenization" as formulated by Zabus. The strategy employs the two methods that aim at "naming and identifying the gap between mother tongue and other tongue without necessarily bridging it: 'cushioning,' . . . tagging a European-language explanation onto an African word, and 'contextualization,' . . . providing areas of immediate context so as to make the African word intelligible without resorting to translation."[42]

The reader encounters "indigenization" in practice in the opening lines of Echewa's novel, marking it as one of its signature strategies. In recounting the dramatic, mystifying events of the night before he leaves for America, Ajuzia performs an initial act of translation that affirms to the English-language reader his requisite qualifications as transmitter of this challenging story: "Nne-nne was in a state that night before I left home. *Amuma-Muo*, it sounded like, but the feast of Ngwu, the spirit that possesses people in our area, was long past, and besides I had never known Nne-nne to be possessed before."[43] Ajuzia's in-betweenness and sense of defamiliarization enable him to render an opaque situation "intelligible" without "resorting" to the literal meaning of the term *Amuma-Muo*. As the story unfolds, Ajuzia is seen struggling to make sense of a situation that, for whatever set of complex reasons, does not present itself as immediately available to his understanding.

Nne-nne provides a vision of history made by men and a subversion of that history voiced by women, in which women figure as agents, not objects, of history—colonialist or otherwise. Echewa delineates a precolonial backdrop against which women's economic independence and the political impact of women's associations were part of the fabric of indigenous social structures; this narrative underscores the claims of feminist and African scholarship that colonialism, far from liberating African women, curtailed the prerogatives and rights they had formerly exercised.[44] How this occurred was seen most patently under the British system of indirect rule, Lord Lugard's dual mandate doctrine, transferred wholesale by the British in 1922 from India, where it had "succeeded," to Nigeria, where it was an abysmal failure. Unlike the French, whose assimilationist policy aimed at producing cultural clones, the British were interested only in producing dutiful British subjects. From a distance, the colonial administration imagined it was maintaining indigenous political social institutions across diverse regions by placing local warrant chiefs in charge, rather than British administrators. These generally corrupt surrogates for British colonial power were deeply resented by both men and women and not seen as vested with legitimate authority. Moreover, these institutions bore no relation to the traditional political or social structures, which differed from province to province, often from village to village. The dual-sex model of dispersed and shared economic and political responsibility and authority yielded to a single-sex model, in which women had to struggle to exert influence, often instead of the Nigerian men, who did not protect their interests.

The most dramatic example of resistance by African women to their loss of influence and status was the brief and violent struggle called *Ogu Umunwanyi*, or the Women's War, by the Igbo, in which women demonstrated against the British for the right to be consulted on matters that directly affected them. The British, who named the conflict the Aba Riots, were victorious, and they wrote an official history according to the colonialist script. Nne-nne's rendition of the events fills in the blanks of the elided version, challenging decades of British scholarship that neglects to mention that the Igbo give a different name to this revolt. Some British and

Nigerian histories even remove women entirely from the action. Nne-nne's act of resistance to British appropriation and Ajuzia's textualization of her narrative illustrate Pierre Nora's distinction between memory and history:

> Memory and history, far from being synonymous, appear now to be in a fundamental opposition. Memory is life, borne by living societies founded in its name. It remains in perpetual evolution, open to the dialectic of remembering and forgetting, unconscious of successive deformations, vulnerable to manipulation and appropriation, susceptible to being long dormant and periodically revived. History, on the other hand, is the reconstruction, always problematic and incomplete, of what is no longer. Memory is a perpetually active phenomenon, a bond tying us to the eternal present; history is a representation of the past.[45]

The historian Judith Van Allen traces the imperial act of translation that underwrote the name "Aba Riots." She argues that, whereas "Women's War" stresses the prominent role of women and the idea of a grave assault on an enemy, the British term localizes, diminishes, and diffuses the impact of the revolt, which ranged over most of southeastern Nigeria. Indeed, the term "Women's War" provides the crucial discursive framework for reading Echewa's rendering of this female incursion into male history-making. "Making war," also called "sitting on a man," was an institutionalized form of punishment used by Igbo women against a man who excessively mistreated his wife, violated the women's market rules, or persistently allowed his cows to eat women's crops. The punishment consisted of gathering at the man's compound at an appointed time and dancing, singing scurrilous songs detailing the women's grievances against him (and often insulting him by calling his manhood into question), banging on his hut with the pestles used for pounding yams, and, in extreme cases, tearing up his hut. The women would stay until he repented and promised to reform. Thus, as Van Allen explains, "Women's War" connotes an extension of women's traditional collective method for settling grievances with men who had acted badly toward them, a method considered to be the ultimate recourse available to women for reinforcing their judgments (61–62). The Women's War was the collective expression of a collective judgement: the Igbo women identified or associated colonialism with the exercise of illegitimate male power.[46]

In Van Allen's account, the British decided in 1925 to introduce direct taxation in order to create a Native Treasury, whose purpose it was "to pay for improvements in the Native Administration, in accordance with the British imperial philosophy that the colonized should pay the costs of colonization" (71). Responding to high prices in the palm trade, the British raised taxes tax on men and collected without trouble. However, in 1929 a zealous British assistant district officer, apparently acting on his own initiative, decided to "tighten up" the census registers by recounting households and property. Despite his assurances to the warrant chiefs that there was no plan to increase taxes or to tax women, the counting of women and their property was read by women as a sign that they were to be taxed, and the rumor spread quickly through their communication networks.[47]

In the novel, Nne-nne tells us that two months before the Women's War started, there were terrifying omens: "Together they marked a turning point in the seamless history of the times, and as some people would say later, a turning point almost as significant as the sighting of the first White man in the area." The war began, in Nne-nne's version, when Akpa-Ego, a pregnant woman kneeling by a vat of palm mash, was approached by Sam-el, the counter, with his notebook and pencil and list of questions. After he asked her her name and how many children, goats, sheep, and chickens she had in her chicken coop, she turned on him and asked, "Has your mother been counted?" In his outrage, he traced the line of authority from himself to the king of England. Who was she, an illiterate village woman, to set herself against the king of England?

The story of what had happened between Akpa-Ego and Sam-el was retold again and again. . . . "Is there not anyone who is safe anymore?" the hearers exclaimed. "Is there not anyone who is considered sacred and untouchable? Not even a pregnant woman? Why is it so important for them to count women, if it is not to tax us?" From the possibility of a tax, the complaints grew to include everything that was wrong with their world—death of children, infertility of soils, the blighting of crops, the cost of things sold in the market.[48]

On November 23, it is said, tens of thousands of women mobilized to get rid of their warrant chiefs and the Native Administration itself. They sounded the alarm: "*Ndom Amapu* is at war with the Government. *Ndom* is at war with the White man."[49] The women appeared at the Native Administration centers in loincloths, carrying sticks wreathed with palm fronds, their faces smeared with charcoal or ashes and their heads bound with young ferns. The British were unaware that this dress and adornment signified war, the

sticks being used to invoke the power of female ancestors. The women
chanted, danced, sang songs of ridicule and insult, and demanded the warrant chiefs' caps of office. At some locations, they broke into prisons and released prisoners; of the sixteen native courts they attacked, most were
burned or destroyed. The British quelled the rebellion only by using large
numbers of police and soldiers, and on one occasion Boy Scouts; they fired
on the women, leaving more than fifty dead and fifty wounded, many of
whom were clubbed or whipped. None of the British were seriously injured.

Nne-nne's stories recount women doing inconceivable things, and always in the context of absolute, compelling inevitability; incorporated are
the women's battle cries and songs of solidarity. One of the chants is *Oha
Ndi Niom*, "the spirit of womanhood," a formulation that uncannily resembles Julia Kristeva's maxim "woman can never be defined":

> What makes you a woman?
> What makes a woman is imponderable!
> Uncountable!
> Unfathomable!
> How many women are there in the world?
> *Nnu-kwuru-nnu! Igwe!* Innumerable!
> What is a woman?
> A knot that is impossible to untie!
> A river that no one can swim!
> A knot in a tree that no one can cut through![50]

Translation and Ethnography

While the oracular power of Nne-nne's stories and proverbs testifies
to the Igbo women's sense of the universal spirit and eternal solidarity of
women, made emblematic during the Women's War, the novel's intriguing
chapter on ethnography, entitled "Woman to Woman: Ugbala and Elizabeth Ashby-Jones," focuses on the race-gender divide as it figures in colonial relations, disrupting the effects of the "female universal" (*Ndom*) articulated elsewhere in the text. In this central episode in Nne-nne's testimony,
Echewa explores the notion of positionality and the ethical and epistemological implications of cultural relativism by reframing the ethnographic
experiences represented, by destabilizing the roles of subject and object,

and by staging the postcolonial return of the anthropological gaze. This narrative also illustrates the ways race can structure both difference and sameness in a number of varied contexts, while literacy/illiteracy remains an unequivocal global signifier of difference among women.

I Saw the Sky Catch Fire stresses how fundamentally the ethnographic project is a project of translation.[51] From its inception in the nineteenth century as a field and a discipline—an unequally distributed mode of knowledge production—theorists of anthropology endeavored to render the culture of "unknown" peoples into the "meaningful" terms of the West. Edmund Leach characterizes the social anthropologist's methodological and conceptual enterprise as "a problem of translation, of finding categories in his own ways of thought which can be fitted to the complex of observed facts that he records."[52] Even as Echewa's novel conveys how imperative and yet how conflicting the mutual claims of translation between generations (and across gender) within the same culture are, it conveys just as insistently that intercultural translation is an act of exchange in which what is different cannot be "simply" transposed univocally or unilaterally into another cultural context or social space without great risk and loss of specificity. Indeed, Talal Asad's contention that intercultural translation is embedded in relations of power—"professional, national, international"— resonates throughout the novel. By embedding both Ajuzia's and a white woman ethnographer's observations, "personal ruminations and conjectures" into Nne-nne's larger narrative, Echewa represents intergenerational transmission and intercultural translation dialectically and narratively, and, by doing so, implicates each mode of translation in the other. Intercultural translation figures doubly in this narrative, which is simultaneously a cautionary tale about the potential seductions of foreign exchange and a critique of British anthropology's complicity with colonialism (the latter being a priori not a mode of exchange but of domination). If the ultimate sobering effect of the Ashby-Jones affair is to reinforce the reader's awareness of what Asad terms "the inequality in the power of languages," how that power is effected and diffused is a crucial part of Nne-nne's story.[53]

Early in the novel, Nne-nne disrupts the launching of her story about the ethnographer when she suddenly leaves Ajuzia and goes into her bedroom, returning with a small piece of cloth tied into a knot. Inside the cloth is a smaller, older, yellow piece of fabric, in the center of which is a strand of hair and a single pearl. These, Nne-nne explains to Ajuzia, "came from the dress of the White woman [*Nwanyi Bekee*]. This is her hair and this pearl came from her necklace. We cut off her hair and darkened her skin with indigo and gave her wrappers like ours so she wouldn't stand out so much." The White woman was Elizabeth Ashby-Jones, an English-woman who had been traveling and observing "native women" when the war broke out. The women of Ikputo Ala, where she was at the time, had kidnapped her. Nne-nne participated in guarding the famous hostage; the last group of women to hold Ashby-Jones, as Ajuzia narrates, "divided among themselves not only the locks from her hair and kerchiefs from her frock, but handwritten pages from her notebook, as mementos of their historic encounter." Five years later, after the death of his grandmother, Ajuzia finds more than a dozen pages of Ashby-Jones's notebook among Nne-nne's possessions. The chapter about Ashby-Jones recounts her endless interrogations of and activities and engagements with the women and their reactions to her, which sometimes consisted of their turning the tables and asking her questions. It also includes excerpts from her notebooks, set apart from the rest of the text by italics. Organized thematically, the notebook entries are labeled "Nakedness," "Farming," "Waterpots," "Census," "Parables and Proverbs," "Oratory," "A Garden?" and "Tragedy!!!"[54]

Ashby-Jones's critical commentary on what she regards as the strange habits of the women is matched by their returned gaze. Not only do those who were once only written about now talk back, they also create an ethnographic portrait of the white woman and their interplay with her from their point of view. Nne-nne's caricature of the anthropologist writing portrays a woman whose hand flew across the pages, who could write "faster than anyone could dance, faster it seemed, than her interpreters could talk. Even when no one was talking, she continued writing."[55] If the women marveled at how much she wrote, they bemoaned how little she listened to them when they tried to convey to her "the burden of life" that was falling too heavily upon them. They tried to express to her their hope that as a "Fellow Woman" she could understand their grief. Much devolves from the sustained distinction between Fellow Woman and White Woman.

Nne-nne's epithet for Ashby-Jones, "White woman," implicitly challenges the designation that British women of empire used—"Europeans"—for themselves. According to Helen Callaway, the colonial terms "African" and "Native" eventually changed to "Nigerian," and "European" became "ex-

patriate."[56] The eliding of race and the privileging of geography in the imperial lexicon contrasts sharply with Echewa's representation of the colonial
subject's understanding of white and outsider as being roughly equivalent.
At the close of a particularly tense episode between the women and Ashby-
Jones, in which her notebook and writing instrument are derided (one of
the women uses her pages as toilet paper), they indict the collaborative en-
terprises of anthropology, colonialism, and racism:

"White woman, why did you come here? Why did you not stay in your own
place? I mean *you* personally, not just the Government, because the same spirit
must have driven you to come here as drove them. You said you came here to find
out about us, woman to woman. Have you found out everything that needs to be
found out about everything in the place where you have your home, and the only
thing left to be found out about was us?"[57]

By the time the women finally decide to bring their "historical encounter" with Ashby-Jones to a conclusion, that is, to let her go without
harming her, the only bond they share with her—gender—pales before the
overriding difference of race (signifying but also including culture here).
Their final invocation is especially poignant and revealing as a tacit affirmation of how culture-bound their "universal" notion of *Ndom* is. This
scene crystallizes the challenge of "reading" other cultures and compels the
reader to ask outright: What if the idea of the universal autonomy and solidarity of women is not a universal?

> "'*Iyah! Iyah!*' the other women said.
> "'This woman!'
> "'*Iyah! Iyah!*'
> "'This woman, whose skin is without color, hair is like corn
>   tassels, and eyes are like shiny glass beads!'
> "'*Iyah! Iyah!*'
> "'But nevertheless a woman!'
> "'*Iyah! Iyah!*'
> "'Dumb and speechless, but nevertheless a woman!'
> "'Barren, but nevertheless a woman!'
> "'Be the judge between us and her!'
> "'She came to us, not we to her!'
> "'We did not seek her out to harm her!'
> "'The war that now engulfs us has been made by her husband
>   and her people!'

"'Ala, make a woman out of her!'
"'*Iyah! Iyah!*'
. . .
. . .

"'Let her feel our grief!'
"'Let her feel Women's Grief!'
"'Let the burden of our grief sit before her eyes!'
"'And sit on her tongue!'
"'And make her fingers limp, so that she cannot pick up a writing
     stick and write with it!'
"'If she writes, let her write the truth about us!'
"'If she speaks, let her speak the truth about us!'
"'If she should fail to speak the truth about us, if she should fail
     to write the truth in her writing, let this wine that we all
     drink together, this wine of our joint womanhood, conse-
     crated to Ala and Edoh and to Efanim, let it intoxicate her
     into a state of madness that no one can cure! Let this wine,
     which contains the blood of our wombs, seal her womb in
     this incarnation and in all her future incarnations.'"[58]

Posed in Benjamin's terms, what is at stake here if not the foreignness of
language and experience, over and across relatedness: what are the conditions of translation? To consider this as anything but a rhetorical or metaphysical question requires attending to the subject position of each character. Whose foreignness and in what context? Each position in *I Saw the
Sky Catch Fire* is, by definition, limited and partial: Ashby-Jones is an
ethnographer, but hardly a feminist; Ajuzia, an enlightened metropolitan
and a native informant translator of a Third World text, is not a woman;
arguably, the Igbo women, represented by Nne-nne, are ethnographers,
despite their lack of conventional critical tools. Indeed, as Asad contends,
invoking Benjamin's notion of translation as harmony of intention with
the original rather than reproduction of it, "it could be argued that 'translating' an alien form of life, another culture, is not always done best
through the representational discourse of ethnography, that under certain
conditions a dramatic performance, the execution of a dance, or the playing of a piece of music might be more apt."[59]

The Igbo women—who esteem above all else their female voices,
their agency, and their fertility—curse the white British woman with silence, madness, and sterility should she betray them in translation. Their

curse is an enactment of desire and an affirmation of the power of language to remake the world, a performative utterance. It acknowledges both kinship and distance, difference within apparent sameness: she is a woman, but certainly not a woman like us. Yet even in their increasing sense of alienation from her, from her practices and forms of life, by recognizing what is dear to her—her writing stick (and not only as an instrument to be used against them)—the Igbo women attempt to resist and relativize the distance between them and the strange foreign woman. Something meaningful, if terribly disappointing, happened in this interpretive space of translation, on both sides—but especially from the point of view of the indigenous women, whose projections and expectations far exceeded what Ashby-Jones was able or inclined to fulfill. That disappointment is intensified if we modify our frame of reference momentarily and think not in anthropological terms but in affective ones. Something more complex and ambiguous than resentment or mere "anthropological" fascination with the white woman as exotic Other must have motivated them to take and keep her things, including her handwritten pages; these possessions are traces, artifacts, even fetishes of what surely can be called a failed romance. Meaning may be migratory, but it also binds. The Igbo women's act confirms Nora's notion that "memory, insofar as it is affective and magical, only accommodates those facts that suit it; it nourishes recollections that may be out of focus or telescopic, global or detached, particular or symbolic. . . . Memory takes root in the concrete, in spaces, gestures, images, and objects."[60]

"The Politics of Translation," Gayatri Spivak's practical and theoretical reflections on the task of the feminist translator, offers acute insights into the nature of the encounter between the Igbo women and Ashby-Jones. An experienced translator, Spivak locates her critique in individual practice, directing her commentary most pointedly at a literary critic-ethnographer of sorts, the Western feminist translator of Third World women's texts. Faintly echoing Benjamin, Spivak advises this practitioner that "translation is the most intimate act of reading. Unless the translator has earned the right to become the intimate reader, she cannot surrender to the text, cannot respond to the special call of the text."[61] From Spivak's delineation of the feminist political issues at stake in "surrendering one[self] to the linguistic rhetoricity of the original text," a model emerges that defines the power of the relation to the other as a matter more of eros than of ethos.

Dismissing all benevolent intentions grounded in a presumption of women's global solidarity, Spivak argues—literally—for multilingualism as the first order of commonality or identification:

Rather than imagining that women automatically have something identifiable in common, why not say, humbly and practically, my first obligation in understanding solidarity is to learn her mother-tongue. . . . This is preparation for the intimacy of cultural translation. . . . If you are interested in talking about the other, and/or in making a claim to be the other, it is crucial to learn other languages. . . . We must also remember that not all the world's women are literate. There are traditions and situations that remain obscure because we cannot share their linguistic constitution. It is from this angle that I have felt that learning languages might sharpen our own presuppositions about what it means to use the sign "woman." If we say that things should be accessible to us, who is this "us"? What does that sign mean?[62]

Ashby-Jones, hopelessly monolingual, a poor listener, and an obsessive counter, is unable to decipher Igbo facial expressions, as she puts it, to grasp why the Africans resist externally imposed structures of "understanding, order, and control." She cannot discern connections among their linguistic, social, and aesthetic practices. She believes them to be incapable of abstractions. Her observations, though replete with thick description, remain nonetheless opaque. Are we meant to take her narrative at face value? The moment announces itself as the perfect narrative opportunity for an ethnographer-critic—so inclined or so able—to make what Bhabha describes as a shift "from the cultural as an epistemological object to culture as an enunciatory site, [a shift that] opens up possibilities for other 'times' of cultural meaning (retroactive, prefigurative) and other narrative spaces (fantasmatic, metaphorical),"[63] to undo what Sherry Simon refers to as "the myth of pure difference."[64] Is Ashby-Jones an untranslatable figure, a straw white woman, the reader wonders—that is, either a setup or an inside joke, and, if so, at whose expense, to achieve what end, to pursue what point?[65]

In Ashby-Jones's journal entry on parables and proverbs, a pervasive mode of Igbo expression, all the issues involve translatability. She is stuck inside her symbolic system of references and cannot move beyond it. The genteel ethnographer's lack of reflexivity seems so outrageous that in places it approaches parody. How should this failure in translation be read? What information is not being exchanged in this projected encounter? Is this an

African writer's imaginary of a Western ethnographer's unmediated reflections? Or a rendering of an African writer's fantasy of a Western ethnographer's private journal, a journal meant, of course, for her eyes only? In either case, the ethnographer's rhetorical range is not unimpressive: it moves from unintended irony when she takes flight toward figurative, oblique expression to pathos when she devolves into patronizing, ethnocentric, essentialist comparison:

I have heard more proverbs and parables in the last few weeks among these people than I ever care to remember. They toss them out at the proverbial drop of a hat. Most of them are only marginally meaningful—at least in translation. Otherwise *obscurans obscurantis!* What is somewhat irksome is the habit of circumlocution that spawns these proverbs, the misdirection, obliquity, and intentional obscurity. . . . The African mind has a tendency to go around in circles. . . . It sometimes tries one's patience to no end to get a straight answer from these people! The problem . . . is the difference between complexity and obscurity, between the rhythms . . . which make up a complex musical composition and the random notes that may suggest but assuredly do not constitute a Bach concerto. What the African ceremoniously disguises as deep thinking is to genuinely deep and complex thought what a baby's babblings are to a great poem. (N.B. This probably sounds harsher than I intended and possibly reflects the frustration I feel at this moment. Generally I have a kindly disposition towards these people, especially the women, and believe there is something "noble" in the very simplicity of their lives, but . . .).[66]

Unable to work her way out of an evolutionary scheme in which "intentional obscurity" (i.e., unintelligibility, resistance to translation) can be measured only unfavorably against deep complexity, Ashby-Jones, her anxieties and frustrations openly declared, reaches some melancholy conclusions about the limited possibilities of intercultural translation. Her imperial apologia dramatizes the impotence of monologic thinking and thus demands to be historicized, for here the colonial context has overriding implications. Asad's remarks again resonate: "[T]he interesting question for enquiry is not whether, and if so to what extent, anthropologists should be relativists or rationalists, critical or charitable, toward other cultures, but how power enters into the process of 'cultural translation,' seen both as a discursive and as a non-discursive practice."[67]

Deemed remote and inferior, reduced to nature and a timeless, ethnologized synchronic present—their precolonial past denied the status of history—the Africans were "othered" by the Europeans.[68] Ashby-Jones's interpretive impasses resemble the "abysmal gulf" described by Dorothy Hammond and Alta Jablow in *The Myth of Africa*. Their study identifies four hundred years of British writing about Africa as producing a series of images that result in a conceptualization of Africa "as a world apart . . . too alien to be encompassed within the normal rubrics of civilized under-standing, of their languages, their cultures, their mentality as an entirely different order of humanity . . . , of the core of African character as so enig-matic that it is simply unintelligible to the European."[69]

The story of Elizabeth Ashby-Jones, fictional British woman ethnog-rapher traveling around eastern Nigeria in the late 1920s, closes part 1 of the novel. If her figurative function, thematically and rhetorically, in *I Saw the Sky Catch Fire* appears circumscribed, it is inescapably allegorical and metatextual in significance, a commentary on its own status as a postcolo-nial translation of the colonizer's misreading of the Other. The white woman's incursion into the Igbo women's space and the effects of her pres-ence become an ineluctable part of their collective memory of their lives before, during, and following the Women's War. And yet, because the novel resumes in part 2 with Ajuzia and Stella's complicated domestic in-trigues, the heavy legacy of Nne-nne's death, and the coming to terms on all sides with Ajuzia's predicament, a reader might presume that the expe-riential impact of the Women's War was felt only by the participants. In fact, the impact was far-reaching.

Although the historical, political, and theoretical implications of the Women's War exceed the boundaries of Echewa's text, they lie well within the interests of this study: the processes and practices of translation, colo-nialism, and anthropology converge in the massive 1929 uprising of Igbo women in eastern Nigeria against the colonial state and its policy of indi-rect rule. This event marked a historical divide in colonial administrative practice: the British were horrified and stunned by what had happened and what it represented—how little they knew their subjects. And the gender twist only added, as it were, "insult to injury." According to Helen Lack-ner's case study on the tie between social anthropology and indirect rule, "a long-lasting revolt by thousands of *women* (anywhere) who were neither accompanied nor led by men was a totally unheard of and outrageous phe-nomenon for a colonial government."[70] In the aftermath of an urgent and thorough investigation into the underlying causes of "the Riots" by a commission of enquiry, the colonial government set about reorganizing native administration and began to dedicate considerable resources to the development of anthropological studies in eastern Nigeria. For decades afterward, missionaries and colonial administrators were aided in their endeavors by anthropologist-translators doing fieldwork in the name of God and the empire.

One significant study from this period was Sylvia Leith-Ross's *African Women*, an ethnography devoted exclusively to the structures of Igbo women's lives. The wife of a colonial officer under Lugard in the British protectorate in northern Nigeria, Leith-Ross first came to Nigeria in 1907. Later widowed, she returned to Nigeria often, in many capacities: in 1925, she accompanied her brother, the lieutenant governor of the southern provinces of Nigeria, who was responsible for introducing indirect rule there. Leith-Ross wrote seven books describing different aspects of life in Nigeria. *Stepping-Stones: Memoirs of Colonial Nigeria, 1907–1960* recounts her experiences in the bush and refers to material she gathered for *African Women*, including her unpublished "scribbled notes." Lackner characterizes Leith-Ross "as speaking in the voice of an enlightened administrator . . . paternalistic and extremely ethnocentric."[71] Is the resemblance between Ashby-Jones and Leith-Ross more than coincidental?

And what would an affinity suggested by the letters *a* and *j* in the names Ashby-Jones and Ajuzia signify? This self-reflexive project in translation comes to realize that lines of descent and affiliation—cultural genealogies—get drawn in surprising and unpredictable ways. At the end of *I Saw the Sky Catch Fire*, as a mystified and defensive Ajuzia is forced to confront the corrosive effects of his five-year absence on his marriage to Stella, he suddenly identifies with the native men and the British colonial administration in 1929, characterizing their response to the Women's War with the exclamation, "We had no idea you felt so aggrieved!" By positing an analogy between the Women's War and his own domestic conflicts and reducing both rebellions to native untranslatability, Ajuzia is not merely rehearsing the novel's pervasive war theme while clinching, once and for all, the connection between patriarchy and colonialism. He is showing the extent to which his experience of postcolonial dislocation has defamiliarized his perceptions. Now he recalls and even empathizes with some of Ashby-Jones's ethnographic comments about "the diffuseness and intractableness of native culture and of her efforts to find structure in it," going so far as to observe, ironically, that "if the natives had been sensible enough to govern themselves through some easily identifiable administrative structures, then any foreigner who wanted to colonize and govern them would have had an easier time of it."[72]

But this line of self-defense cannot hold: Ajuzia's estrangement from local codes and modes of expression and his alignment with Ashby-Jones marks a shift in relation and perspective, a move toward positioning himself as another kind of cultural translator. Of course, it was Nne-nne who provided Ajuzia with the contents of Ashby-Jones's notebooks, making this process of transmission, this transfusion of otherness, both necessary and possible. Her capacious legacy to him included her mementos from the Women's War—Ashby-Jones's things—whose transferential power he could only understand belatedly. As strong as the lure of American academic life is for Ajuzia, equally strong is the weight of Nne-nne's "substantial memory," as he has acknowledged several pages earlier—especially her ways of mastering and defying her "griefs."[73] In the final chapter, "Woman Wins," Ajuzia's personal predicament changes again, as Stella, speaking as if she were the oracle of Nne-nne, refuses to go to America with him, insisting that he make a choice. In the presence of that ancestral spirit, Ajuzia remembers Nne-nne's "eerily fateful nocturnal memoir" delivered on the eve of his departure for America,[74] a performance intended to ensure that he would remain home and, after her death, stay to preserve the compound.

Certainly, the call to translate Nne-nne's story is inseparable from Ajuzia's decision to hold America off indefinitely, to defer. But at the same time, there is more than one "scene of inheritance" in the novel. The British colonial ethnographer's legacy of failure as an intercultural translator opens up a space for the postcolonial heir-translator to assume and perform the kind of crucial intervention Lawrence Venuti terms in *Rethinking Translation* "resistant translation strategies." Such strategies, he says, "help to make the translator's work visible, inviting a critical appreciation of its cultural political function . . . and help to preserve the linguistic and cultural difference of the foreign text by producing translations which are strange and estranging, which mark the limits of dominant values in the target language culture and hinder those values from enacting an imperialistic domestication of a cultural other."[75] Although Venuti refers to a set of specific discursive practices perceptible on the level of the utterance, I would build on that notion by arguing that Echewa's ensemble of narrative strategies in this rich and textured novel, in particular its foregrounding of the complicitous relationship between translation and ethnography, is a kind of "resistant translation." Invoking both Benjamin and Asad, Arnold Krupat discusses the same strategy, which he terms "anti-imperial translation," among Native American authors writing in English.[76] As part of a much larger project, Krupat identifies this practice as performing ideological work that parallels that of postcolonial fiction across the globe. Its goal is to emblematically reappropriate the concept of translation, long an instrument of colonial violence, as a means of retaining, literally and figuratively, the "Indian" in the text.

*

The responses of Claude in *Chamberet* and Ajuzia in *I Saw the Sky Catch Fire* recall Derrida's image of translation as a contract infinitely negotiated by way of the most fleeting contact, remnants, detours, diffusion, and dispersions of meaning: "Benjamin names the subject of translation, as an indebted subject, obligated by a duty, already in the position of heir, entered as survivor in a genealogy, as survivor or agent of sur-vival."[77] That genealogy, as I have attempted to show, is always multiple. This conception of translation enjoins a view of history manifested in the second thesis in Benjamin's "Theses on the Philosophy of History." Benjamin invokes the (nameless) dead who claim, above all, to be remembered: "The past carries with it a temporal index by which it is referred to redemption. There is a secret agreement between past generations and the present one. . . . Like every generation that preceded us, we have been endowed with a *weak* Messianic power, the power to which the past has a claim. That claim cannot be settled cheaply."[78] Reading Echewa and Morhange-Bégué, we are reminded that each generation rewrites its relations with the past in the hopes of inscribing a future, that to translate and to be translated is to be saved from oblivion. It also prompts us to recognize that the difficulty of translation derives no less from the violent and volatile inequality between languages than from the inherent nonequivalence of languages. Translation's intersecting temporal and spatial processes underwrite acts of intergenerational transmission, operating as the crucial means by which imperiled narratives are passed down, received, and survive in memory.

Only by being deemed worthy of translation can a text be assured of living on outside of its own context: its capacity to be translated is a sign of its aesthetic and political significance. Thus, the original is indebted to its future translation. The translator, as an inheritor, is indebted to the original because it imposes the task the translator must try to fulfill: the translator assumes a responsibility for the survival of the original by taking on that task, by responding to its claim, though, as we shall see, not without reservations or re-vision. Under these conditions, cultural narrative and tradition can be said to be on a continuum, subject (especially at moments of perceived crisis) to the rigors of reinterpretation from within as well as from without—that is, to translation as an intrinsic as well as extrinsic operation. What links the tasks of the translator of a cultural narrative and those of the inheritor of a tradition, what governs the conditions of reception, is that neither simply receives a static repository of information or knowledge; rather, both undertake a mission, enter a contract, to engage in a self-critical, dynamic, transformative process, to change and be changed— or die a certain death.

4

The Memorialist as Translator

JORGE SEMPRÚN

> Autobiography is . . . an interplay, a collusion, between past
> and present; its significance is indeed more the revelation of
> the present situation than the uncovering of the past.
> —Roy Pascal, *Design and Truth in Autobiography*

In this final chapter, I focus on the inscription of loss in autobiography as an act of translation—more specifically, on the place of memory
and mourning in textual acts of testimony and transmission.[1] The various,
entangled aspects of "living in translation"—literary, philosophical, cultural, and historical—that I have traced in this book converge in the long,
rich literary and political career of the bilingual Spanish exile and revolutionary intellectual Jorge Semprún. Although relatively unknown to North
Americans, he is a familiar figure in the European cultural landscape. Semprún's life is a stirring example of a sustained, embattled engagement with
some of late modernity's most contested grand narratives of liberation
from fascism and tyranny: the Spanish Civil War, the French Resistance,
and communism. His experiences—a venerable catalogue of transnational
cataclysm and catastrophe, displacement, struggle, and loss—are emblematic of twentieth-century Europe's distressed, reverberating history. His
longing for justice, freedom, and international solidarity, and his multifaceted, persistent, and principled attempts to ground a body of political
convictions in real possibility, merit scrutiny by those inheriting this con-
founding and fraught legacy. Since the day of his return to France after his
internment in a German concentration camp, Semprún has assumed strategies of resistance and self-disclosure. At its most acute points, his almost

preternatural capacity to fight and make sacrifices for his political ideals, though not at the cost of suspending his critical judgments, has drawn fierce responses. Ultimately, Semprún's elegant articulations of lament, rage, and despair about lost lives and lost causes designate him an exemplary survivor and witness.

Semprún's survival narrative, and the means he uses to both translate and transmit his ongoing story, are the result of densely layered factors—age, geography, sensibility, education, and ideology. In 1937, the teenage Semprún and his family fled the Spanish Civil War for France, where he joined the Communist Party. In 1940, at the age of seventeen, he joined the southern branch of the French Resistance, the Maquis. Caught by the Gestapo in 1943, he was tortured and deported as a political prisoner to Buchenwald, where he was interned until liberation on April 11, 1945. Upon liberation, Semprún returned to France as an *apatride*—a stateless person—and struggled, with extraordinary difficulty, to begin life again. As he puts it in his book *The Long Voyage*, "In order to survive, the organism has to adhere closely to reality, and reality was actually this totally *un*natural world of the prison of death. But the real shock occurred when I returned from this voyage."[2] For the Spanish Red (*Rotspanier*) who returns after the war from his "long voyage" not to Spain but to France, both liberation and exile were experienced within a complex set of relations. The goals of the Resistance appeared on the surface to have been achieved, but the revolution was a depressing failure; moreover, despite the grotesque crimes perpetrated and the massive upheavals suffered by millions in Hitler's war, as well as the rearranging of the global political map by the Allies, fascism in Spain had, nonetheless, survived.

In Buchenwald, Semprún had—for the first time since his exile—associated with Spaniards, with whom he could speak Spanish; perhaps most important, he met members of the Spanish Communist Party.[3] In the sixteen-year interim between liberation and the writing of *The Long Voyage*, Semprún engaged in parallel and interrelated political and psychological struggles. He engaged in political work full-time, joining the illegal, Paris-based Spanish Communist Party (PCE), in which he served in important positions from 1952 to 1962 as a key organizer of underground operations aimed at overthrowing Franco's fascist regime. However, during the Stalinist purges of the early 1950s, Semprún began to question and criticize the PCE's rigidity and corruption, implicating its entrenched political culture, and he and the Marxist theorist Fernando Claudin were expelled at an international conference held in a Bohemian castle in Prague in 1964. Saying farewell to his comrades signified the end of "the most important period of my life, the one that had brought me the greatest adventure and the most experience," he wrote (*AFS*, 215). And yet he reports that there were other contradictory emotions, for he felt "the intimate satisfaction of having been faithful to my most profound convictions to the very last, of not having betrayed that Communist freedom that had brought me to the party at the age of eighteen and that now, in obedience to an identical need for rigor and consistency, was driving me from the party" (215). Not long before he was expelled, in an all-consuming rush, he had written *Le grand voyage*, the book that "wrote" him, which won him two literary prizes, the Prix Formentor and Prix littéraire de la Résistance. Semprún had already completed the book when the leaders of the Party castigated him as an object of suspicion, as an ambitious writer with priorities outside the Party. Except for the years between 1988 and 1991, when he returned to Spain to participate in the post-Franco debates about the transition to democracy and served as minister of culture, he has lived in Paris.

The three autobiographical texts by Semprún that are the touchstones for my analysis were written over almost a thirty-year period: *The Long Voyage* (titled *The Cattle Truck* in England), an autobiographical novel written in 1963; *The Autobiography of Federico Sanchez* (translated in English as *Communism in Spain in the Franco Era: The Autobiography of Federico Sanchez*), an *autobiocritica* written in 1976; and *Literature or Life*, a metamemoir written in 1991.[4] Just as *The Autobiography of Federico Sanchez* and *Literature or Life* are commentaries on *The Long Voyage*, seen from the governing perspective of mourning and memorializing in autobiographical writing, *The Long Voyage* and *Literature or Life* may be regarded as bookends for *The Autobiography of Federico Sanchez*. I have selected these texts because they are at once three generic variations on a theme and three thematic variations on a genre—and because they offer temporal and conceptual markers elucidating Semprún's remarkable life course. In a different discussion, one might carefully delineate and elaborate on the generic variations and innovations among these autobiographical narratives, but for my purposes here, the overarching rubric of self/life/writing is most pertinent.

The Long Voyage recounts a five-day mental and physical journey from Compiègne, France, to Buchenwald in January 1944 from the perspective of its twenty-year-old Spanish narrator—philosopher-poet, communist, and member of the French Resistance. Part 1 consists of the mental journey, the narrator's thoughts and recollections of his Resistance activity, capture, torture, deportation, and liberation (mirroring Semprún's own experiences); the narrative centers on the power of the imagination to offset what is physically transpiring inside a dark, claustrophobic cattle car containing 119 political prisoners bound for the German concentration camp. The only direct representation of the camp itself is found in the much shorter part 2, which recounts the transport's delivery at the gates of Buchenwald.

The Autobiography of Federico Sanchez, part confession and part political critique, revisits the day, almost twenty years after liberation, when Semprún was officially denounced and expelled from the Spanish Communist Party as an intellectual heretic. Semprún's expulsion from the PCE recapitulated his original exile from Spain, all the more painfully because he found himself rejected and reviled by those with whom he had shared his deepest hopes for the post-Franco era. Exclusion from the PCE's militant activities permanently changed his political and personal life, helped redefine the real and symbolic boundaries of Buchenwald for him, and redirected his writing career. *The Autobiography* polemicizes against his former comrades, provides testimony about a series of specific events, and analyzes their implications for the Party and for himself.

Literature or Life covers roughly the period from 1940, Semprún's last year as a student at the prestigious Lycée Henri-IV in Paris, just before he joined the Maquis, to 1992, after his only return visit to Buchenwald. Perhaps most significantly, the book is a testimony to the oscillating effects of his experiences in Buchenwald and a philosophical investigation into how such an account can be narrated. Indeed, *Literature or Life's* greatest contribution to Holocaust literature may be its anguishing approach to, and startling analysis of, the problem of survival: whether and how to translate the experience of life-in-death or death-in-life. Divided into three parts, the text is organized both structurally and thematically around repetition and return, juxtaposed and transposed memories, and embedded stories. As Semprún shows by example, and my own reading practice here will reinforce, these densely intertwined memories, reconstructions, and reflections are linked by association and do not pretend to observe any linear chronological dictates, though they are driven by the demands of history.

Because writing confers its own ontological and performative status, virtually all writing is a form of memorializing—if not in intention, then certainly in effect. The more purposeful agenda of autobiography is to translate, by any means necessary, the ephemera of a life into narrative, and in the process to resurrect and retain, in altered form, what otherwise might be lost to the autobiographer, as well as to future readers.[5] Autobiography creates a legacy through memorialization and claims a space in life for death and loss—striving to reconfigure the terms of meaning that mortality imposes on representation. Critics of autobiography have increasingly redirected their attention away from specific strategies of recollection and re-creation and toward memorialization as a primal feature or motive for more recent autobiographical writing. Of course, many notable autobiographies, from St. Augustine's *Confessions* to Vladimir Nabokov's *Speak, Memory*, postulate on the methods and motives for textualizing memory, analyze its intricate workings, and exhibit their own specific self-reflexive memorializing technique as strategies of compensation and consolation for loss. Nonetheless, the ways in which, most recently, autobiographers and readers strenuously bind memory to catastrophic trauma and loss in particular, signal a shift, which I address in this chapter. My reading of Semprún's testimonial narrative of survival encompasses and engages his lifetime of shocks and losses: historical, political, and psychic.

Why Write?

Semprún's account of his lifelong dance with death and its dialectical relation to political struggle is astounding for its intensity and variety of expression. Semprún implies that his anguishing memories of Buchenwald had more or less lain dormant because he was so preoccupied with political work. The pattern was established soon after the war. "The murderous language of writing" was impossible, so, as he puts it, he chose to forget: "After that spring of 1946, having willingly joined the collective anonymity of a postwar life glittering with all sorts of possibilities for the future, I lived more than fifteen years, the historic span of a generation, in the blissful fog of this amnesia." By writing, he believes, he was "refusing to live"—for retelling was reliving everything he had struggled to keep in abeyance—a mode of existence Semprún calls "this studied schizophrenia" (*LL*, 226). As the narrator testifies early in *The Long Voyage*, the novel recounts many terrible events, but little about the camp experience itself: "For sixteen years I've tried to forget this voyage, and I did forget this voyage. No one around me thinks any more about my having made this voyage. But the fact is that I forgot it while realizing full well that one day I would have to take it again" (*LV*, 24).

Only when he had the time and the imaginative space to reflect on what haunted him did the memories of his Buchenwald experience emerge; and they took shape slowly and artfully. Semprún's self-characterization in *The Autobiography of Federico Sanchez* as "the instrument, the translator, of this anonymous work of memory" (*AFS*, 185) that was "revived" by listening to another survivor's testimony, illustrates a phenomenon common to survivors of collective catastrophic events. In listening silently, over a series of evenings, to a comrade describe the horrors of imprisonment in Mauthausen, the clandestine militant Semprún recognized the dominant features and elements of every concentration camp story, including his own. Although surprised by the act of disclosure itself and reminded of the horrors he himself had suffered and witnessed, Semprún was nonetheless not shocked by its content. And yet, the effect of his comrade's testimony and its message—the violation of one's humanity, the affront to all humanity— moved Semprún to write his own story.

Semprún provides ample evidence of memory's dependence on external stimuli. Involuntary memories, as extensively elaborated in philosophy and literature by Bergson and Proust, are metonymically associated and rooted in the sensorial and the unexpected—a flash of color, a particular smell, the strains of a song. For Semprún, by contrast, what I would call "motivated" memories are more often provoked or solicited by the speech acts of others, and are thus dialogical and metaphorical in nature: the oral testimony of a fellow survivor, La Pasionaria's proclamation of his expulsion from the Spanish Communist Party, the radio announcement of the death of Primo Levi. Semprún links the genesis of *Literature or Life* only hours before the radio announcement of Levi's death and his memory of that moment to the last revisions seven years later of the very book the reader is reading. By doing so, he suggests a structural similarity with the dialogical genesis of *The Long Voyage*, which emerged in response to another survivor's testimony, and also inscribes himself in the particular genealogy of Holocaust survivor testimony. Although Semprún explains the circumstances that finally produced the writing of *The Long Voyage* sixteen years after liberation, he never explicitly states by what means of self-selection the act of writing this text fell to him. What compelled Semprún's individual intervention seems to be the self-justification of transforming "disjointed and repetitive stories" (*AFS*, 185) into an aesthetic object, of shaping disparate memories into a literary narrative. Put another way, Semprún wrote *The Long Voyage* not only because he again "remembered" he had a story to tell—hence the imperative to tell it—but, perhaps more important, because he knew he had the capacity to refashion it with aesthetic aplomb and political acuity.

In *The Autobiography of Federico Sanchez*, written shortly after he was expelled from the Communist Party, Semprún adamantly refutes the Party leaders' charge that his politics and his writing life were in conflict and that his writing had begun to preempt his politics. Despite his rage at being cast out by the Party, Semprún waited to publish the book until more than a decade later, after the death of Franco and the legalization of the PCE in Spain.[6] Among the many governing ironies of his life at that time, the publication of *The Long Voyage* brought him a life-changing, worldly success that he describes as having been paid for "with the brutal return of past despair" (*LL*, 226). Thus, by the time *The Autobiography of Federico Sanchez* appeared, Semprún was a well-known figure, though he continued to suffer from a Buchenwald-induced despair provoked by writing; nonetheless, he continued to write otherwise, across genres, and always autobiographically and politically.

A glance at Semprún's relatively short but distinguished run as a screenwriter of notable political films reveals not so much an escape from Buchenwald as the site of traumatic memory as a delving into the more diffused problematic of whether, in Sartrean terms, writing is a form of political commitment. More specifically, all the films—Alain Resnais's *La guerre est finie* (1965); Costa-Gavras's *Z* (1968), *The Confession* (1969), and *Stavisky* (1977); and Joseph Losey's *Les routes du sud* (1978)—whatever their expressed subject matter or historical framework, convey his profound disappointment and frustration with postwar European internecine leftist politics. This is seen most patently in the protagonist of *La guerre est finie*, a middle-aged revolutionary whose political life is defined by his experience in the Spanish Civil War. The film depicts the tragedy of Spanish history after 1936 as an intergenerational conflict, as well as a conflict between theory and praxis, myth and reality. Any spectator familiar with Semprún's personal history recognizes crucial elements of his story in the representation of the betrayal of revolutionary dreams and ideals by the PCE.

Whatever the context, Semprún's textual moves all take place at the margins of autobiography; throughout his career, he has never ceased to experiment with the forms and techniques of the genre. Not only does he keep writing his autobiography, interminably as it were, but he also keeps finding different genres and media through which to work through the problems that he struggles to elude and yet must confront. In *The Autobiography of Federico Sanchez*, he violates the pact between author and reader that Philippe Lejeune regards as the defining convention of autobiography—that is, that the signature of the author and the name of the protagonist are the same.[7] How, then, to write an autobiography, not in one's own name, but in the name of another? And, more to the generic point, why do so? Despite the surface similarity of their titles, Semprún's text differs fundamentally from, for example, *The Autobiography of Alice B. Toklas*, Gertrude Stein's inside twist on the relationship between textual subjectivity and identity.[8] Toklas and Stein are two different people, and Stein is ventriloquizing her own story through Toklas, but Sanchez and Semprún are the same person. Structurally and narratively, Semprún's technique here more closely resembles Christa Wolf's in her memoir about growing up in Nazi Germany, *Patterns of Childhood*.[9] In that text, the adult autobiographer, seeking to maintain a respectful distance masked by the conventional use of the autobiographer's "I," refers to herself as a child as "Nelly" and addresses her as "you." Federico Sanchez was one of several of Semprún's noms de guerre during his career as an underground militant; clearly, Semprún wants to split their textual and narrative identities, just as they had to be in reality, precisely so as not to collapse the distinction between the man writing the memoir in the mid 1970s and the man whose life and activities are being depicted in the immediate postwar period under scrutiny, the man expelled and silenced by the Communist Party.

In theory, the identity of the clandestine militant Federico Sanchez died that day in Prague and the identity of the writer and intellectual Jorge Semprún emerged in full view. Thus there is a double and fitting irony to Semprún's textual reappropriation of his former identity in *The Autobiography of Federico Sanchez*. That critical fiction—the identity split between Sanchez and Semprún—was purposefully collapsed in print a number of years later when the two identities were revealed by his political nemesis, Santiago Carrillo, as belonging to the same person. For Semprún, Carrillo's effort to defame the legacy of both Federico Sanchez and Jorge Semprún for future generations of young communists becomes the pretext for Semprún to reclaim, for his own purposes, both his name and that of Sanchez:

And in 1974 nobody remembered Federico Sanchez anymore. I myself had forgotten about Federico Sanchez. . . . Well, then, now that [Santiago] Carrillo [PCE secretary general] has resurrected Federico Sanchez, now that he has conjured up this specter and rescued him from oblivion, now that he has given him a semblance of reality, he will be obliged to put up with the consequences. He will be obliged to confront his absence of memory of Federico Sanchez. (*AFS*, 202)

Semprún's textual reappropriation of Federico Sanchez reminds us that history is always contested territory; though the past is on some level irrecoverable, it is never completely sealed and thus never truly past.[10] All its traces and ligaments live on through us and in our texts. In this decisive confrontation with the Party and the suffering it caused, Semprún performs a range of interrelated functions of remembering and memorializing simultaneously. As he ponders the differences between history and memory, he clarifies the instrumentality of "direct testimony" and fills in the blanks with the names of the silenced witnesses who need him to speak on their behalf:

Someday, no doubt, researchers will thoroughly analyze this somber period in the history of the Spanish Communist Party. But I greatly fear that even the most detailed analyses will still lack the terrible flavor and vigor of direct testimony. I am very much afraid that the witnesses of that period will never speak. Jesus Monzon is dead. So is Joan Comorera. (*AFS*, 91)

Dispersed throughout his narratives are pages devoted to memorializing the names of communist comrades who gave their lives fighting fascism, either in the underground or in Buchenwald. But in the service of accounting for his own change of heart and break with Party orthodoxy, he reserves his outrage, grief, and guilt for the innocent victims of the spectacular Party trials and other liquidations and assassinations, in particular the hanging of his comrade Josef Frank.

Frank, who had been his comrade in the *Arbeitstatistik* (labor statistics) service in Buchenwald, became a prominent member of the Czech Communist Party and was accused in 1952 of having been a Gestapo agent in the camp. For Semprún, Frank's innocence was certified by the fact that Semprún had survived the camp, making it possible for him at that very moment to be "drinking a cup of coffee and reading *l'Humanité*." Reading about the trials, Semprún reasons that "[i]f Frank had been a Gestapo agent, you would have become ashes and smoke in the crematory of Buchenwald decades ago. What is more, you had collaborated with Frank on several ultraclandestine party missions at Buchenwald. If Frank had been a Gestapo agent . . . he would have taken steps to denounce you." Semprún's salutes and mea culpas to his fallen comrades, each one an incantatory variation on "Go on remembering," culminate in a repeated admission of "shared responsibility" with the leadership of the Spanish Communist Party, not for Frank's death on the gallows, but for "living the lie of the accusation." Critical to this exemplary passage in the *autobiocritica* is Semprún's shame-filled association of Frank's death with his own political advancement. The following spring, in 1953, Semprún addresses Sanchez: "You made your first clandestine trip to Spain. Then a new stage in your life began, remember" (*AFS*, 95, 96–97).

In these ritualized inscriptions of individual loss, memorializing and confessing are inextricably related efforts at self-explanation and rectification in a historical context. Their goal is to reify the bonds of the collectivity at the expense of narrow or partisan self-interest, so as to call attention to the crime committed while not repeating it symbolically. In other words, Semprún's naming of those names that would otherwise be forgotten or forever cut off from their political frame of reference is a designated social, but not abstract or undifferentiated, act of mourning. It is signified, precisely, asserts Dominick LaCapra, by a "specification of the objects of mourning . . . the naming of for whom one mourns."[11]

The twin tasks and burdens of memorializing for the sake of preserving one's symbolic investments in the past and memorializing to redress past wrongs are undertaken, nonetheless, with a diffused set of desires and intentions. Although Semprún values testimony as a historical mode of discourse and believes in its ethical and political significance, he may be too implicated in his own "context of survivorship," in the words of Eric Santner,[12] to benefit psychically from this exercise. As will become increasingly evident over the course of this chapter, even as he mourns the loss of his role in the Party and his faith in its political culture, psychological compensation for pain and suffering has never been either a motive or an effect of writing for Semprún. Several pages later, Semprún again evokes the memory of Josef Frank, "my comrade in Buchenwald," noting that despite repeated public confessions of having remained silent in the face of injustice, "this wound of Stalinism on my own skin continued to burn" (*AFS*, 105). Memorialists like Semprún, who are survivors, seek to inscribe themselves and their stories into history; although these stories are ostensibly about the past, about the already happened, they are always written or rewritten in the present and are directed at and toward the future. Autobiography, both testimonial and testamentary, is a form of scriptural reincarnation—even if of the secular kind. It stakes a claim to one's own afterlife, to the promise of collective remembrance. For if writing is an act of resistance against forgetting, it is also an act of resistance against being forgotten. Every autobiographical occasion is an apologia or defense of one's life or position against another potentially last word on the subject.

This is especially the case with autobiographies whose project of remembrance is patently historical, political, or ideological in nature, in which the moral imperative to remember is conceived as both a responsibility and an opportunity to affect a situation. "The struggle over the historical record is seen from all sides as no less crucial than the armed struggle," Barbara Harlow observes.[13] Although all Semprún's writing serves the causes of resistance and reclamation, *The Autobiography of Federico Sanchez* deploys repudiation, refutation, and rectification as its means to "settle accounts" or "set the record straight" against the forces of denial and repression—for posterity. Although we do not often conceive of them as such, Holocaust and other kinds of testimonial narratives constitute a subset of the kind of autobiographical writing in which historiography and memory are encoded as being at odds with one another, and the political and/or ideological function of writing as counterdiscourse is foregrounded. As an attestation of loss, *The Autobiography of Federico Sanchez* is a manifestly political text with a not-so-latent psychic dimension. Certainly, its autobiocritical approach to the problem of selective memory as a political tool affirms "the uses of psychoanalytical interpretation in understanding the shape and meaning of historical event and narrative."[14]

The Long Voyage is Semprún's most acclaimed novel. Its events are told in the present tense from the perspective of the narrator, Gérard, although the real present of the narration is not the time of the deportation journey but sixteen years later, when the narrator is remembering it. The two time frames have always been linked, however, because what Peter Brooks calls "the inchoate intent to tell"[15] has already been born in the cattle car:

Four days, five nights. But I must have counted wrong, or else some of the days must have turned into nights. I have a surplus of nights, more nights than I can use. . . .We're advancing . . . toward the fifth night, the sixth day. But is it we who are advancing? We're motionless, stacked in on top of one another, it's the night that is advancing, the fourth night, advancing toward the motionless corpses we are destined to be. I burst out laughing. . . . "Save your strength," the guy says. (*LV*, 9)

What Terrence Des Pres calls "the language of ultimate concern,"[16] offset by this tone of mordant irony, fuels the dialogical exchange between the narrator and his new comrade, "the guy from Semur," around which this existential(ist) novel is structured. With so much to remember, and so much to say, and the destination or resolution all but predetermined, five days in the cattle car is both too long and not long enough. Since this is a survivor's tale, all the tension in this taut narrative is strung between the drive to live and the movement toward death. As Brooks puts it, plot is what deviates, digresses, from this straight line.

Brooks's argument for a Freudian poetics locates in *Beyond the Pleasure Principle* a model for the way narratives work and reads our interpretive schemas as themselves products of the ways stories of the psyche get narrated. In Freud's text on the theory of the drives, we find, Brooks says,

a dynamic model that structures ends (death, quiescence, non-narratability) against beginnings (Eros, stimulation into tension, the desire of narrative) in a manner that necessitates the middle as detour, as struggle toward the end under the compulsion of imposed delay, as arabesque in the dilatory space of the text. The model proposes that we live in order to die, hence that the intentionality of plot lies in its orientation toward the end even while the end must be achieved only through detour.[17]

This model helps us conceptualize what is a survival mechanism of the most profound and exquisite kind, implemented under the direst of conditions: the freedom of the imagination to refuse the inevitability of death. Indeed, whereas "the guy from Semur" wants to survive the trip so that he can return from it—seemingly unconcerned about what is at the end of the line (that is, between "the voyage" and "the coming back"), the narrator is already attaching the will to survive to the imperative to tell about it. In their first of many conversations on the subject, they assume their assigned subject positions, each providing different yet interchangeable commentary on how best to stay on those parallel tracks on which trains, narratives, and lives run. "The guy from Semur" initiates:

"We have to hold out."

. . . .

"Hold out for what? So we can tell about this voyage?"
"Of course not, so we can come back from it," he says sternly.

. . . .

"Don't you think we ought to tell about it?"
"But there's nothing to tell. A hundred and twenty guys in a box car. Days and nights of traveling. Old men who go off their nuts and begin screaming. I'd like to know what there is to tell."
"And at the end of the line?" I ask him. (*LV*, 25)

Through the course of the young Spaniard's meditations, remembrances, and projections, the reader learns that the unnamed Frenchman from Semur, with whom he banters and feels a desperate solidarity, will die suddenly at the gates of the camp and that the narrator will struggle, in full-blown ambivalence, for sixteen years to tell this story—in novelistic form: the very one the reader is reading. As a commentary on what elicits this narrative, the fundamental question, of course, is not what there is to tell, but how and why to tell it. The problem of what constitutes the promise of a meaningful—not to mention gratifying—story for Semprún's protagonist is rehearsed, repeated, anticipated, and revealed partly through the fractured chronology that flashes back and projects forward, as the narrative moves inexorably toward "the end of the line," the point at which there will be nothing more to say, or, at least, no way to say it.

When the cattle car reaches Buchenwald—with only some of its human cargo still alive—the narrator is forced to abandon his pal from Semur. The loss of the comrade who served as the crucial repository of his memories is described as a primal severing of the narrator from his own past experience. Threatened now with symbolic effacement—the possibility of not being remembered—he links the imperative to transmit the story of this voyage with his only chance for survival: "the laying down of his body on the floor of the car as though I were laying down my own past, all the memories linking me to the world of the past. Everything I had told him during these days and endless nights, everything my life used to be is slated to disappear, since he is no longer here" (*LV*, 216–17).

The feature of repetition in a testimonial narration reflects the compulsion to return to the scene of traumatic events, which in turn masks the fear of doing so. Thus to say that repetition and return link the memoir and the novel, both as formal strategies and thematic structuring devices, is to indicate that repression, a mode of unconscious evasion, is but another kind of return. One very painful and powerful five-page passage in *The Long Voyage*, using stylistic repetition and rendered in excruciating detail, performs or enacts a precise event that appears to have been blocked or concealed until the telling. As trauma theorists attest, the act of witnessing the death of other people is an elemental part of trauma. However, such an encounter with death, though overwhelming, is never absolute or total, because that would be too threatening to the organism; rather a delicate psychic economy is maintained, an unstable combination of how much is taken in and how much one keeps out. For Semprún's narrator, who has recounted the deaths of close comrades, as well as of others he did not know, again and again, this act of witnessing exemplifies what has been called the "survivor mission." Carrier of a singular charge long withheld, the event belongs to another order of atrocity, calling for a special act of transmission:

And maybe I shall be able to tell about the death of the Jewish children, describe that death in all its details, solely in the hope . . . that these children may hear it . . . to tell of their death . . . that story which has never been told, which has lain buried in my memory like some mortal treasure, preying on it with a sterile suffering. Perhaps it is out of pride that I have never told anyone the story of the Jewish children, come from Poland in the cold of the coldest winter of the war, come to die on the broad avenue leading up to the camp entrance. . . . As if I had the right or the possibility, to keep it to myself any longer. It's true that I had decided to forget. . . . All right, I had forgotten everything, from now on I can remember everything. I can tell the story . . . not as a story that happened to me especially, but above all one that happened to the Jewish children from Poland. That is, now, after willful oblivion, not only am I able to tell this story, I feel compelled to tell it . . . not in my own name . . . in the name of the Jewish children. The story of their death on the broad avenue which led up to the camp entrance, beneath the stony gaze of the Nazi eagles, surrounded by the laughter of the S.S., in the name of death itself. (*LV*, 162–63)

The day he saw the Jewish children die crystallized for him the categorical difference between those who had been deported to the camp either as political enemies or as undesirables, to work under slavelike conditions, and those who were on their way to extermination.[18] However much he and his comrades had suffered at the hands of the Nazis, a causal explanation for their situation and pride associated with it existed. As a *Rotspanier,* he was the fascists' self-declared political enemy, and his actions as a resister had expressed this, whereas in this transport of Jews, which included about fifteen children between the ages of eight and twelve, the narrator witnessed the purest expression of genocidal brutality. His description of the children's otherworldly innocence sets this act of testimony apart from all others in the narrative, and not only because it is steeped in disbelief and horror. What is most curious about this aspect of Semprún's testimony is his disclosure that it may be "out of pride" that he has not told this story sooner. What would "pride" have to do with it? The unspoken word here,

I would suggest, is pride's opposite: shame. "The death of the children" is an agonizing reminder to Semprún that despite his and his comrades' special positions in the camp, they were nevertheless prisoners and in no position to prevent such atrocities without jeopardizing their own lives. What does this say about the syndrome of survivor guilt?

The overarching significance of this particular act of witnessing is marked above all by its harrowing psychic effects; but it is also useful to note that there were larger postwar political stakes in the distinction drawn so painfully in this long passage. That Semprún is often referred to as a "Holocaust" writer because he is a survivor of a concentration camp merits clarification. "Concentration camp" and "Holocaust" are commonly used as synonyms, as if "Holocaust" were interchangeable with the "World War II" or "National Socialism," both of which were, of course, related but separate events or entities.[19] Just as having been interned in a concentration camp does not make one a victim of the Holocaust, not all targets of Hitler's Final Solution necessarily suffered in a concentration camp. In reinforcing this distinction, my point is not to essentialize or hierarchize the victims or victim groups of the Nazis or of wartime suffering in general. Rather, I am reinforcing a political and historical distinction that has great bearing on Semprún's interpretation of himself as a survivor.

As Semprún signals in the passage about the Jewish children and elsewhere, the full range of differences among the prisoners in the camp was an incontrovertible fact of life and death. Moreover, the systems of classification inherent in the concentration camp universe did not end with the war; they were used to promote specific postwar political agendas and revised nationalist narratives. Indeed, for decades following liberation, the issue of how the various victims of Nazi persecution were represented took on disturbing importance in the postwar narratives of every country that had been under Nazi occupation. Questions about returning deportees asked which camp, why they had been interned, how long they had been there, how they were treated, and what their intended trajectories were. If the differences not only *within* but *among* the various camps assumed importance after the war as a means of self-identification for the deportees themselves, those differences also became the means, though for differing reasons and ends, by which the dead were classified and commemorated by their compatriots and respective governments. Regarding those who did not return, where and how they died took on paramount importance.[20]

Part 2 of *The Long Voyage* is only fifteen pages long, functioning both as a coda and a prologue: "the long voyage" to the camp has ended, and the narrator has physically survived that ordeal. Semprún's narrator recounts the long march from the train platform to the camp itself. What might be called the "transition" or "shift" between the two parts—the first written in the first person, the second in the third person—is actually a rupture or break that occurs, almost imperceptibly, in the middle of the last sentence of the first part. The shift from first to third person is introduced by the self-identification of the narrator as Gérard, which was, in fact, Semprún's nom de guerre in the Resistance. "The guy from Semur is dead and I'm alone. . . . Maybe he had said, 'Don't leave me alone, Gérard,' and Gérard jumps down onto the platform, into the blinding light" (*LV*, 216). The first sentence of part 2 begins with a kind of strange irony that characterizes Semprún's entire relationship to his own survival: "By chance he lands on his feet" (*LV*, 221). This narrative shift registers what is both a psychic and physical leap from the awful shared intimacy of that cattle car into pure alienation and objectification, from life into the concentration camp universe of death.

Thus it is a jarring revelation in *Literature or Life* when Semprún announces that "the guy from Semur"—who had engaged Gérard in conversation throughout the fateful voyage until the very end, and thus helped him survive it—was an invention. But the creation of this comrade with whom the narrator could share the voyage was no mere literary device, however brilliant; it was the only way he could return to the experience, sixteen years later, and survive it a second time. The "guy from Semur"—who is also Semprún—dies so that Gérard can "live." That is the coda, the end of the line, his survival of the voyage. But the memory of entering the camp is still another matter. That trauma is so great that the first-person narrator must split off from Gérard as well—from Gérard, who is "not the same person" as himself.

On the final page, at the end of the voyage, "Gérard tries to engrave all this in his memory," as he marches to the lively music on a cold, clear January night, already imagining the possibility that "the impending death of all the spectators may efface forever the memory of this spectacle" (*LV*, 236). He announces, invoking Dante, that he is "leaving the world of the living." In every Semprúnian text after *The Long Voyage*, the narrator has left "the world of the living," and his status as a survivor is a constant internal renegotiation, as well as a reengagement of, the meaning of survival in the outside world. Lawrence Langer presents this as a crucial feature in oral testimonies by survivors: "For the witnesses, the Holocaust is at once a 'lived' event and a 'died' event: the paradox of how one survives a died event is one of the most urgent . . . topics of their testimonies."[21]

Thirty years after completing *The Long Voyage*, Semprún opens *Literature or Life* with a description of April 12, 1945, the day after the liberation of Buchenwald, with the newly freed, twenty-year-old Semprún seeing the horror of his own gaze reflected in the eyes of three young British officers. Here Semprún revisits the experience of "liberation" yet again (the word "liberation" may be the most semantically charged in Semprún's entire survivor lexicon). There is an enormous difference between the representation of the liberated survivor with the young British officers in *Literature or Life* and the scene that takes place one day later in *The Long Voyage*. In *The Long Voyage*, Gérard, the traumatized young survivor, shows two young, attractive women from the French Mission around the crematorium at Buchenwald. He is both sufficiently self-aware to register the irreconcilable gap between the visitors and the survivors and sufficiently self-possessed to want to jolt the women out of their blissful ignorance, however futile he may know the gesture to be. Seeking narrative control of the situation and exercising a bit of macho malice in the process, he actively seeks to shock them. Although the purpose of the tour of the crematorium may be to provide a political, moral, or historical lesson, Gérard seems to derive a certain degree of sadomasochistic pleasure from seeing how far he can push the graphic limits of the situation to elicit some desired effects from his audience. In fact, he shows how few words are required to accomplish his task.

The thematic power of the scene derives from his retelling of the story; reporting the tour calls attention to the performativity of this act of translation from first-degree testimony to second-degree testimony, from the visual to the verbal. Semprún's narrator embeds the *showing* of primary, documentary evidence of atrocity within a narrative that recounts the *telling* of the *showing*; and one of the ironic effects of Semprún's technique is to make the reader momentarily complicit in that process, as if the reader shared with the narrator both the consciousness of death and the unbearable knowledge of the camps. Here the young women are outside—on the other side, on the unequivocal side of the living. But, ultimately, a false sense of complicity has been created. Semprún's point is precisely that although language has the capacity to record, report, or even reimagine what transpired in the crematorium, physical, even temporal proximity will not bring anyone closer to the event, which is experientially untranslatable on any level, from any remove.

Sixteen years after the end of the war, in *The Long Voyage*, Semprún's self-depiction as a survivor stresses his resistance in the camp and on an embattled political stage. Almost fifty years after Liberation, in *Literature or Life*, Semprún emphasizes instead the loss of agency and feelings of abjection that he experienced, suggesting that perhaps, over time, Semprún lost faith in what precisely his resistance stood for. However we conjecture the reason for the marked contrast between the two representations of the newly liberated concentration survivor, both scenes ultimately convey the same message about the subject position of survivor as Other. Both encounters reinforce the existential difference between survivors and the rest of the human race. In *Literature or Life*, Semprún depicts the scene of "liberation" as a moment of naked horror reflected in the expression of the other: "They stand amazed before me, and suddenly, in that terror-stricken gaze, I see myself—in their horror" (*LL*, 4). This moment frames the survivor's immediate situation, but, more important, it projects forward to its prolonged implications and the overarching theme of the book. This condition has no tenable resolution. The expressions on the young soldiers' faces shock him into recognizing that in his eyes they see death, and that for the survivor, death is no longer "on the horizon, somewhere straight ahead, the unpredictable end-all of fate. . . . Death is already in my past. But I have not really survived death. . . . I have not escaped it. I have, instead, crossed through it, from one end to the other. All things considered, I am a ghost" (*LL*, 14–15). Having "crossed . . . from one end to the other" brings with it a labyrinthine complex of self-imposed expectations, but already he expresses doubt about "the possibility of telling the story." Although such an admission will not be surprising to contemporary readers familiar with Holocaust survivor narratives, what distinguishes Semprún's Wittgensteinian approach to the problem of speaking (or writing) unspeakable horror is precisely that he doesn't consider such horror to be unspeakable. The problem with articulating or transmitting trauma lies, in Semprún's rather dissident view, not in the intrinsic inadequacy of language, but in the nature of the experience itself and its subsequent effects:

Not that what we lived through is indescribable. It was unbearable, which is something else, something that doesn't concern the form of a possible account, but its substance. Not its articulation, but its density. The only ones who will manage to reach this substance, this transparent density, will be those able to shape their evidence into an artistic object, a space of creation. . . . Only the artifice of a masterly narrative will prove capable of conveying some of the truth of such testimony. The "ineffable" you hear about is only an alibi . . . language contains everything. . . . You can tell all about this experience. . . . Even if you remain caught up in it, prolonging death, if necessary—reviving it endlessly. . . . Even if you become no more than the language of death, and live at its expense, fatally. (*LL*, 13–14)

For Semprún—at least in this passage which can be seen as a retrospective commentary on his entire literary career as a survivor—the problem of transmission is not metaphysical, but rhetorical and psychological; language is not transcendent, but immanent—on both sides of the writing/reading, telling/listening divide.[22]

Semprún alters Hayden White's notion that "narrative is a meta-code, a human universal on the basis of which transcultural messages about the nature of a shared reality can be transmitted."[23] Semprún asks: How can one communicate to the world outside the camp what it cannot otherwise possibly fathom, such as the quotidian smell of crematory smoke against the seeming eternal expanse of snow, and then the memory of the smell of burning flesh as it impinges on a perfectly glorious spring day in Paris many years after the war? What Semprún calls "the radiant horror of absolute evil," however, is on the other side of even that abyss.

Even if one had given evidence with absolute precision, with perfect objectivity (something by definition beyond the powers of the individual witness), even in this case one could miss the essential thing. Because it wasn't the accumulation of horror, which could be spelled out, endlessly, in detail. One could recount the story of any day at all, from reveille at 4:30 in the morning to curfew—the fatiguing labor, the constant hunger, the chronic lack of sleep, the persecution by the Kapos, the latrine duty, the floggings from the SS, the assembly line work in munitions factories, the crematory smoke, the public executions, the endless roll calls in the winter snow, the exhaustion, the death of friends—yet never manage to deal with the essential thing, or reveal the icy mystery of this experience, its dark, shining truth. . . . What's essential . . . is the experience of radical Evil. . . . Besides the essential thing about this experience of Evil is that it will turn out to have been lived as the experience of death. (*LL*, 87–89)

This passage is rhetorically stunning, because even as Semprún posits, and in so doing performs, what he claims to be the failure (or irrelevance) of

testimony—the accretion of details as the ultimate cataloguing of atrocities—it also points to what is beyond a certain kind of totalization. Semprún's declared preference for the recasting of evidence into "an artistic object" suggests that the initial choice to employ fiction as his medium was
a source of gratification with surplus value. Like the *Fort/Da* game played
by Freud's grandson, he re-creates the traumatic experience—endlessly, it
would seem—so as to exert the very control or mastery over his life that he
lacked during the traumatic experience itself, of course. Only over time—
through more living—did he come to realize that having been so close to
death, having come back from it, as it were, did not put death behind him.
Mortality was not something he had beaten when young and would never
face again; rather, knowledge of death was something he inhabited, that
would inhabit him forever. Here Freud's description of the drive toward
death as being not life's opposite, but its other, is apt.

The acute relation between trauma and survival has been closely examined by Robert Jay Lifton, whose clinical practice and theoretical research have focused on the psychology of the survivor. Lifton describes the
survivor as one who has come into contact with death in some bodily or
psychic fashion and has remained alive. For these survivors, "The death
imprint consists of some radical intrusion of an image-feeling of threat or
end to life. . . . To be experienced, the death imprint must call forth prior
imagery either of actual death or of death equivalents. In that sense every
death encounter is itself a reactivation of earlier 'survivals.'"[24] Lifton puts
the encounter with death, the knowledge of death, at the center of the
traumatic experience. He contends that the confrontation with death is a
life-transfiguring process in which structures of meaning and images in relation to death are not only repeated, but also reformed and recontextualized, along a life-death continuum.

The metamemoir *Literature or Life* encompasses and comments upon
The Long Voyage, situating the writing of the novel—"the confrontation of
death through writing"—within the life and career of its author (*LL*, 243).
Consequently, the reader of the memoir *Literature or Life* is constantly sent
back to the novel *The Long Voyage*, written thirty years earlier, and not
because the memoir resumes where the novel leaves off, at the gates of
Buchenwald. Nothing so linear or systematic occurs in *Literature or Life*.
Rather, the dialectic of the certainty of that terrible knowledge and the fear
of remembering it is played out in the space between the two texts. *Litera-*

ture or Life as testimony, as meditation, shuttles elliptically between the recounting of Semprún's and other inmates' experiences in Buchenwald— the anatomy, the organization of concentration camp life, its daily regime—and the crippling difficulty of calling up and writing about those experiences, the loss of comrades, the terrors, and their aftermath.

Literature or Life is saturated with political and philosophical observations, but most of all with literary references, notably relating to the reading and reciting of poetry. These are not perfunctory points on an intellectual's intimate itinerary; the primary coordinates of Semprún's existence, they are not displays of erudition, but sources of sustenance and stimulation. And yet, although it would be easy to conflate "literature" with "writing" in this text (as, in fact, the title of the translation in English mistakenly suggests), the difference between these terms has a significant bearing on how we understand Semprún's struggle. The memoir makes clear that "literature" was itself a lifeline in the camp, not only an antidote to the dehumanization of the concentration camp universe, but also a mode of communication, solidarity, resistance, restoration, and appeal.[25] Semprún's love for literature has remained integral and instrumental to his identity. Although he insists that the act of writing is not a lifeline, Semprún keeps engaging the question of whether his lifelong, endless vocation is surviving or writing; he discovers again and again, to his anguish and surprise, that despite the testimonial imperative, he neither writes to survive nor survives in order to write.

The Language Question

Semprún is an inveterate translator, the ultimate infiltrator. As a bilingual writer whose sensibility was forged and formed in exile, he has an approach to identity, nationality, culture, and language that is, not surprisingly, contrarian, perversely contradictory, and not amenable to external pressure of any sort. Almost without exception, wherever Semprún lived, and whatever the literary content of his writing, he wrote in French. And yet, although an *homme de lettres françaises*, he refused to renounce his Spanish citizenship to be elected a member of the Académie française. In *The Long Voyage*, the narrator confides that while he doesn't consider France to be "home," he speaks French without a foreign accent, because it is the "surest way to preserve my status as a foreigner, which I cherish above all. If I had an accent, my 'foreignness' would be constantly apparent, it would become something banal, exteriorized. Personally, I would get used to the banality of being taken for a foreigner. Similarly, being taken for a foreigner would then no longer be any problem, it would no longer have any meaning. . . . In a certain sense, being a foreigner has become an internal virtue" (*LV*, 100). For Semprún, bilingualism may obscure the traces of origin, but the opposite of "foreigner" is not "native," nor does he want it to be. To press the problem of Semprún's nationality as if it were primarily an internal, existential issue is to miss its broader implications. Semprún's "identity" is at the crux of a much more extensive, complex, and fraught postwar issue, which he treats with a tone of absurdist rancor in a scene that follows a few pages later in *The Long Voyage*. Having expressed pride at being a Spanish Red, or *Rotspanier,* in Buchenwald, the narrator describes arriving in repatriation camp after the war and being denied his allowance of eight packs of Gauloises cigarettes and a 1,000-franc note because he wasn't "really French." He counters by showing respect for the category, if not the process. Not only is he not French, he explains with careful deliberation, but he didn't fight for France in the war; he was in the Resistance. He therefore hadn't been "repatriated" at all (*LV*, 111–12), and as a nonrepatriated person, he was entitled to money for transportation and lodging until he arrived "home." Out of sympathy, the administrators let him have the cigarettes anyway. Gérard explains to the reader that the rules actually helped him to rediscover a very significant reality: he was "going from one foreign country to another foreign country. That is, I'm the one who's a foreigner" (*LV*, 113). "Foreignness" ensures a productive perspective on politics that Semprún is loath to give up.

For Semprún, exile is first lived as a binary condition and conventionally framed as a suspension between two points—Spain and France. Over time it becomes a more diffused and abstract condition. In "Vous avez une tombe aux creux des nuages . . . ," a speech Semprún delivered in Frankfurt in 1994 upon receiving the German book trade's Friedenspreis, he elaborates on his view of exile by contrasting it with that of Thomas Mann, who after becoming an American citizen declared his true homeland to be, not Germany, but the German language. Semprún's position on such matters is irreducibly multiple.

[L]a langue espagnole n'a pas été ma patrie en exil. Elle n'a pas été la seule, en tout cas. Au contraire de Mann, je ne me suis jamais exilé de ma citoyenneté espagnole, mais de ma langue maternelle, si. A une certaine époque, j'ai cru que j'avais découvert une nouvelle patrie, en m'appropriant la langue française. . . . Cela n'est pas non plus vrai. Du point de vue de la langue littéraire . . . je suis apatride, à cause de mon bilinguisme invétéré, de ma schizophrénie linguistique définitive. . . . De toutes façons, l'idée de la patrie ne m'a jamais hantée. . . . Liberté, justice, solidarité avec les humiliés et les opprimés. . . . En fin de compte, ma patrie n'est pas la langue, ni la française ni l'espagnole, ma patrie c'est le langage.

The Spanish tongue was not my homeland in exile. It was not the only one, in any case. Contrary to Mann, I never exiled myself from my Spanish citizenship, but from my mother tongue, yes. There was a time when I believed that I had discovered a new country/homeland, by appropriating the French language. . . . But that is not true either. From the point of view of literary language . . . I am without a country, because of my inveterate bilingualism, my definitive linguistic schizophrenia. . . . The idea of a homeland has never haunted me. . . . Liberty, justice, solidarity with the humiliated and the oppressed. . . . All told, my country is not a specific language, neither French nor Spanish, my country is language.[26]

Semprún's translative, transnational orientation cannot be disaggregated from his politics, which has never endorsed a parochial, protectionist, chauvinist view of identity. For Semprún, language is to be liberated from its nationalistic constraints, while maintaining the fluidity of difference.[27]

It is worth noting, given Semprún's standing as a French-language writer and his remarks about the contingent relation between language and nation, that he wrote *The Autobiography of Federico Sanchez,* exceptionally, in Spanish. For politically pragmatic reasons, to stress his Spanish connection and to ensure that the book would reach its destined audience, he may have considered it necessary to take on the Spanish Communist Party in Spanish. The symbolic significance of this unique textual event connects, ironically, to a strange occasion that Semprún recounts in *Literature or Life,* when he was awarded the Prix Formentor in 1964 for *The Long Voyage.* During the ceremony, Semprún was offered a commemorative copy of the book in every language into which it had been translated. When he was handed the Spanish edition, it was explained to him that due to censorship in Franco's Spain and printing problems in Mexico, only the cover of the book was available. The rest of the book was blank. Arguably, the missing text was itself a testimony to the exile from Spain that set into motion

Semprún's literary career in French. As I discuss above, the publication of *The Long Voyage* was soon followed by Semprún's expulsion from the Communist Party. It seems reasonable to say that Semprún—censored on the one hand by the Falangists and nearly expunged on the other by the communists—reinscribed his Spanish identity in the interstices, restoring his mother tongue to its original, suspended place in *The Autobiography of Federico Sanchez*.

Semprún's multiple crossings exhibit an ongoing relation to translation as the dominant, transcendent, cosmopolitan modality in his life, one that he has, repeatedly, chosen to renew in every context. Arguably, this modality chose him and became his destiny. He implicitly ascribes his position, and possibly, even his survival, in Buchenwald to his knowledge of German; as the only Spanish deportee who knew German in an international group of prisoners, he did clerical work in the camp's internal administration, the *Arbeitsstatistik*.

Revising Trauma and Mourning Sites

The narrative of Semprún's survivor experiences reads like a litany of Europe's greatest tragedies; and his twenty-two months in Buchenwald as a young man clearly marked him more than anything else. During the course of his writing career, Semprún has devoted more pages and expended more energy on that subject than on any other. In a larger context, Buchenwald continues to resonate as a defining site for considering the Holocaust, cultural memory, and the conflation of physical landscape and catastrophic event. Even as Buchenwald's meaning as a representative Holocaust site is consolidated, its complex history continues to disperse multivalent sedimented meanings. Wulf Kirsten, a poet from the former East Germany who grew up virtually next door to the ruins of the Nazi concentration camp, resurrects Buchenwald ("Beechwood"), built around Goethe's beloved tree on the outskirts of Weimar, as doomed, permanently unsettled scenery in his poem "Bleak Site: A Triptych":

I

bitter day at a bleak site, up-hill,
earthward black streak of clouds,
the roistering storm sloughs across

copse and swamp, it clutches
at the wood, sets up a clash and a clank
in the forest of death, snowdrift
scours in slanting direction,
sounds of drumming and whistling,
what tearing and turmoil among the leaves that cover the
    skullyard,
abruptly lifted up into the sky, ready to fly
and light as a feather: Buchenwaldweather.

2

iron-hoops on the steep slope,
destroyed sheet metal,
rust-corroded utensils,
violently scattered in spiny scrub
which grows abundantly on dumps,
cornel runs up the slag-heap
free-handed like me,
plates broken in two, bowls,
white china, trademark Rosenthal,
a leather shoe crumbling away
before my eyes, up there
were barracks, barracks, occupied
by totenkopf divisions,
ever-scheming barbarians,
who dispersed
and took to headlong flight, satan
disappeared, as man of honor
he rose again, peaceable,
never even hurt a fly,
useful member,
without memory though.

3

flotsam and jetsam, *limebrow's darkened soul,*
stricken from the rock, quarryman
Poller, upward the steep slope's winding road
shoulder-sore and tortured,
as if the *millstone of fate*
is crushing him, on earth's slate write the names

of the dead, who ran into the chain of guards,
here Scholem went, there Minister Winterstein,
unfree in nature, an endless succession
of names, defenselessly exposed,
a somber day that makes me restless, no
one else is following the perceptual paths
along the leafless young plantation, below the fringe
some footholds, neck-breaking they are in the shell-
lime, *the mass of tyrants like chaff*
blowing away, from this barrack on whose outline
I stand, the kapos jumped, thrashed
with shovel sticks until they broke to pieces.
rising lines, moss-covered
domes of the hills, above motionless bodies
the leveled-off quarry, abandoned,
as if nothing had happened.[28]

Kirsten's tour of Buchenwald emphatically brings the reader to the bleak site of the title. The poem identifies and rescues tangible, everyday objects from the abstraction of wholesale death and willful oblivion, while hinting at the intermingling of competing historical narratives among its debris. Buchenwald served for many around the world as the first exposure to the array of atrocities committed by the Nazi regime; televised newsreels, still photos, and film footage taken at the camp's liberation by the U.S. Army made it one of the earliest visual representations of the horrors of the Holocaust.[29] Yet despite its representative status, how and why Buchenwald signifies so powerfully in Semprún's life is not as straightforward as it may appear, because today "Buchenwald" neither conveys a single criminal legacy nor represents a singular site of haunting or mourning. Despite its permeating presence in Semprún's overarching narrative, each time Buchenwald figures in another discursive context, its meaning shifts. In fact, "Buchenwald" provides the strongest argument for conceptualizing "survival" not as a unique and completed event after which everything else is a postscript, but rather as "survivorship"—an ongoing, inconclusive, shifting experience whose finality comes only with death.

To reconceptualize "survival," we must also recontexualize "trauma," a term that became a nearly ubiquitous catchall in the 1990s.[30] In *The Language of Psycho-analysis*, J. L. Laplanche and J.-B. Pontalis define psychic trauma as "an event in the subject's life defined by its intensity, by the subject's inability to respond adequately to it, and by the upheaval and long-lasting effects that it brings about in the psychical organization. In economic terms, the trauma is characterized by an influx of excitations that is excessive by the standard of the subject's tolerance and capacity to master such excitations and work them out psychically."[31] The problem is how precisely to master "the amounts of stimulus which have broken in and of binding them, in the psychical sense, so that they can then be disposed of,"[32] so that the organism can in theory return to its desired innocuous and unthreatened state. Traumatic memory, powerfully invasive in its own right, is characterized by the uncanny repetition of those events; that is, the recreation of the traumatic experience, what Freud calls the "return of the repressed" or "repetition compulsion" in *Beyond the Pleasure Principle*.

The discourse of trauma has been the operative referent in all Anglo-American and European-language literary and clinical discussions of Holocaust survivor testimony, which serves as the extreme limit case of the psychoanalytic paradigm. Semprún's corpus is treated accordingly.[33] Angel Loureiro reiterates this common viewpoint in his study of the autobiographical subject in modern Spain: "In Semprún's case, it all begins with trauma, and the key will be to understand it, to comprehend what was going on at the camp, so that the event can be stored in oblivion and thus be safely remembered."[34] While "trauma" is indeed a dramatic structuring device in Semprún's writing, I question its usefulness as both an originating and explanatory principle for the totality of his project and hence am also opposed to the working assumption that the "Buchenwald trauma" is the interpretive "key." I hope, as a result of rethinking the case of Semprún, that a more dynamic approach to the categories of trauma, mourning, and survival will emerge, one that illuminates the relation between traumatic event and site of mourning, between survivorship and memorialization. I contend that the trauma of Buchenwald is inextricably intertwined with another trauma in Semprún's life, that of his gradual disillusionment with and break with the Spanish Communist Party, which recontextualizes Buchenwald within a larger narrative of personal and political loss. That disillusionment and divestiture of faith, in my view, reflects an overarching loss of meaning in the narratives that defined the great struggles of the twentieth century.

This alteration in perspective should help us understand why, if the deleterious psychic effects of a concentration camp experience appear to require little elaboration, the particularly complex political history of Buchenwald certainly warrants elucidation. Buchenwald, with its elegiac pastoral name, has had two diametrically opposed lives, with manifold implications for understanding Semprún's successive experiences of loss. Arguably, "the crisis of commemoration" spawned by the camp's legacy is inseparable from Semprún's own, stressing an interplay of competing temporally and spatially charged meanings. From 1937 to 1945, Buchenwald had special symbolic currency as a "political" camp, established at Weimar as a principal destination for Hitler's opponents—social democrats, communists, and clergy. As the war progressed, deportees from annexed and conquered countries were added, with Jews remaining a small minority of the camp population. In 1941, thousands of Soviet war prisoners were sent to Buchenwald. Jews were for the most part sent east to Poland to the extermination camps. Indeed, whereas "Buchenwald" figures centrally in both Germany's and Semprún's memorial networks—though for entirely different reasons—"Auschwitz" is the signifier par excellence of the Holocaust.

At the beginning of April 1945, with the approach of the Allies, the Germans began to evacuate the camp, leaving about 20,000 inmates to their fates. On April 11, there was an insurrection organized by a group of Spanish internees, made up of communists and members of the Resistance, who seized German weapons and occupied strategic positions in the camp. (The powerful symbolism of an internal network of communist resistance within a Nazi concentration camp for Semprún and his comrades cannot be overstated. Semprún's participation in the insurrection is mentioned in *The Long Voyage*.) After putting up a short battle, the Germans fled, leaving the camp in the control of the prisoners. U.S. troops under the command of General George S. Patton Jr. arrived shortly after, disarmed the prisoners, and liberated the camp.

Following Liberation and the defeat of the Third Reich, Buchenwald became part of East Germany and was reinaugurated as the site of the founding narrative of the victory of communist-led resistance, even of self-liberation, over fascism. After the German Democratic Republic collapsed and Germany was reunited, the opening of Russian archives revealed that from 1945 to 1950, Buchenwald had served as a Soviet internment camp, where the NKVD incarcerated, initially, Nazi collaborators, considered

enemies of the state, but subsequently also communists and even some social democrats who had been previously imprisoned by the Nazis. The discovery of mass graves from the Stalinist period generated explosive debates
about Buchenwald as a contested "site-based memorial" with a "double
history." It is not for lack of either allegorical or literal evidence that we
have such difficulty "resolving" a problem that is, of course, unresolvable.
How many competing stories of suffering can be accommodated in a single site, and in such a relatively brief period of time? Barely had the Nazi
atrocities been linked to this specific space before the same ground was
turned over to reveal new victims. However discomfiting such evidence
may have been for those who had cannily chosen to forget that human
beings had been obliterated en masse in their midst, as well as any memory
of them having ever existed, for others who disclaim responsibility in the
name of either Hitler or Stalin, this layered legacy may prove to be ultimately comforting. They would prefer that no distinctions be made among
Germany's victims. But because remembering, like forgetting, is not an inert or neutral function, but one that always has a particular object in mind,
or it will have no historical or ethical value at all, "neutrality" or "neutral-
ization" are not viable responses to such a troubling and complicated issue.
To acknowledge memory's malleability only makes the mandate all the
more important. How to memorialize, even contain, these two pasts, without relativizing or equating them, in the same symbolic and physical landscape?[35] What constitutes appropriate, respectful, responsible commemoration of the history of each regime, without confusing or conflating their
respective crimes?

In the acceptance speech Semprún delivered in Frankfurt in 1994
upon receiving the Friedenspreis, he attaches Buchenwald to the burden
and mission of Germany—as the only nation to have internalized the two
totalitarian experiences of the twentieth century:

Buchenwald est toutefois le lieu de mémoire historique qui symbolise au mieux
cette double tâche: celle du travail de deuil qui permettra de maîtriser critique-
ment le passé, celle de l'élaboration des principes d'un avenir européen qui nous
permette d'éviter les erreurs du passé.

Buchenwald is, however, the site of historical memory that best symbolizes this
double task: that of the work of mourning that will permit the critical mastery of
the past, that of the elaboration of principles of a European future that will permit us to avoid the errors of the past.[36]

It is ironic, in light of the camp's postwar memorial history, as well as of the Nazi mania for classification, that the motto on Buchenwald's gates was "Jedem das Seine" ("To each his own"). As an implicit reminder that both memorial work and mourning work are selective and partisan, Semprún exhorts Germany to "remember" its past, and the full range of human loss for which it is responsible, so that Europe can avert a catastrophic future. Invoking Buchenwald as the fitting site of Germany's unresolved mourning for its losses as well as its crimes, Semprún reiterates that "critical mastery of the past" is a constructive process that does not mean covering over tragic remains or collapsing the past into the present. Every tragic remainder prepares the way for, invites, and compels new tasks for the translator.

Mourning Becomes Memory

Semprún's writing offers a chance to mark the distinction between the experience of trauma—and the resultant psychological return to that event—and the reality of living with ongoing loss. Just as most commentary on Semprún centers on the theme of trauma in his writing, it also presumes a neat separation between the trauma of his experience in the camp and "the rest"; that is, his activities as a clandestine antifascist militant following the Civil War in Spain, a resister during World War II, and a clandestine militant communist organizer following that war. Semprún's own disquisitions on his Buchenwald experience and his need "to forget" in order to overcome it may have initially contributed to this tendency to disconnect what happened in the camp from the politics of postwar Spain, France, or even Germany, for that matter. But what Semprún's writing shows is precisely that his memories of that experience had to compete and be reconciled with others, not only as a personal, psychological problem, but as a historical reality. A review of his career reveals that after the war, when writing (i.e., remembering) was impossible, he actively resumed the anti-Franco struggle, and when party politics betrayed him, he returned yet again to writing; and writing remained his ultimate nonclandestine act of bearing witness to the loss of his greatest symbolic investment: republican Spain. Clearly, Semprún did not conceive of politics and writing as mutually exclusive vocations; rather, violently, the opposition was ideologically imposed on him by others. His response to their reification of belief and practice was to confront and reinterpret his repeated survivals and their consequences.

Understanding Semprún's exemplary experience with loss, beginning with the loss of homeland and eventuating in disillusionment with a cherished set of political and social beliefs to which he had committed all aspects of his life, enables us to think about how the mourning of lost meanings may be the most pervasive condition of our time. Peter Homans defines the process of mourning as "a complex response to object loss, in which the 'objects' that are 'lost' are social and cultural objects and not only familial and intrapsychic objects."[37] Both the thematic content and the arc of Semprún's career attest that there is no mourning without memory and, in many cases, no memory without mourning. Mourning is not only a response to the loss of a beloved object, but, as Freud formulates it in "Mourning and Melancholia," also a response to a loss of belief. "Mourning is regularly the reaction to the loss of a loved person or to the loss of some abstraction which has taken the place of one, such as one's country, liberty, an ideal, and so on."[38]

I draw support here from the allied projects of Dominick LaCapra and Eric L. Santner.[39] Santner is concerned not to blur the distinction between "narrative fetishism," otherwise called "the inability or refusal to mourn," and mourning, "both of which are responses to loss, to a past that refuses to go away because of its traumatic impact." The "work of mourning," as described in condensed terms by Santner, is "the process of elaborating and integrating the reality of loss or traumatic shock by remembering it and repeating it in symbolically and dialogically mediating doses; it is a process of translating, troping, and figuring loss."[40] Santner's definition of what is involved in the work of mourning shares in the general tendency to pair trauma and loss as almost interchangeable terms; minimally, it suggests that loss itself is "traumatic."

I concur with Santner's linking of the process of mourning as mediation to processes of translation, as well as the linking of mourning and survivorship, but I question the presumptive practice of conflating trauma and loss: Is there not a useful theoretical distinction to be made between the traumatic encounter with death and a sense of grave loss? What are the implications of applying the term "trauma" almost automatically, as I think is often the case, when other kinds of experience are equally pertinent? Surely, what defines a crucial aspect of the experience of modernity is that of "cataclysmic, unassimilable shocks to the organism," the definition of trauma. But we experience late modernity just as forcefully as the cumulative and collective experience of living beyond our expectations or in spite of certain historically produced limits or constraints, as when the things or persons one has loved or cherished have disappeared or have been divested of symbolic significance and nothing of equivalent value exists to replace them. From a psychoanalytic perspective, our goal is to preserve ourselves and our libidinal attachments: thus, our identities are tied to what we cannot bear to lose, often precisely because those love objects reflect back to us an idealized image of ourselves and define who we are.

In reference to the experience of survival, its inevitable, most enduring, and conscious consequence is a sense of dynamic, actual loss; that is, the wound. I am concerned here with the shattering event (or events) that produces shock initially, but whose legacy is sorrow and grief for a historically specific, destroyed political or ethical structure of relation. I argue here for a critical framework in which we would no longer be afflicted by an undifferentiated discourse of "trauma" that subsumes or incorporates loss within it, as if the condition of loss were itself the unresolved trauma. Rather, trauma and loss would be understood to be distinct conceptual terms, signifying and implicating different forces.[41]

From this stance, I return to Semprún and the problem of loss and mourning by way of LaCapra. Freud's distinction between mourning and melancholia rests, according to many of his interpreters, on the difference between actual and ideal loss, the latter considered pathological, because the loss of the idealized, beloved object is never overcome. Its absence is transcendental, a permanent, constant aspect of a personal or cultural psychic landscape. LaCapra has elaborately argued that absence and loss should not be conflated. LaCapra's insistence on maintaining a distinction between lack—which is metaphysical, ontological, and transhistorical—and loss—which is contingent, specific, and historical—has a homologous relationship to his distinction between structural and historical trauma. In line with LaCapra's thinking, I maintain that what most accurately characterizes Semprún's emblematic experience is not structural trauma, but repeated and repetitive, politically produced, historical loss. Not ideal loss, but the actual loss of an ideal.[42] By viewing the various ways in which Semprún has represented his concentration camp experience, one begins to understand that survival, as another kind of death, has a complex and very unstable relationship to temporality. This also resonates with the approach of David Eng and David Kazanjian, editors of *Loss: The Politics of Mourning*, who affirm a productive rather than reactive mourning: "The politics of mourning might be described as that creative process mediating a hopeful or hopeless relationship between loss and history."[43] We need to take up Semprún's identity as a survivor of Buchenwald against the interrelated personal, political, and historical losses he continued to suffer after the war. Those losses, which, I argue, override the return or reification of trauma for Semprún, are what he translates into more politics, and always—despite his assertions of its stultifying impact—more writing. Both his politics and his writing engage an unfinished future in relation to a past that can never be safely dismissed, discarded, or put to rest.

Death's Call

If what defines trauma is the awareness of having come perilously close to death without dying, then those who survive a traumatic event must continue to live with that embodied knowledge of their own and others' mortality. In the camps, one was surrounded by death, by the smell and sight and fear of it, and sometimes, no doubt, by the lure of it as an escape from intolerable pain and exhaustion. Certainly, one was subjected to witnessing the death of others, but there was also the constant, incomprehensible possibility of one's death, the constant threat of finally leaving the camp "through the chimney." And yet, it is the unfathomable nature of that reality—not the actual possibility of dying, but the terrifying inability to comprehend one's own death—that constitutes the trauma. "For consciousness, the act of survival, as the experience of trauma, is the repeated confrontation with the necessity and impossibility of grasping the threat to one's own life," Cathy Caruth asserts. "It is because the mind cannot confront the possibility of its death directly that survival becomes for the human being, paradoxically, an endless testimony to the impossibility of living."[44] "Survival" means not only that one has lived beyond one's own death, but that one has lived through the death(s) of others. Semprún brings the long view to a set of very complex and perturbing questions about survivorship, the status of the survivor as a multivalent figure and the complex role testimony plays in contemporary culture.[45] Although it appears to be virtually impossible for survivors to separate the miracle of their survival from the shame and guilt of having survived, Semprún demonstrates the reductiveness of that formulation, and echoes Primo Levi's assertion that the only witness worthy of the name is one who perished: "The worst survived, that is, the fittest, the best all died."[46]

Semprún's twist on Levi's paradox comes in the early pages of his memoir *Le mort qu'il faut* (2001) and is a mordant response to an ambiguous, heavily charged phrase he has heard many times over the years from those who were not there: "On peut dire, que tu en as de la chance, toi" ("It could be said that you are lucky, eh"; my trans.). To belong to the group or category of persons who endured and survived the camps is one thing, living through/with the experience afterward another; being told by others, from the outside, what it means or what message it should convey is yet another. Semprún hears traces of animosity and suspicion in their attribution of "luck" to his having survived a concentration camp. This elicits from him an acerbic commentary:

Certes, le meilleur témoin, le seul vrai témoin, en realité, d'après les spécialistes, c'est celui qui n'a pas survécu, celui qui est allé jusqu'au bout de l'expérience, et qui en est mort. Mais ni les historiens ni les sociologues ne sont encore parvenus à résoudre cette contradiction: comment inviter les vrais témoins, c'est-à-dire les morts à leurs colloques? Comment les faire parler?

Certainly, the best witness, the only true witness, according to the specialists, is the one who hasn't survived, the one who went to the end of experience, and who died from it. But neither the historians nor the sociologists have managed to resolve this contradiction: how to invite the true witnesses, that is to say, the dead to their colloquia? How to get them to speak?[47]

Semprún's bitterness is palpable and seemingly targeted. His resistance to the perverse idea that he should feel at once lucky for having survived (*survécu*) and guilty for being lucky is a pervasive motif in his testimony. For Semprún, no moral virtue is to be attached to either the living or the dead: being here rather than there is merely a matter of "chance."[48] And if being a survivor is a dubious distinction for those from the outside, for survivors themselves, the line between the living and the dead is, in many cases, very tenuous. Nevertheless, a crucial factor in Semprún's survival of Buchenwald was the fact that the political prisoners held the key posts in the camp's administration, and that he received a certain protection as an intellectual in the Communist Party organization. Is his status as a "survivor" compromised, and is he defending it? To whom is he speaking? How has the passing of time modified his image of himself and his experience in the camp and as a deportee?

Certainly, survivors of catastrophe represent something to the outside world, often in spite of themselves; at the same time, to repeat, one of the motivations for survivor testimony beyond telling "the story" is the perhaps belated claiming of interpretive space in a realm of competing image projections. Without question, survivors also represent something to one another. If much of Semprún's literary performance is characterized by a kind of defiant pride in his "fatal singularity" (*LL*, 230)—his existential solitude—it is no less defined by his sense of fraternity and solidarity with other survivors of this massive collective catastrophe, despite differences in their individual experiences. And yet, since what survivors share is a special relationship to death—"the fraternity of death," Semprún calls it—and to the ongoing struggle against its pull, this bond is close but precarious.

The underlying assumption of Cathy Caruth's formulation that "trauma thus requires integration, both for the sake of testimony and for the sake of cure"[49] would appear to be supported by *The Long Voyage*'s necessarily belated emergence. And yet, the repetition compulsion at work in Semprún's oeuvre, while succeeding in fulfilling its testimonial function, calls into question the ultimate therapeutic value of writing, bringing in this case neither consolation nor closure. In the career of Jorge Semprún, writing and therapy are inimical. Reflecting on the entire enterprise of reintegrating overwhelming memories in *Literature or Life*, Semprún, in the most adamant of terms, rejects redemptive notions about the feasibility of achieving psychic mastery over trauma through language, or by extension, the creative act. Indeed, he insists that despite repeated attempts to find through writing a link to "the world of the living," a means of restoration or recovery from his horrific remembrances of Buchenwald, writing only thrusts him back into death.

Ultimately, Semprún testifies that the choice is not between writing or death, as the binary opposition is usually understood, but rather between "writing or life." Drawing on a counterexample to argue his point that no ontological certainty underwrites a claim such as "I have survived," when "I am surviving" more accurately describes one's ongoing condition, he reflects on the life of his soul mate Primo Levi and their opposite trajectories. Levi began writing about his experience in Auschwitz immediately after the war in fall 1945 in *Se questo è un uomo* (*If This Is a Man*; unfortunately, better known in English by the title *Survival in Auschwitz*). In contrast to Semprún, he felt "that he was returning, literally, to life."[50] When Levi died, Semprún was profoundly affected, as if it signified the inescapable intimacy and power of the "original void" that nothing can overcome. Moreover, there is another personal dimension to this loss: each survivor's death has real collective (and not only symbolic) consequences, because each aging survivor is a carrier, bodily, of memory of the Holocaust. Each death depletes the world of a variant of that shared experience and makes the world a much lonelier place for those who remain. The gap between survivors and others inevitably widens when no common reference points exist.

What Still Remains

The Autobiography of Federico Sanchez and *Literature or Life* include extended commentaries on the writing of *The Long Voyage*. The reader learns from those digressive, crosscutting, spiraling, relentlessly intertextual and metatextual narratives about survival and survivorship that it was the "confrontation with death through writing" that initially suppressed the Buchenwald story, the necessary story Semprún could not write for so many years. Semprún takes up this problem repeatedly—in *Literature or Life* most pointedly—and often interrogates the relation between the word "survivor" and its experiential referent. Semprún's attempt to define what it means to have survived is presented as a problem of interlingual as well as intersemiotic translation. Recounting watching the May Day demonstrators at the Place de la Nation in Paris, he has difficulty situating himself in relation to both the living and the dead. His ambivalent, confused meditation on survival assumes the form of a highly mediated play on words, especially in English translation, as though the linguistic and the existential were inseparable realms, and the untranslatability of the word were a function of the impossibility of being "here" or "there," either "now" or "then":

I've never understood why one should feel guilty for having survived. Anyway, I hadn't really survived. I wasn't sure of being a true survivor. I'd crossed through death, which had been an experience of my life. There are languages that have a word for this sort of experience. In German, the word is *Erlebnis*. In Spanish, *vivencia*. But there is no single French or English word that means life as the experience of itself. You have to find periphrases. Or use the word *vécu*, which is only approximate. And questionable. A bland, flabby word. First of all, and above all, it's passive, this word for what is "lived through" or experienced. And it's in the past, as well. But the experience of life, which life makes of itself, of oneself in the midst of living it—is active. And in the present, inevitably. In other words, this experience draws on the past to project itself into the future. (*LL*, 138; trans. slightly modified)

Semprún's narrative strategy is manifested in his obsessions with temporality and language; as he probes this unrelenting existential problem, its philosophical, political, and moral implications suffuse the immediate postwar landscape. What does survival mean and what does it entail? Neither at the moment of its occurrence nor at any point thereafter is it a completed action or experience. To have "survived" is not to be in a circumscribed realm, but in an afterlife within life that includes death. A parade of returning deportees in their uniforms and a brief, but violent, snowstorm signify that survival does not mean escape from—but a repeated return to—death. Semprún closes this emblematic passage on survival and translation by explaining that it is the persistence of (involuntary) memory rather than the glorification of survival that dominates a beautiful spring day after the war. The war may have ended, but for him, it is still not over; its effects are everywhere. Over and over again, Semprún shows that what may ultimately threaten survival is memory; and yet, without memory, of what kind of survival do we speak?

Let us return to the scene in *The Long Voyage* that takes place on April 13, 1945, two days after the liberation of Buchenwald. Gérard (the name, it should be noted, Semprún used in the French Resistance) contrasts the jarring vision of the visiting young Frenchwomen, these "living dolls," with his own and his fellow deportees' appearance, referring to himself and his comrades as "Russian and German, Spanish and French, Polish and Czech skeletons." The young women, brimming with obscene ripeness, have heard of the concentration camp's horrors and have come to witness them. When Gérard shows them to the big square where roll call was taken, he sees, as if for the first time—now, from the outside— the camp that was the setting for his former life, which formally ended only two days before. Despite the immeasurable difference between then and "today," he realizes that there is a link between his two lives. The link is death.

"But it really doesn't seem all that bad," one of the women says, and Gérard decides to show them inside the two-story crematorium—hooks, lifts, ovens. Speechless as they leave the ghastly place, which the women at first mistake for a kitchen, they come upon a pile of corpses in the interior courtyard—"skeletons which they haven't yet had the time to bury." Gérard reports:

I'm thinking that in the Little Camp the elderly, the ill, and the Jews are still dying. For them, the end of the camps will not be the end of death. Looking at these wasted bodies, with their protruding bones, their sunken chests, these bodies piled twelve feet high in the crematorium courtyard, I'm thinking that these were my comrades. I'm thinking that one has to have experienced their death, as we have, in order to look at them with that pure, fraternal expression. (*LV*, 75)

At first mention, Semprún's rather surprisingly inclusive reference to both the living and the dead as "skeletons" indicates that the camp inmates share more than a physical similarity, their "wasted bodies": what they have in common is a solidarity of suffering, the experiential fraternity of death. Anyone who has seen photographs of concentration camp prisoners taken during and immediately following the war can conjure up Semprún's image of the living dead alongside the dead. And yet, Semprún is neither obscuring the distinction between death and life, the border that separates them, nor sponsoring a kind of abstract symbolism. Rather, he is positing that, in the netherworld of a "liberated" concentration camp, what has transpired is an exchange between the living and the dead that transcends corporeality. The space in between the two, death in life, life in death, wherever that may be, is where the survivor lives thereafter. "Can these bones live?" certainly comes to mind, but where to put the stress—on "bones" or on "these"? Whose bones? As long as the dead are recalled and remembered, they are not truly dead. This entreaty to the living to gather the bones and carry over the dead by remembering them is also an open-ended address to the survivors who have shared the experience of death—indeed, shared a space and a place with the dead—that living with death is its own way of life.

What is perhaps most stunning and perturbing about Semprún's oeuvre is its unswerving defiance of the idea that life triumphs over death through art. Indeed, it mounts a formidable challenge to received notions about the "narrative cure," and the enabling and disabling effects of rendering trauma in language over the course of a lifetime—what Caruth calls "the double telling, the oscillation between a crisis of death and the correlative crisis of life: between the story of the unbearable nature of an event and the unbearable nature of its survival."[51] As a corrective to the desire that writing not only remake the world but repair it, Semprún compels us to question whether, under what conditions, and to what extent, writing can enable one to achieve mastery over traumatic experience, to recover from so much loss. Though history may be haunted by the dead, it belongs to the living; thus, de facto, the autobiographical enterprise, though fundamentally redemptive in nature, is also ardently appropriative. These two interrelated facets of autobiographical writing, redemption and appropriation—and their role in memorializing processes—underscore the contiguous relation between translation and survival. This is powerfully theorized in Michel de Certeau's reformulation of Freud's return of the repressed:

But whatever this new understanding of the past holds to be irrelevant—shards created by the selection of materials, remainders left aside by an explication—comes back, despite everything, on the edges of discourse or in its rifts and crannies: "resistances," "survivals," or delays discreetly perturb the pretty order of a line of "progress" or a system of interpretation. These are lapses in syntax constructed by the law of a place. Therein they symbolize the return of the repressed, that is, a return of what, at a given moment has *become* unthinkable in order for a new identity to *become* thinkable.[52]

For Semprún, the injunction to insert his story into history ultimately overrides the desire to forget what is most devastating about that story. To write is to rewrite history; every revolutionary endeavor seeks to overwrite what has preceded it, but in the process the past is retrodden and reread along the designs created by its own, perhaps unconscious partisan current interests.

Of the myriad cultural forms available to transmit the losses of the past, all involve the act of translation. The memorialist especially is preoccupied with the legacy of historical loss as it is manifested in lost battles, lost illusions, lost lives. In their broadest embrace, textual acts of mourning and memorialization are dialogues with death, in which relief, rage, guilt, and shame are enmeshed with grief, both collective and personal. More pointedly, they speak on behalf of the dead, the missing, and sometimes even in their name—for the dead, by definition, can no longer speak for themselves and are often consigned to anonymity and oblivion, as well as to silence. Indeed, the memorialist is steeped in the work of mourning both for others and for oneself, a complex, potentially interminable transaction, a "reckoning with the dead."[53] Translation is an impetus to forestall loss, it is a response to impending loss, and it is a sign itself of the consequence, as well as the consciousness, of loss.

Surviving Survival

Is "survival" the translation of death into life? What are the borderlines of a life, a language, a text? The line that distinguishes purposeful survival from survival for its own sake? Semprún's repeated interrogations of survival and survivorship resonate with Derrida's interlingual metacommentary on translation and translatability, the work of mourning, and the meaning of survival. In "Living On: Border Lines" (1979), which appeared first in English—that is, in translation—Derrida examines, primarily in English but also in French and German, through the practice and performance of translating, the "on" in "living on," which is another way of asking, what does "living on," or "sur-vivre," mean? What about, as Derrida says, "super," "hyper," "over," *über*, and even "above" and "beyond"? His elliptical approach decenters normative conceptions of the translatability of cultural values and meanings, as he calls the entire presumptive weight of the injunction "to live" into question:

Who said that we had to live? But, who's talking about living? Must we live, really? Can "living," "live," be taken as an imperative, an order, a necessity? Where do you get this axiomatic certainty that we (or you) must live? Who says that living is worth all the trouble? That it's better to live than to die? That, since we've started, we have to keep on living?[54]

The provocative tone of this passage opens the text's discussion of indeterminacy, of survival as a problem to be raised in language, as it momentarily drives a wedge between a word and its associated meanings, its almost infinite textual permutations. Derrida's questions both engage and displace a philosophical (metaphysical) inquiry whose intention is to assume the essence of life or being and then move on to other problems and themes. Echoing both Nietzsche and Freud in this transvaluation of what is presumed to be the highest value—life—Derrida disentangles concepts from terms, figurative from literal meaning. Here he seeks to locate the differ-ence between "living" and living "on"—at the borderlines, at the edges and peripheries, on the horizon, on the always co-implicating margins of life and death. He wants us to keep in mind that life and death are not polar opposites but rather contiguous; they share an intimate kinship.

Seeking to demystify the hypostasizing business of ascribing a deter-minant or underlying principle to "life," "Living On: Border Lines" affirms the ambiguous relation of language to language and the incessant con-fronting and renegotiating of conceptual limits and linguistic borders, in-evitably recrossing what it uncrosses. In an exemplary passage later in the text, Derrida signifies, without naming it as such, that translation is the form through which mortality is challenged and a language survives—not as perpetuation in the biological or physical sense, but as historical and cultural renewal: "This enduring, lasting, going on, stresses or insists on the 'on' of a living on that bears the entire enigma of this supplementary logic. Survival and revenance, living on and returning from the dead, liv-ing on goes beyond living and dying, supplementing each with a sudden surge and a certain reprieve."[55] "Survival and revenance, living on and re-turning from the dead" are clearly to be distinguished from other more self-contained and self-justifying forms of survival. Only in Derrida's sub-sequent writing on translation, in *The Ear of the Other* and "Des Tours de Babel," can it be seen that from the distinction between kinds of survival an entire theory of translation unfolds. Although Derrida makes no refer-ence in either *The Ear of the Other* or "Des Tours de Babel" to the other text, it is most useful to read them along with "Living On: Border Lines," as complementary.

In "The Task of the Translator," Benjamin employs the two terms for survival in German interchangeably. (Derrida notes, again, as a point of se-mantic as well as rhetorical interest, that in German two different words with two different meanings are translated by the one French word *sur-vivre*, which in English is translated as "to survive, to live on.")[56] *Überleben* means above life—that this life referred to exceeds nature, biology, organic corporeality alone—whereas *Fortleben* means the prolonging of life. *Über-setzen* means, not surprisingly, translation. Of the link between translation and living on, Benjamin explains:

Just as the manifestations of life are intimately connected with the phenomenon of life without being of importance to it, a translation issues from the original—not so much from its life as from its afterlife [*Überleben*]. For a translation comes later than the original, and since the important works of world literature never find their chosen translators at their time of origin, their translation marks their stage of continued life [*Fortleben*]. The idea of life and afterlife in works of art should be regarded with an entirely unmetaphorical objectivity. . . . The concept of life is given its due only if everything that has a history of its own, and is not merely the setting for history, is credited with life. In the final analysis, the range of life must be determined by history rather than by nature. . . . The philosopher's task consists in comprehending all of natural life through the more encompassing life of history.[57]

*

To read Semprún is to appreciate an indefatigable intertextuality. Every Semprúnian text refers implicitly and explicitly to every other one in his corpus, as well as to memories and events previously represented differently, because they are subject to profound and repeated rethinking over historical time. Semprún's textual project is involved intuitively, viscerally, and critically with the literature and philosophy that make up his intellectual formation; fittingly, every text addresses the implications of its own ontological status in the world. And yet Semprún writes passionately and effectively against "the writing cure," against the prevailing belief that self-expression clarifies, consoles, or compensates for or recovers what is lost. Semprún insists that writing is not necessarily on the side of life; sometimes it brings us closer to death.

But the impulse or the imperative to translate that characterizes Semprún's position suggests that both life and death are in some fundamental way inconclusive—open—and that formal and psychological closures are neither attainable nor ultimately desirable. Every translation has its own inherent limitations—surely, limitations that can potentially be overcome only by another translation. In my exploration of translation as the medium that revives the dead by re-presenting from within language ever-new possibilities for recoding the future as well as the past, I have offered Semprún as a fascinating and important case study. Semprún's writing again and again challenges on its own difficult terms the conventional depiction of survival as an achieved state, a static, unchanging condition with a fixed point of reference and a statute of limitations. Semprún demonstrates, in all his writing, that survival and survivorship are ongoing. They do not demarcate achieved success or mastery over a life-threatening event now completed but are ever-renewable responses to shifting circumstances experienced over the course of a lifetime.

Throughout *Can These Bones Live?* my objective has been to show that translation is at the nexus of our most critical cultural operations and spheres of thought and practice. I have suggested, through a range of readings that address slavery, sexuality, death, and the afterlife of texts, that all efforts to marshal the subversive and transformative power of translation to serve one interest or another are futile and misplaced: translation serves every interest. But because translation is never final or authoritative, just as the original was not, it promises nothing but another chance, the promise of yet another way: for words continue but nothing remains. Whatever one's position or status, the current order of interpretation, the state of things, the arrangement of the bones will yet yield—for better and for worse—to otherness and change. To respond to the vocative dimension of translation, in the spirit of Benjamin and Derrida, is to recognize the primacy and dynamism of difference in language and in history. To attend to the effects of translation's call is to pursue a way that is redemptive, but never triumphalist, to find in every turn of phrase the overture to another.

"THE HOME OF THE PHOTOGRAPH IS THE CEMETERY":
A SECOND-GENERATION HOLOCAUST NARRATIVE

In the summer of 1987, my Holocaust-survivor parents, Ludwik and Pola, took my younger siblings, Charles and Gayle, my husband, Henry, and me on a trip to Poland, their birthplace. In our family, "Poland" was a realm so mythically charged that as a child I could not imagine it as a physical place where my parents had actually lived as young people and where they would have continued to live, quite gladly, had Hitler not so monstrously intervened. "Poland" was the reason I had no grandparents. For a displaced child of refugees growing up in the late 1950s and 1960s in Fort Lauderdale, Florida—a mythical realm of another sort, certainly, but too, too real to me as I struggled almost against all odds to transcend the smug monotony of endless palm trees and shopping malls—there was nothing as remote in time and space as Poland. And yet, as foreign as it seemed, I was the only child culturally imprinted "European," since I was born in Munich, where my parents met after the war ("European" was a term whose connotations in the xenophobic, assimilationist environment outside our home were nothing but negative). My otherness took the elusive form of a sensibility, a disposition that had internalized difference, and could not evade it because already inhabited by it. I was struck by the fact that our neighbors' and friends' houses held no dark mystery, had nothing cryptic or recessed about them, nothing to hide or protect. Everything in sunny, segregated South Florida seemed to be no more than a flat, shiny surface, concrete and accessible to immediate sensory perception. By contrast, Poland was a void. Throughout my childhood the only vital, if somber, visual association I could conjure up of eastern Europe was a leap into fancy by way of Chagall's paintings: I was convinced that in Poland there was no ice cream and that cows walked blithely on the roofs.

So, when my father asked me in his usual, singularly directive manner as we sat together in a LOT airplane bound for Warsaw, "Why do you think I decided we should all travel to Poland now?" I answered, "Because you wanted to show us where you and Mom came from, after all these years." And to my surprise, he said, "No, that's not the reason. It's because I want to say good-bye." Even as a woman in her mid-thirties with two children of her own, I lived in constant dread of my father's departure from this world; this was not a reassuring statement. Tears flooded my eyes. He continued, "I have waited a long time to bring this chapter of my life to a close and I have prepared myself. You see, I have brought my father's pocket watch, which was safeguarded for Uncle Jacob and me during the war should we ever return, and this photograph of my sister." He recounted the saga of the watch, whose ultimate destiny as a male artifact, I knew, lay with my brother. The oval-framed photograph of the girl, his only sister—it was impossible to conceive of her as someone who would otherwise have become my aunt—was very familiar to me; I had seen it virtually every day of my life at home; it occupied a central place on my father's desk, among his papers and books. Her image is deeply etched in my memory, partly because I always felt there was a physical resemblance between us (although this was more likely some elected symbolic association, since I was my parents' oldest child, born in Europe, and their bridge to the past), partly because the object itself had special status, as one of very few family relics that had mysteriously survived the devastation. I sensed that by carrying these remnants of his lost loved ones back to Poland with him, my father was completing a crucial physical connection, restoring some kind of continuity where there had been only rupture. That my father might have any more specific intentions regarding either the watch or the photograph eluded me; and, in any case, I was so overwhelmed by everything about the trip that I was unable at the time to absorb anything else.

Our visit to Poland lasted a little over a week. We spent time in Kraków, made an excursion to Chopin's birthplace, and spent a chilly, awful day in Auschwitz-Birkenau. After breakfast on the penultimate day of our stay in Warsaw, my father announced that he was having trouble finding a way of getting to his hometown of Radomsko, about eighty miles from Warsaw, near the pre–World War II German border, quite close to the Catholic shrine of the Black Madonna at Czestochowa. We couldn't hire a taxi because regulations restricted the number of passengers allowed in one; and no buses or trains could deliver us there in a reasonable period of time.

FIGURE 2. Portrait of my father's sister, Guta. Photographer unknown.

As a last resort, my father had decided to comb the municipal parking lot across the street from our hotel in hopes of finding an acceptable vehicle and a willing driver. Having enjoyed a late night out on the town, my brother opted out of this activity and went back to his room to sleep, while the rest of us trundled after my father. Once my father located a minivan in the parking lot that he thought would fit the bill, he scribbled something in Polish on a piece of paper and left it on the windshield. Upon our return to the hotel that afternoon from sightseeing, we were greeted by my near-hysterical brother, who had been roused from a deep sleep by heavy knocks on the door and loud voices speaking Polish (a language whose sounds were not unfamiliar to him, but that on some deep, primal level clearly filled him with fear, especially under the circumstances). Convinced that the KGB (probably conflated somewhere with the Gestapo in his unconscious) had been following him and were planning to arrest him for some virtual or real infraction, he had refused to open the door and had remained paralyzed until our return. A few minutes later, we were able to make sense out of this mystifying episode, whose comic elements made it resemble a Slavic *I Love Lucy*. The men at the door came back again, their purpose being to respond in the affirmative to the advertisement for a driver they had found on their van. Fifty American dollars to take six people to Radomsko was an offer they could not refuse.

The following morning, one of the men met us outside our hotel and the six of us piled into the van, which did not exactly have passenger seats, but rather two wooden benches, one on each side. It was generally used to transport mining equipment, coal, and coal miners, so the ride was in no way cushioned. All the better, as far as I was concerned, because I wanted to experience this entire trip in as hypersensitive a state as I could. I need not have worried about it living up to my emotional expectations. Every moment since our arrival had been exquisitely tormenting, intense, adventurous, mournful. If it was almost impossible to believe that our family had "gone back" to Poland, it was all the more extraordinary that we were on our way "back" to Radomsko. The driver was, loosely speaking, a member of my generation, probably approaching forty, born in postwar Poland. He did not speak or understand English. I have absorbed a good deal of Polish, but my speaking repertoire is limited to *Ja cię kocham* ("I love you") and the first few lines of the Polish national anthem—an oddly affectionate legacy, I confess. Throughout the ride, my parents and the driver exchanged superficial, cordial words in comfortable colloquial Polish; he clearly knew that we had come from America and that they were of Polish origin. But, beyond that—I was dying to know—had he thought further about who we might be? I had the strong sense that he had no idea. It is hard to imagine now, but even in the late 1980s, it was unusual to see groups, large or small, of Jewish-identified tourists—anti-pilgrims, of sorts—traveling around Poland in search of their roots or of history in the manner that has since become rather common. It was especially rare to see Americans at all outside of Warsaw, Kraków, or Auschwitz. This was not too long after *Shoah* but before *Schindler's List*. Our group—obviously a family?—had no official or organized function; were we on a vacation? It seemed to me that, lacking explicit points of reference—and some degree of imagination or curiosity—our Polish driver could not have surmised who we were or why we would want to travel to Radomsko.

I was acutely aware of the enormous gap that separated him from us, as well as of the experiences that divided us, the second generation, from our parents, people who had a primordial, yet forever ruined, relationship to Polish soil, to the Polish language, to this geographical and cultural landscape. But I was as interested in his perception of us as I was in our own purposeful private journey; indeed, all of the strands were completely entangled for me. What did he see when he saw us? Why did I care so much, why did it matter what he knew or thought? What did he represent? What form of recognition was I seeking, what kind of acknowledgment? Why did I fear his indifference most of all? What was his role in our family drama? What kind of communication would I have liked to forge, given the opportunity, the necessary tools? What impression did I want to leave him with?

After a couple of hours on the road, we arrived at the central square of Radomsko, a very small town. There were a church, the town hall, and a park with a playground. As we started to walk down the streets and alleyways, my father described what seemed to be the plan for the day: we would be visiting the town and would meet the van again at around 2:00, at which point, I assumed, we would return directly to Warsaw. We spent the next two hours or so guided by my father, who showed us everything of personal or civic importance. We entered the large apartment house his family had owned and even gained entrance to the apartment in which they had lived and spoke to the current occupants. They were perfectly accommodating. My father pointed out with pride what had been family property, and what still belonged to them under Polish law; he found his mother's family name, Naijkron, clearly evident on signs on buildings and in courtyards. Occasionally, he would stop someone of a certain age and ask a question or seek corroboration of some sort. Sometimes there was a sign of mutual understanding or remembrance, sometimes a mere shake of the head would be enough to stop the flow of words. The strangeness of our family eating a typical lunch in a local restaurant was exceeded only by my father's wanting to buy me a piece of crockery in a small shop next door as a souvenir from Radomsko to bring back to New York. And everywhere we went, we attracted attention and were followed by bands of kids, as if the circus were in town.

Our tour of Radomsko over, we strolled back to the van. I continued to wonder what constituted normalcy in a situation like this. What did it mean to have been singled out for extermination and to have survived? Did the townspeople, some old enough to remember my father's family in some way or another, think that the Jews had come back to haunt them, or perhaps to reclaim what had been taken from them during the war, almost fifty years ago? Did they feel menaced, were they shocked or surprised or angry? Were there any sentimental traces of a bygone era, the disappeared world of the Jews? Was it a not altogether unpleasant experience, receiving a visit from Jews from America and their now-grown children, who, let's face it, had done pretty well, after all? As we climbed back into the van, I heard my father tell the driver that he wanted to make one more stop before going back to Warsaw; the driver nodded, no problem. And then my father said that he wanted to go to the Jewish cemetery. When I saw the expression on the man's face I realized that all my questions, worries, doubts, and anxieties had not been misplaced, and that those two words—*Żydowski cmentarz*—explained everything to him. Suddenly, he knew exactly who we were and why we were there; it would not be an exaggeration to say that it was a moment of revelation. The cemetery was, of course, on the outskirts of town, and it took less than twenty minutes to get there. As we drove there, my father told us that this was the cemetery where his sister was buried. I thought, how perversely fortunate for people who have been deprived in wholesale fashion of the luxury of burials and funerals, of final farewells and resting places, of knowledge and certainty, to know where a loved one had been murdered and to be able to go there—even if "there" is a mass grave. It was preferable to walking on the ashen earth at Treblinka looking for the anonymous remains of your parents.

Along the way, my father told us his younger sister's story. After he and his elder brother Jacob, two young men in their twenties, had crossed the border and fled into Russia, their parents, awaiting imminent deportation to a destination they could not have envisioned, arranged for their twelve-year-old daughter to be hidden in a farmhouse outside the town, along with a dozen other children, where, it was hoped, they might be safe. It was prearranged that on certain nights, the children would sneak into town and get provisions from people they knew and trusted. The local pharmacist, who incidentally had also held the pocket watch, was one of the contacts. After the war, when my father and uncle returned from the Russian labor camps to Radomsko to search for family members who might have survived—parents, sister, grandparents, aunts, uncles, cousins—the pharmacist described the Jewish liquidation and deportations and recounted the events in which their sister and the twelve other children had been killed. One night, when the children were in town making their pickups, one of them was spotted by a Gestapo agent, who followed her and discovered the hiding place. The following morning, the Gestapo showed up, rounded up the children, and shot them all on the spot. Many years later—helped by the daughter of people who had known my grandparents—my father, uncle, and other relatives of the murdered children had donated money to the cemetery to have a proper collective grave made, with each child's name inscribed on the tombstone. Their financial support, they hoped, would ensure that the cemetery in general would not be neglected and that the grave site would be maintained.

Not surprisingly, like most Jewish cemeteries in eastern Europe, the cemetery was in abject condition, a big field terribly overgrown with tall weeds and underbrush and some wildflowers, with markers of rough-hewn stone sticking out of the ground in all directions like crooked teeth. I remember my mother picking a rose from a bush at the house across the street and carrying it with her as we began our search for the grave. There was a very nonchalant, beret-clad caretaker, with whom my father spoke; he did not seem particularly concerned or well informed about where specific graves were located. My father was visibly distressed. We set out on our own to find the grave, and eventually we did. Although my father's hopes of a presentable tombstone had already been dashed, when we came upon it, I was surprised and relieved that it actually existed and that all of the etched names were legible. I had never seen my family name—so exposed— on a tombstone. Stunned, we watched my father run his fingers over the letters of his sister's name—GUTA BRODZKI—and take out a skullcap and the photograph of Guta, which he had, of course, brought with him expressly for this. He placed the photograph on the stone next to her name and motioned to his wife and grown children to stand next to him there as he said Kaddish, the prayer for the dead. He sobbed quietly, as I had seen him do many times in his life; he was not a man who was embarrassed to express his emotions, tears of joy and pride, as well as of sadness. He had cried openly at my wedding as we walked together down the aisle, and I cried with him, in some deep complicitous gesture. Now, eleven years later, he asked my husband, Henry, who served throughout this trip as photographer and chronicler, to take a picture of the five of us standing—with the photo of Guta—at her grave. I don't know how long we stood there. It was unbearable. The feelings of pain and impotence and loss were overwhelming. We couldn't bear to watch our father suffer, and we could not share his suffering with him. Eventually, my father asked Henry (who was no doubt relieved) to come with him as he made his way through the weeds, as if on a scavenger hunt, to look for other graves: markers with names he might recognize, some of them those of long-dead rabbis, some of spirits he could not name but would have liked to summon. My mother went off by herself to wait for them. We three siblings, as if liberated from hell, bolted as fast as we could in the other direction—toward the van. One of us spontaneously reached for and handed the surprised driver a U2 cassette we had brought; we wordlessly passed around a pack of cigarettes, and the four of us started to smoke and sway furiously to the beat of *The Joshua Tree*. The tension inside the van and its release were palpable. As inheritors of something we could not have articulated, we shared an extended moment of absolute communion. No translation was necessary.

Passing On

What I could not know then and understand only now, made terribly clear by his death in 1995 and by the passage of time, is that my father's "good-bye" to Poland made possible—perhaps made necessary—my own open address to the part of my parents' past that I had vainly (in both senses of the word) kept at a safe intellectual and psychological remove throughout most of my adult life. My childhood was another story. The truth is that being the child of survivors—before that was an identifiable syndrome—pervaded my childhood; "the War" was the silent referent, the reflexive explanation for everything that couldn't be accounted for in my microcosmic universe. Because of "the War" I understood perfectly well how causality and chaos could converge at infinity: to me being a child of survivors meant that anything was possible at any time, nothing really mattered and my real life was elsewhere. It was the most determining aspect of my identity, and I was fully conscious of that fact from an early age, and, I thought, of its ominous consequences. In fact, being "fully conscious" meant that I was always aware that I would have to both protect and seek escape from that private source of shame and honor, whose paradoxical implications perturbed me. It was dangerous knowledge, not to be shared.

Now when I remember that trip to Poland in all its starkness and in-
tricacy—especially the scene at the Radomsko cemetery, which re-presented
my parents' survival amid millions of deaths, while prefiguring my father's
passing (on)—I marvel at his directorial acuity and am grateful for my
husband's skill with a camera. As a professor of literature and a specialist in
autobiography, I appointed myself family scribe for this trip to Poland.
The reflections that follow, while irreducibly personal, have been steeped
in scholarly brew; they are composed within some sort of analytical framework. But before I return to the scene of inheritance, a scene marked by
the shocking intensity of the moment as experience and by the inevitable
temporal delay that makes possible understanding (not by chance did it
take me ten years to begin the task of writing about it), I want to explore
the terrain.

How does a commemorative rite—captured as photographic event,
crystallized in a photo of the living (present) flanking a photo of the dead
(symbolically present) at the site of a mass grave—function as a mode of
(intergenerational) transmission? What does it mean to shoot a family portrait among the ruins? How to render the nature of that legacy? When did
the second generation cross the line—pass—from being witnesses to being
participants (even ambivalent ones) in this process? What is the image's relation to the moment it seems to document or represent, for the photographer, the subjects, the viewer? What is the evidentiary status of this photograph? What role did my father's sister's *image* perform in this reenacted
narrative of both individual and collective trauma and survival (the one my
father mastered so well)—of rupture and continuity, loss and restoration,
exile and redemption, mourning and reaffirmation?

The portrait of my father's sister is a formal close-up in sepia tones
against a white background, grainy in texture. Her features are very distinct and she is looking directly into the camera. Visible are a polka-dot
bodice that fades out at the edges of her silhouette and a dark bow that
holds back her dark hair. Although I know she must have been approximately twelve years old at the time, perhaps because of the surrounding
blankness that matches the whiteness of her face, she seems strangely age-
less, almost an abstraction. There is nothing intrinsically evocative about
this photograph, except possibly its vintage quality; it derives its power and
poignancy because not long after the picture was taken, this adolescent girl
suffered and died violently, one single life annihilated in the Holocaust.

Her tragic destiny as part of the Final Solution is inscribed into the image, and our knowledge of that reality cannot be dissociated from the representation. Moreover, since it is the only extant picture of her, her image is forever frozen in it. As Susan Sontag reminds us, every photograph of a person participates in a symbolic economy of death: "Photography is the inventory of mortality. . . . Photographs state the innocence, the vulnerability of lives heading toward their own destruction, and this link between photography and death haunts all photographs of people."[1]

The photograph rescued my father's sister from oblivion. Her mute image had lived among us, inscribed in our domestic landscape of a family of survivors and their children, performing its haunting work silently. It is perhaps ironic that whatever its singular status in our family, as an isolated, individual portrait, it does not qualify as a family photograph per se, according to Julia Hirsch, who asserts: "A person whose photograph decorates a desk, a wall, a wallet, a gravestone, may command family devotion. But we cannot be sure that this photograph is a family photograph because it does not itself show a blood tie."[2] In other words, family photographs have documentary as well as symbolic value: they attest to relationality. "Through photographs, each family constructs a portrait-chronicle of itself—a portable kit of images that bears witness to its connectedness," Sontag says.[3] How, then, to read this photograph? In and of itself, the portrait of my father's sister is not a Holocaust photograph; it does not belong in the category of photographs that indexes, invokes, portrays, or "captures" prewar eastern European Jewish life in any graphic or oblique way. It is connected to the Holocaust, to paraphrase Marianne Hirsch, by its context and not by its content.[4] However, the genocidal context is overriding and overdetermining, and its effects at once sustain and obscure the distinction between those who survived and those who did not. "The destruction had been such that not a single image survived from pre-War Jewish life that was not now stained, marked by death," Nadine Fresco observes.[5] In the complex entangled set of relations that survivorship creates with the dead, the imperative to remember and the infinite need to mourn coexist with feelings of terror, guilt, shame, resentment, betrayal, and abandonment. I suspect that, for my father, the photograph of his sister—lone material remnant and visible daily reminder of exile, destruction, absence—was pressed into particularly heavy (and lonely) service as the bearer of visual and symbolic associations that extended beyond its immediate referent toward other empty spaces and suspended narratives. No doubt, her image stood in for the irretrievable images of all the other family members who had disappeared, had never returned. However antithetical my parents' modes of compensation and sublimation and the diverse effects these produced upon us, it seems to me that not a day passed in their post-Holocaust existence when they did not consciously remember, if only for a fleeting instant, what they had experienced and how much they had lost. A vehicle of memory, the photograph sitting on my father's desk enabled him to maintain a material connection with the "once was," the "having been there."

My father's sorrowful act of carrying across, of transporting the photograph of the lost object (the missing person, if you will) to the grave constituted a privileging of its metaphorical over its metonymic status or axis of meaning, its substitutive rather than referential or indexical function. The graveside ceremony, in which the photograph was featured so prominently, substituted for the funeral that never took place, for all the funerals that never took place, for all the bodies that were never recovered. Even as photographs represent absence by invoking presence, they preserve the absolute disjunction between "what was" and "what is not." After all, the photograph of the dead one is only a photograph. Unlike a hair ribbon or a piece of jewelry once worn by the person, for example, there is no physical, sensual, or "organic" relationship, no sense of contiguity between the subject and the representation. And yet, of course, if the photograph served primarily to reveal who was missing from the scene through symbolic substitution, the narrative attached to the photograph by survivors and other members of the family—the suffering and final destiny of its subject—assumed full referential meaning there in the desolate cemetery, in its ultimate context, as it could nowhere else. What the photograph could not accomplish by itself, it performed on-site.

Because my father was the only one among us for whom the photograph had personal, acute meaning—affective power—the ceremony at the cemetery was a theater of signs and memory, producing "a scene of inheritance" in which my parents' cumulative legacy was inscribed and passed on. Such scenes stage their own reception, even if belatedly; indeed, that may be their very purpose—to impress the present upon the past and the past upon the present, that is, to create memories, to turn witnesses and spectators into participants, to make us part of the story, to include us in its embrace. Without such shared memories, the past does not exist and there is no possibility of a future.

The inherited photograph of my father's sister brought our family to the cemetery and the photograph of us taken there turned the symbolic event into a "scene of inheritance." As our photographer, my husband was indispensable in recording the trip; and his insider/outsider status generally opened up the play of family dynamics in a highly beneficial way. But he was put at a special kind of remove that day. Behind the camera, silently calling the shots, he was witness to our angst, but his displacement kept him outside the immediate family circle and gave him a measure of protection against the emotional power of the experience, and, I would argue, many of its fleeting and sustaining images. I have no doubt that he considered this a reprieve. For me, the result of his being excluded from this process of transmission, while being crucial to its production, is a cluster of mixed feelings. If, as it is said, we frame memories as if they were photographs, Henry's photographic eye framed the photographs that to a great extent have become my memories. I must sometimes remind myself of this significant fact, because even though I know his physical presence was integral to the entire event, he is, by necessity, absent from those pictures.

If this had been a traditional family portrait, of course, the photographer would have taken greater care to make everyone stand in a coherent arrangement and look in the same direction. These are broken, or at least slightly skewed, ranks. Though sadness pervades the image, it doesn't look as if we are all concentrated on the same activity or have the same agenda: the striking difference between my parents and us is that my parents are staring straight into the camera. My father's hands are clasped in front of him; my mother, slightly in back of him, is holding his left arm. They are a unit. They could constitute their own separate picture. My sister is looking down at the mottled gravestone, the fingers of her left hand actually resting on it. I am wearing sunglasses and looking down as well, leaning in on one leg, with my hands folded across my chest. Although it was sunny that day, I am wearing a jacket. My brother is also shielded by sunglasses, and it is hard to know whether he is engaging the camera or looking down obliquely; his hands are behind him. My parents are standing so solidly, squarely, and resolutely; their direct and purposeful expressions say to

FIGURE 3. Family portrait at children's tomb. Photograph by Henry Issenberg.

the photographer, "Record this momentous occasion for posterity, that we were here and that we came back," while my siblings and I appear uncomfortable and uncertain.

When I study the photograph now, I am shocked by the insight that what our disparate expressions and postures register is not only the disjointed character of the scene, but also our categorically different relationships to the Holocaust. Our parents' identity was secure in this context. They had suffered differently from each other, but they had survived, and still endured; the trauma was theirs. Through the course of our lives, we, their children, had been intimate witnesses to the toll this experience had taken on them and on ourselves, but we were nonetheless always one step removed, spared personal experience of the Holocaust itself. What is captured in the photograph in the cemetery is the second generation's malaise at being neither here nor there. In that scene, our parents literally know where they stand—they know who they are and what they are doing; and we are clueless, disarmed. Hence our flight. "Photographic images, then, whatever their apparent subject, are images *in crisis*," Regis Durand writes. "Something in them is always trying to run off, to vanish. Even when staged or posed, photographs always relate to a sense of disaster, of catastrophe, to the infinitely short instant when something collapses, turns around, becomes undone, or undergoes a transformation."[6]

*

It is not for rhetorical effect that I have ended my remembrance of our visit to Radomsko, to the Jewish cemetery, inside the van with our Polish driver and the words "No translation was necessary." Have I indulged in willful self-deception, a fantasy, imagining transparent understanding, imposing psychological and narrative closure, where, of course, there could be none? I think not. I am only bearing witness to an extraordinary moment, one that at the time I felt traversed all manner of difference. What made it so exceptional was precisely that it was extraverbal and beyond translation, indeed that this very point was what mattered, because we were holding at bay a certain idea about Poland. That said, I want to underscore what Walter Benjamin has shown to be inherently paradoxical about translation and translatability, that even as the exercise of translation renders, recasts, assimilates the foreign into familiar terms, the process also produces the opposite effect: it calls attention to itself, making strange the apparently familiar, in this case, the familial. The "scene of inheritance" in the cemetery, in which our legacy as children of Polish Holocaust survivors was ultimately inscribed and passed down was, of course, a process of vertical transmission. But what is it that was actually transmitted to us? Surely, something more fractured than intact. If it looks as if my sister, my brother, and I had sought refuge from our parents' past in an unlikely place—that van—we did so with full knowledge that we were only temporarily escaping the weight of our family legacy. Perhaps that's what made it sublime. What remains most significant for me is that our default language (both common and transcendent) was postwar global popular culture—we were identifying ourselves generationally and internationally (horizontally), just as my parents were identifying themselves in their circumscribed way. While they were reclaiming their history, their identity, we were claiming ours. Even though we certainly came from them, we were not the same. We felt fortunate to be in the position to exercise our capacity (or was it our right?) to redraw our boundaries, to choose how much concentrated exposure to our parents' trauma we could tolerate. And I, for one, did not want to stay stuck back there: I knew I was too susceptible. But it was already late for that, even if I did not want to recognize it then. A lifetime of sustained exposure to repetitions of their original trauma has convinced me that, in fact, their past is not just proper to them, and that it is the inherent otherness of our connection that makes my translation of their survivorship both necessary and possible.

The linchpin of our spectacular trip to Poland was the taking of that family portrait among the ruins, my parents and their grown children flanking the grave on which the photograph of my father's dead sister—with its profoundly estranging effects—had been placed. By virtue of its being staged, contrived, forced, and posed, by calling attention to itself as wholly strange and nonconsensual, the family portrait clinched a historical and genealogical connection between my parents' past and our futures and then historicized it as event—so that we would have not only the memory of the experience but its visual representation as well, a graphic reminder of the intertwining of history and memory. Nonetheless, although the photograph seized, in Benjamin's idiom, both my parents' intentionality and our ambivalence as we stood there that day, its meaning has shifted over time. "From memory we proceed easily to memorials, which both represent an originating act of remembrance and serve to invoke the act of remembrance in those who view the memorial," Linda Haverty Rugg observes.[7]

If remembering is a "motivated" symbolic practice and photographs are always already haunted, then aren't memorial practices primarily prospective strategies designed to ensure the linking of traces of the past to the future as well as to the present? Might these practices rehearse a death that hasn't occurred yet, even as a photograph evokes the scores of named and nameless deaths that have? It is the death of my father that frames this narrative.

In the productive work that mourning performs (and that melancholia resists), the lost object comes to be seen as particular and belonging to a past that can be differentiated, overcome, and relinquished in favor of the present, even for a present in which the loved object no longer exists, as Freud elaborates in his essay on the paradigmatic responses to loss, "Mourning and Melancholia."[8] In the contest between the death drive and the life force, mourning is allied with the latter—it is dynamic, resilient, forward-looking; in deference to reality, it accepts the death of the Other, and demonstrates the subject's capacity to reengage with object substitutes. Marsha Lynne Abrams's description of this trajectory confirms my enduring sense that my father was a successful mourner:

A life-affirming response to loss depends . . . on an act of *transformation*, enabled by a reparticularization in space/time, by which a suspended state of solipsistic absorption becomes a twofold dialectical *process*: a movement through the past on the way to a movement beyond it, joined with a "spatial" movement between subjective and objective worlds. This process, ongoing in that loss is a constant feature of human existence, reflects the workings of Eros as an instinct of progressive complication.[9]

I could not know then that even there—in that desolate, unforgiving cemetery, especially in that cemetery—Eros was nonetheless in the ascendant. Indeed, my father was preparing us to live without him, precisely by having so deeply involved us in his own strivings to move beyond, to overcome.

Thus, this very project of translation is an expression of gratitude and an act of commemoration, just as it is also a staking out of my own testimonial space. As Shoshana Felman puts it, echoing Benjamin: "The way in which the translator can bear witness to *what actually happens* in the original is, however paradoxically, not by imitation but only by a new creation, a creation that, although it ensures the literal survival of the original, is itself only the testimony of an afterlife."[10] Eduardo Cadava presses this point further in a study of the ways in which Benjamin articulates his conception of history through the language of photography. I invoke the photograph of my father's dead sister, Guta, once more, with Cadava's words in mind:

Photography is a mode of bereavement. . . . The disjunction that characterizes the relation between a photograph and the photographed corresponds to the caesura between a translation and an original. . . . In order to be faithful to what is translatable in the original, the translator must depart from it, must seek the realization of his task in something other than the original itself. . . . If an original can only live on in its alteration, it is no longer alive as itself but rather as something other than itself. To say that "a translation issues from the original—not so much from its life as from its afterlife"—is therefore to say that translation demands the death of the original. Or more precisely, like the photograph that names both the dead and the survival of the dead, translation names death's continued existence. The original lives beyond its own death in translation just as the photograph survives its own mortification in a photograph. If the task of translation belongs to that of photography, it is because both begin in the death of their subjects, both take place in the realm of ghosts and phantoms. . . . The home of the photograph is the cemetery.[11]

I bring this epilogue and this book about translation, survival, and cultural memory to a close, at the threshold of the literal and the metaphorical, in that strange, mournful but generative space in which the living and the dead exchange ever-renewable meanings. It was the death of my father, in 1995, eight years after our trip to Poland, that framed this story: my debt, my gift, my task.

REFERENCE MATTER

Notes

INTRODUCTION

Epigraphs: Ezekiel 37:1–6, in *The Jewish Study Bible*, ed. Adele Berlin, Marc Zvi Brettler, and Michael Fishbane, Jewish Publication Society, TANAKH translation (New York: Oxford University Press, 2004); Walter Benjamin, "The Task of the Translator," in *Illuminations*, trans. Harry Zohn, ed. Hannah Arendt (New York: Schocken Books, 1968), 73; Clea Koff, *The Bone Woman: A Forensic Anthropologist's Search for Truth in the Mass Graves of Rwanda, Bosnia, Croatia, and Kosovo* (New York: Random House, 2004), 13.

1. See *Theories of Translation: An Anthology of Essays from Dryden to Derrida*, ed. Rainer Schulte and John Biguenet (Chicago: University of Chicago, 1992), which effectively constructs a tradition of translation theory that begins in the late eighteenth century. For a selection of recent collections that treat translation as a critical organizing principle, see *On the Translation of Native American Literatures*, ed. Brian Swann (Washington, D.C.: Smithsonian Institution Press, 1992); *Rethinking Translation: Discourse, Subjectivity, and Ideology*, ed. Lawrence Venuti (London: Routledge, 1992); *The Translator's Invisibility*, ed. Lawrence Venuti (New York: Routledge, 1995); *The Translatability of Cultures: Figurations of the Space Between*, ed. Sanford Budick and Wolfgang Iser (Stanford: Stanford University Press, 1996); *Postcolonial Translation: Theory and Practice*, ed. Susan Bassnett and Harish Trivedi (London: Routledge, 1999); *Changing the Terms: Translating in the Postcolonial Era*, ed. Sherry Simon and Paul St. Pierre (Ottawa: University of Ottawa Press, 2000); *Translation and Power*, ed. Maria Tymoczko and Edwin Gentzler (Amherst: University of Massachusetts Press, 2002); *Nation, Language, and the Ethics of Translation*, ed. Sandra Bermann and Michael Wood (Princeton, N.J.: Princeton University Press, 2005).

2. As Marc Redfield puts it, in its heyday, theory itself became a kind of language event, first marked as "hyperforeign" and considered a European import, now considered a refashioned American export. "Introduction: Theory, Globalization, Cultural Studies and the Remains of the University," *Diacritics* 31.3 (2001): 5. Barbara Johnson's characterization of theory and translation as fellow travelers,

without using the term, stresses the important point that the undomesticated quality of theory inevitably implicated translation. That is, for all critical intents and purposes, the translation of theory also produced the theory of translation: one could not be thought (or read) without the other. "It is not just that theory involved a mad impetus to translation, but that the theory that transformed literary studies utterly transformed the practice of translation." *Mother Tongues: Sexuality, Trials, Motherhood, Translation* (Cambridge, Mass.: Harvard University Press, 2003), 32.

3. Benjamin, "Task of the Translator": see source note to epigraph above.

4. Jacques Derrida, "Living On: Border Lines," in *Deconstruction and Criticism*, ed. Harold Bloom et al. (New York: Continuum, 1979); id., *The Ear of the Other: Otobiography, Transference, Translation* (Lincoln: University of Nebraska Press, 1985); id. "Des Tours de Babel," in *Difference in Translation*, ed. Joseph F. Graham (Ithaca, N.Y.: Cornell University Press, 1985).

5. Derrida, *Ear of the Other*, 104.

6. For an exemplary study of the transformation of translation practices and policies in a globalized and technologically defined economy, see Michael Cronin, *Translation and Globalization* (New York: Routledge, 2003).

7. J. Hillis Miller, "Literary Study Among the Ruins," *Diacritics* 31.3 (2001): 57–66; quoted from 65.

8. For a still timely assessment of current anxieties and polemics within the field of comparative literature, especially in relation to the broadening of boundaries and the shifting of paradigms, see *Comparative Literature in the Age of Multiculturalism*, ed. Charles Bernheimer, especially the essays "Multiculturalism and Global Citizenship," by Mary Louise Pratt, and "In the Name of Comparative Literature," by Rey Chow. Regarding the changing fortunes of comparative literature in relation to translation studies, in 1993 Bassnett and Lefevere pronounced: "Comparative Literature as a discipline has had its day. . . . We should look upon translation studies as the principal discipline from now on with comparative literature as a valued but subsidiary subject area" (161). Stanley Corngold opens his essay "Comparative Literature: The Delay in Translation," in *Nation, Language, and the Ethics of Translation*, by considering the claim that "comparative literature is a kind of translation . . . that it should take translation as its model" (139). The 2006 ACLA report on the state of the discipline, edited by Haun Saussy, reflects the paradigm shift from multiculturalism to globalization. See also *Translation, History, and Culture*, ed. Susan Bassnett and André Lefevere (1990; reprint, London: Cassell, 1995). In *The Translation Zone: A New Comparative Literature* (Princeton, N.J.: Princeton University Press, 2005), Emily Apter has argued that translation studies should be the basis for "a new comparative literature."

9. Maxine Hong Kingston, *The Woman Warrior: Memoir of a Girlhood Among Ghosts* (New York: Vintage Books, 1989), 209.

10. In *Cultural Haunting: Ghosts and Ethnicity in Recent American Literature* (Charlottesville: University Press of Virginia, 1998), Kathleen Brogan identifies the construction of the ghost as another figure of translation in recent ethnic literature. Her notion of "cultural haunting" links, as I do here but with different emphasis, the experience of mourning and the transmission of cultural memory.

11. Benjamin has also written about this in "Excavation and Memory," in *Walter Benjamin: Selected Writings*, vol. 2, *1927–1934*, trans. Rodney Livingston et al., ed. Michael W. Jennings, Howard Eiland, and Gary Smith (Cambridge, Mass.: Harvard University Press, 1999), 575–76.

12. Benjamin, "Theses on the Philosophy of History," in *Illuminations*, 255.

13. Christopher Joyce and Eric Stover, *Witnesses from the Grave: The Stories Bones Tell* (Boston: Little, Brown, 1991), and Koff, *The Bone Woman*, 17. Clyde Snow is quoted in Eric Stover, *The Graves: Srebrenica and Vukovar*, with photographs by Gilles Peress (Zurich: Scalo, 1998), 94. See also Michael Ondaatje's novel, *Anil's Ghost* (New York: Knopf, 2000).

14. In an essay that traces the fate of the epistolary correspondence of Abelard and Heloise, Cecilia Feilla retrieves early English and French meanings of the word "translation" to demonstrate the intimate connection between the physical and the literary act. From the twelfth to the eighteenth century, she explains, "*translation* indicated the transfer of both words and bodies from one language or place to another," especially the removal of saintly remains from one grave to another. "Translating Communities: The Institutional Epilogue to the Letters of Abelard and Heloise," *Yale Journal of Criticism* 16.2 (2003): 363–79.

15. Salman Rushdie, *Imaginary Homelands: Essays and Criticism, 1981–1991* (London: Granta, 1991), 17.

16. Richard Terdiman, *Present Past: Modernity and the Memory Crisis* (Ithaca, N.Y.: Cornell University Press, 1993).

17. David Damrosch, *What Is World Literature?* (Princeton, N.J.: Princeton University Press, 2003), 289, 292.

18. Venuti, *Translator's Invisibility*, 1–2.

19. Lawrence Venuti, "Genealogies of Translation Theory: Schleiermacher," *TTR* 4.2 (1991): 125–50.

20. For an insightful overview of translation's ethical, political, social, and cultural imperatives, see Anuradha Dingwaney, Introduction, "Translating 'Third World' Cultures," in *Between Languages and Cultures: Translation and Cross-Cultural Texts*, ed. id. and Carol Maier (Pittsburgh: University of Pittsburgh Press, 1995), 3–15. For translation issues and their current global implications presented in stark relief, see James Clifford's *Routes: Travel and Translation in the Late Twentieth Century* (Cambridge, Mass.: Harvard University Press, 1997), especially the remarks and discussion that make up the chapter entitled "Traveling Cultures." On the intersection of the ethical and the metaphysical, see also Antoine Berman, *The Experience of the*

Foreign: Culture and Translation in Romantic Germany (Albany: State University of New York Press, 1992): "For translation is not a mere mediation. It is a process in which our entire relation to the Other is played out. Translation . . . is the carrier of knowledge sui generis on languages, literatures, cultures, movements of exchange and contact, etc." (180, 181).

21. I draw on Mieke Bal's succinct definition of "cultural memory" as "memory that can be understood as a cultural phenomenon as well as an individual or social one." The "memorial presence of the past [can] mediate and modify difficult or tabooed moments of the past—moments that nonetheless impinge, sometimes fatally, on the present" (vii). In *Acts of Memory: Cultural Recall in the Present*, ed. Mieke Bal, Jonathan Crewes, and Leo Spitzer (Hanover, N.H.: University Press of New England, 1999), 9.

CHAPTER I. FIGURING TRANSLATION: LOVERS,
TRAITORS, AND CULTURAL MEDIATORS

Epigraph: James Clifford, *Routes: Travel and Translation in the Late Twentieth Century* (Cambridge, Mass.: Harvard University Press, 1997), 7.

1. *Translators Through History*, ed. Jean Delisle and Judith Wordsworth (Amsterdam: John Benjamins, 1995), xiv.

2. Cynthia Ozick, "Envy; or, Yiddish in America," *Commentary* 48 (November 1969): 33–53; Italo Calvino, *Se una notte d'inverno un viaggiatore* (Turin: Einaudi, 1979), trans. William Weaver as *If on a winter's night a traveler* (New York : Harcourt Brace Jovanovich, 1981); Barbara Wilson, *Gaudí Afternoon* (Seattle: Seal Press, 1990); Philip Roth, *The Professor of Desire* (New York: Farrar, Straus & Giroux, 1977). Other recent texts that incorporate or employ translation into their narratives and feature the practice or role of the translator are Julio Cortázar, *A Manual for Manuel*, trans. Gregory Rabassa (New York: Pantheon Books, 1978); Abdelkebir Khatibi, *Love in Two Languages*, trans. Richard Howard (Minneapolis: University of Minnesota Press, 1990); Nicole Brossard, *Mauve Desert*, trans. Suzanne de Lotbinière-Harwood (Toronto: Coach House, 1990); Thea Welsh, *The Story of the Year of 1912 in the Village of Elza Darzins: A Novel* (Brookvale, NSW: Simon & Schuster, Australia, in association with New Endeavour Press, 1990); Ward Just, *The Translator* (New York: Houghton Mifflin, 1991); Ursule Molinaro, *Fat Skeletons* (London: Serif, 1993); Lydia Davis, *The End of the Story* (New York: Farrar, Straus & Giroux, 1995); Banana Yoshimoto, N.P., trans. Ann Sherif (New York: Washington Square Press, 1995); Nicole Mones, *Lost in Translation* (New York: Delacorte, 1998); Leila Aboulela, *The Translator* (Edinburgh: Polygon, 2001); Suzanne Glass, *The Interpreter* (South Royalton, Vt.: Steerforth Press, 2001); Paul Auster, *The Book of Illusions* (New York: Holt, 2002); Imre Kertész, *Kaddish for a Child Not Born*, trans. Christopher C. Wilson and Katharina M. Wilson (Evanston, Ill.: Northwestern University Press, 2002); John Crowley, *The Translator* (New

York: Perennial, 2002); Monique Truong, *The Book of Salt: A Novel* (Boston: Houghton Mifflin, 2003); Hugo Hamilton, *The Speckled People* (New York: Fourth Estate, 2003); Suki Kim, *The Interpreter* (New York: Picador, 2003); Sheila Kohler, *Crossways* (Princeton, N.J.: Ontario Review Press, 2004). These fictional and autobiographical texts are not only meditations on the art and power of translating itself, but also represent reading, writing, teaching, acting, cooking, traveling, filmmaking, lovemaking, even simply being, as acts of translation.

3. Yiddish, once the medium of everyday communication for millions of eastern European (Ashkenazi) Jews, has, arguably, both functionally and symbolically, traded positions with Hebrew, which was installed in 1948 as the national language of the state of Israel. The decision to make Hebrew a modern, living, vernacular language after 3,000 years of uninterrupted use for predominantly liturgical purposes came, ironically, out of a secular, progressive movement generated by the European Enlightenment; its cosmopolitan, emancipatory ideals represented a radical effort to change the social and cultural definition of a people and, effectively, to replace Yiddish. Hebrew's self-conscious status as a "divinely inspired" living language is shared only with Arabic. After the Holocaust, Yiddish was rejected by the Jewish nation builders due to its bittersweet associations with the ghetto and vulgar, parochial insularity; now its reputation is being rehabilitated in some circles as another kind of "sacred" tongue that must be preserved because it is endangered. In yet other circles, in Germany, for example—but especially in eastern Europe today, where actual Jews are conspicuously absent—there is evidence of a Yiddish cultural revival in the form of Yiddish theater (performed by non-Jewish actors) and klezmer music, both of which enjoy a following among the young. For a history of gendered relations between Hebrew and Yiddish, see Naomi Seidman, *A Marriage Made in Heaven: The Sexual Politics of Hebrew and Yiddish* (Berkeley: University of California Press, 1997).

4. Sephardic Jews' vernacular language of exile is Ladino.

5. It is widely assumed that the career, if not the character, of Ostrover is based on that of Isaac Bashevis Singer. When this story was published, Singer had already accumulated some world-class credentials, but he had yet to be awarded the Nobel Prize in Literature, which he won in 1978. Ozick writes directly from her own experience as a translator of Yiddish. Her translations can be found in *A Treasury of Yiddish Poetry*, ed. Irving Howe and Eliezer Greenberg (New York: Schocken Books, 1976); *Voices From the Yiddish: Essays, Memoirs, Diaries*, ed. Irving Howe and Eliezer Greenberg (New York: Schocken Books, 1975); and *The Penguin Book of Modern Yiddish Verse*, ed. Irving Howe, Ruth Wisse, and Khone Schmweruck (New York: Vintage Books, 1987).

6. Jacques Derrida, "Des Tours de Babel," in *Difference in Translation*, ed. Joseph F. Graham (Ithaca, N.Y.: Cornell University Press, 1985), 171.

7. Irving Howe, *World of Our Fathers: The Journey of the East European Jews to America and the Life They Found and Made* (New York: Simon & Schuster, 1976), 452.

8. Ibid., 452. For a general but rich introduction to the culture of Yiddish, see Benjamin Harshav, *The Meaning of Yiddish* (Berkeley: University of California Press, 1990), whose final chapter, "The End of a Language," is devoted to Glatshtein.

9. Cynthia Ozick, *Art and Ardor: Essays* (New York: Knopf, 1983), 152.

10. Katherine Hellerstein, "Translating as a Feminist: Reconceiving Anna Margolin," *Prooftexts* 20: 1–2 (2000): 191–218.

11. Ibid., 213, 214, 81–82. Anita Norich's piece is appended to Katherine Hellerstein's article (213–18).

12. Ozick, "Envy," 73. While Edelshtein may be a remnant of prewar Yiddish culture, a survivor of an eastern European world now gone, he is not a Holocaust survivor, and this distinction should not be lost on the reader. As chance would have it, Edelshtein escaped the Holocaust; he didn't live through it. His complex identification with "survivor" shame and guilt is evidenced in the following declaration to Hannah: "I have spat on myself for having survived the death camps—survived them drinking tea in New York" (74). His donning of the "survivor" mantle rankles, but it speaks as much of his double displacement as it does of any deliberate misrepresentation of his experience.

13. An extremely pertinent and enlightening theoretical explication of the psychopathology of envy can be found in Melanie Klein, "Envy and Gratitude," in *Envy, Gratitude and Other Works, 1946–1963* (New York: Delacorte, 1975), 176–235. From a Kleinian perspective, it is not Ostrover who is Edelshtein's primary object of envy (and desire), but Hannah.

14. Derrida, "Des Tours de Babel," 182.

15. Sarah Blacher Cohen, *Cynthia Ozick's Comic Art: From Levity to Liturgy* (Bloomington: Indiana University Press, 1994), 59–60.

16. Francine du Plessix Gray, *New York Times Book Review*, June 21, 1981. The intellectual *jouissance* that pervades Italo Calvino's *If on a winter's night a traveler* gives preeminence to the experience of reading above all else, almost as if there were no other roles or activities in life. For three of the novel's critical intertexts, see Michel Foucault, "What Is an Author?" in *Language, Counter-Memory, Practice: Selected Essays and Interviews*, ed. Donald F. Bouchard, trans. Donald Bouchard and Sherry Simon (Ithaca, N.Y.: Cornell University Press, 1977), Roland Barthes, "The Death of the Author," in *Image-Music-Text*, ed. and trans. Stephen Heath (Glasgow: Fontana/Collins, 1977), and id., *The Pleasure of the Text*, trans. Richard Miller (New York: Hill & Wang, 1975).

17. Sexual thematics aside, the rapport between grammar and gender in this text is fascinating, bearing directly on the question of nonequivalence in translation. In the original Italian, the Readers are the sexually marked "Lettore" (universal/generic/masculine, that is, unnamed) and "Lettrice" (feminine, named Ludmilla), respectively, which William Weaver translates as the Reader and the Other Reader. Despite this crucial difference in genderization, in the cases of both English and

Italian, the two Readers, whether they are implicitly or explicitly encoded as such, are still distinguished from each other on the basis of sex and sex roles. For an insightful analysis of the ways "you" functions in this narrative apostrophically—the Reader speaking to himself, to the Other Reader, or to the reader outside the text—see Irene Kacandes, *Talk Fiction: Literature and the Talk Explosion* (Lincoln: University of Nebraska Press, 2001), esp. 181–96.

18. Teresa de Lauretis, *Technologies of Gender: Essays on Theory, Film, and Fiction* (Bloomington: Indiana University Press, 1987), 76–77. Most studies of this novel attend to its formal ingenuity and narrative strategies, ignoring the specificity of its representations; de Lauretis, while celebrating its postmodern panache, derides its retrograde sexual politics, considering none of it to be tongue-in-cheek.

19. "The Third Space: Interview with Homi Bhabha," in *Identity, Community, Culture, Difference*, ed. Jonathan Rutherford (London: Lawrence & Wishart, 1990), 210.

20. *Webster's Third New International Dictionary*. See Elaine Marks, *Marrano as Metaphor: The Jewish Presence in French Writing* (New York: Columbia University Press, 1996), a rich study of crypto-Jewishness and overlapping, contaminating identities in French writing.

21. The mystery reader will immediately appreciate Wilson's sororal nod to Dorothy L. Sayers's *Gaudy Night* (New York: Harcourt, 1936).

22. See Michael Cronin, *Across the Lines: Travel, Language, Translation* (Cork: Cork University Press, 2000), 2.

23. Catalan-Castilian tensions have deep roots. Beginning with the Bourbon dynasty's rise to power, Catalonia has suffered three centuries of linguistic and cultural discrimination in Spain. Although the Catalan language has never had any official status, during the early twentieth century, a regional movement was recognized and Catalonia enjoyed limited self-rule. Under Franco's long dictatorship, Catalonia was singled out for cultural annihilation: use of the Catalan language was prohibited and expressions of Catalan identity punished (Basque received similar treatment). Since the restoration of democracy in 1975, Catalonia has enjoyed a high degree of self-governance, and Catalan social, artistic, and cultural institutions are thriving. Although it is a minority language, over eight million speakers, on every social level, conduct their lives in Catalan. Catalonia's cultural and economic standing within Spain is undisputed and its independence movement is still strong.

24. For a nonfictional account of the creative satisfactions and political challenges experienced by a feminist translator of Latin American fiction written by men, see Suzanne Jill Levine, *The Subversive Scribe: Translating Latin American Fiction* (Saint Paul, Minn.: Graywolf Press, 1991).

25. Derrida, "Des Tours de Babel," 165, 172. The Tower of Babel also figures hubris, as Beverly Curran noted in the audience after my presentation on this novel at the 2004 ICLA in Hong Kong. Curran drew a provocative analogy to the

destroyed Twin Towers, which, in a contemporary macrocosmic geopolitical context, were translated as the American Babel by many others in the world.

26. Cassandra's invocation of "the masquerade" brings to mind a passage in Luce Irigaray's groundbreaking French feminist text *Ce sexe qui n'en est pas un* (1977), trans. Catherine Porter with Carolyn Burke as *This Sex Which Is Not One* (Ithaca, N.Y.: Cornell University Press, 1985): "What do I mean by masquerade? In particular, what Freud calls 'femininity.' The belief, for example, that it is necessary to *become* a woman, a 'normal' one at that, whereas a man is a man from the outset. He has only to effect his being-a-man, whereas a woman has to become a normal woman, that is has to enter the *masquerade of femininity*" (134).

27. For two of the most trenchant philosophical and political expositions on these issues in the field of lesbian and gay studies, see Eve Kosofsky Sedgwick's introduction, "Axiomiatics," to id., *Epistemology of the Closet* (Berkeley: University of California Press, 1990), and Judith Butler's essay "Imitation and Gender Subordination," in *The Second Wave: A Reader in Feminist Theory*, ed. Linda Nicholson (London: Routledge, 1997).

28. Judith Butler, *Gender Trouble: Feminism and the Subversion of Identity* (London: Routledge, 1990).

29. The final twists: April is actually the bisexual drag musician Hamilton's stepbrother Albert, and Hamilton and Ana have decided to have a child. It is left to the reader to surmise whether Cassandra's attraction to April has the subliminal component of April being open to commitment, but absolutely averse to children.

30. For a lively exploration into the kinds of elective affinities and social arrangements that reimagine and reconfigure heterosexual marriage, see Elizabeth Freeman's *The Wedding Complex: Forms of Belonging in Modern American Culture* (Durham, N.C.: Duke University Press, 2002).

31. Only a couple of pages later, as the search for Delilah approaches its most fraught and feverish point, Cassandra reports that, in a telephone conversation with Frankie, she used "the fatal word": mother.

32. Derrida, "Des Tours de Babel," 165. The purloined translation may also invoke by association the newly begun, always interrupted, ever-missing incomplete manuscript of *If on a winter's night a traveler*, but the difference between the one in *Gaudí Afternoon* and Calvino's novel is analogous to the difference between the aborted and the infinitely deferred. In other words, whereas in Calvino's narrative reading/translation is continuously, productively erotic because it perpetuates desire, in Wilson's novel the translation is stalled—at least for the duration.

33. Indeed, Wilson resumes and extends Cassandra's translating exploits in a subsequent book entitled *The Death of a Much-Travelled Woman and Other Adventures with Cassandra Reilly* (Chicago: Third Side Press, 1998).

34. For an insightful study of the psychoanalyst figures, as well as of the representation of psychoanalysis itself, in Roth's fiction, see Jeffrey Berman, *The Talking Cure: Literary Representations of Psychoanalysis* (New York: New York University

Press, 1987). Berman identifies Roth's characters as "the most psychoanalyzed in literature" (239). Although Dr. Klinger plays a minor role compared to some of his colleagues in other Roth novels, his guiding spirit hovers over the narrative.

35. In Philip Roth, *Reading Myself and Others* (1975; reprint, New York: Vintage International, 2001), 147.

36. Wolfgang Iser, *The Act of Reading: A Theory of Aesthetic Response* (Baltimore: Johns Hopkins University Press, 1978), 67.

37. *The Translator's Invisibility*, ed. Lawrence Venuti (New York: Routledge, 1995), 20.

38. The writers showcased in this series include Jerzy Andrzejewski, Bruno Schulz, Bohumil Hrabal, Tadeusz Borowski, Danilo Kis, Witold Gombrowicz, and Milan Kundera. Introductions have been written by such authors as Josef Svorecky, Jan Kott, Joseph Brodsky, Heinrich Boll, Elizabeth Pochoda, and Roth himself. *The Professor of Desire* was published in 1977, a few years after Roth "began to be a regular visitor to Czechoslovakia."

39. Why *Moby-Dick*? What do other cultures/cultural others read in Melville's colossal emblematic novel? In a fascinating turn of the personal, the political, and the theoretical, Paul de Man translated *Moby-Dick* into Flemish in 1945, at the conclusion of World War II. Might there be some correspondence between Roth's Professor Soska and Professor de Man? Eyal Peretz examines Melville's "textual event" refracted through a European prism that sharpens both its singularity and its generalizability. He argues that the novel witnesses and testifies to the crises of national identity played out in the second half of the nineteenth century and "in the wake of the European disasters and catastrophes of the twentieth century . . . brought forth in the name of 'Europe' and its ideals." Peretz, *Literature, Disaster, and the Enigma of Power: A Reading of "Moby-Dick"* (Stanford: Stanford University Press, 2003), 19, 95. For a defense of de Man's damning journalistic activities during the war and subsequent secrecy about them, see Shoshana Felman's chapter on de Man, "the task of translation," and on Benjamin as his "double and brother," in *Testimony: Crises of Witnessing in Literature, Psychoanalysis, and History*, ed. Shoshana Felman and Dori Laub (New York: Routledge, 1992).

40. The poignant representation of the aging survivor who can communicate, however obliquely, the horrors he suffered, can be contrasted with Roth's depiction in "Eli, the Fanatic." In that story, a mute, black-hatted Holocaust survivor in an assimilated New Jersey suburb is the sign of pure untranslatability. Representing terror and trauma, indeed, fundamental religious otherness, he is pursued by his doppelgänger, Eli, who beseeches him, "Say something, speak *English*." In *Goodbye, Columbus* (New York: Meridian Press, 1962), 10.

41. Sigmund Freud, *Beyond the Pleasure Principle* (London: Hogarth Press, 1955).

42. J. L. Laplanche and J.-B. Pontalis, *The Language of Psycho-analysis*, trans. Donald Nicholson-Smith (New York: Norton, 1973).

43. Roth's *The Professor of Desire* was written and published after *The Breast*; however, its action takes place in an earlier time. In the latter text, David Kepesh is transformed into a female breast.

44. Laplanche and Pontalis, *Language of Psycho-analysis*, 102.

45. Ibid.

46. Ibid., 103.

CHAPTER 2. GENRE AND GENEALOGY: THE SLAVE NARRATIVE
TRANSLATED OTHERWISE AND ELSEWHERE

Epigraph: Jacques Derrida, "The Law of Genre," in id., *Acts of Literature*, ed. Derek Attridge (New York: Routledge, 1992), 223.

1. The novels—Charles Johnson, *Oxherding Tale* (Bloomington: Indiana University Press, 1982; Evergreen reprint, New York: Grove Press, 1984), Buchi Emecheta, *The Slave Girl* (New York: Braziller, 1977), and André Schwartz-Bart, *La mulâtresse Solitude*, trans. Stephen Becker (New York: Atheneum, 1960)—also have something else in common beyond what some might consider to be decentered or idiomatic representations of slavery. Each of the texts I treat here can be regarded as the "minor" rather than the major text in their authors' oeuvres. Schwartz-Bart's fame is associated with *Le dernier des Justes* (Paris: Seuil, 1959), trans. Stephen Becker as *The Last of the Just* (New York: Atheneum, 1960); Emecheta is best known for *The Joys of Motherhood* (New York: Braziller, 1979); and Johnson is acclaimed for *Middle Passage* (New York: Simon & Schuster, 1998). But, of course, it is precisely my point that these novels are no less emblematic or significant for being deemed "minor."

2. Of the three texts I discuss here, only *Oxherding Tale* is a "neo-slave narrative" according to the criteria of Ashraf H. A. Rushdy, *Neo-Slave Narratives: Studies in the Logic of a Social Form* (New York: Oxford University Press, 1999), who defines these as "contemporary novels that assume the form, adopt the conventions, and take on the first-person voice of the ante-bellum slave narrative" (3). Rushdy derives his term from Bernard Bell but applies it to slave narratives rewritten in the United States in the 1970s and 1980s; he identifies these texts as screen responses to the racial politics of the 1960s. See also Bernard W. Bell, *The Afro-American Novel and Its Tradition* (Amherst: University of Massachusetts Press, 1987).

3. Hans Robert Jauss, *Toward an Aesthetic of Reception* (Minneapolis: University of Minnesota Press, 1982), 22. In a very influential study, Philippe Lejeune argues that autobiography as a genre functions by virtue of a contract (a "pact") between the writer and reader of a text marked as such by the congruence of identity established by the author and the protagonist's having the same name. See *The Autobiographical Pact*, trans. Paul John Eakin (Minneapolis: University of Minnesota Press, 1989).

4. For a comparative analysis on the history of slavery, see James Walvin, *Questioning Slavery* (New York: Routledge, 1996). His last chapter outlines slavery on an international scale in the nineteenth century. Walvin describes British colonial abolitionist efforts in the twentieth century as being particularly challenging for a variety of reasons, among them being the "ubiquity and durability of slavery," as well as the diversity of practices, some of which were barely perceptible to British vision (172–82).

5. For a rhetorically framed transatlantic, transgeneric study of abolitionist discourse in the nineteenth century, see Dwight McBride, *Impossible Witnesses: Truth, Abolitionism, and Slave Testimony* (New York: New York University Press, 2001).

6. *Slavery and the Literary Imagination*, ed. Deborah McDowell and Arnold Rampersad (Baltimore: Johns Hopkins University Press, 1989), viii.

7. David Brion Davis, *The Problem of Slavery in Western Culture* (Ithaca, N.Y.: Cornell University Press, 1966), 30 (hereafter *PSWC*).

8. *The Slave's Narrative*, ed. Charles T. Davis and Henry Louis Gates Jr. (Oxford: Oxford University Press, 1985), xxii.

9. William L. Andrews, "The Representation of Slavery and the Rise of Afro-American Realism," in *Slavery and the Literary Imagination*, ed. McDowell and Rampersad, esp. 62–67; and "Toward a Poetics of Afro-American Autobiography," in *Afro-American Literary Study in the 1990s*, ed. Houston A. Baker Jr. and Patricia Redmond (Chicago: University of Chicago Press, 1989), 85.

10. Hortense Spillers, "Changing the Letter: The Yokes, the Jokes of Discourse, or Mrs. Stowe, Mr. Reed," in *Slavery and the Literary Imagination*, ed. McDowell and Rampersad, 28–29.

11. Contemporary American novels about slavery, some of which use the slave-narrative model, include Margaret Walker's *Jubilee* (1966), Ernest Gaines's *Autobiography of Miss Jane Pitman* (1971), Ishmael Reed's *Flight to Canada* (1976), Octavia Butler's *Kindred* (1979), Sherley Anne Williams's *Dessa Rose* (1984), Toni Morrison's *Beloved* (1987), Charles Johnson's *Middle Passage* (1990), Edward P. Jones's *The Known World* (New York: Amistad, 2003), and Valerie Martin's *Property* (New York: Vintage Books, 2003). Gayl Jones's *Corregidora* (1975) is dominated by the memory of slavery.

12. *Slave's Narrative*, ed. Davis and Gates, introduction, xii–xiii.

13. Maria Tomyczko, "Translation and Political Engagement," *The Translator* 6.1 (2000): 23–47.

14. For a study that utilizes translation as a conceptual tool for examining translated texts about gender, race, and slavery, see *Translating Slavery: Gender and Race in French Women's Writing, 1783–1823*, ed. Doris Y. Kadish and Françoise Massardier-Kenney (Kent, Ohio: Kent State University Press, 1994).

15. Feminist critics have taken up the contentious history of genre politics as patently exclusionary; for an enlightening analysis of how women poets have been exiled by both traditional male critics and feminists for not meeting different

canonical criteria, see Celeste Schenck, "Exiled by Genre: Modernism, Canonicity, and the Politics of Exclusion," in *Women's Writing in Exile*, ed. Angela Ingraham and Mary Lynn Broe (Chapel Hill: University of North Carolina Press, 1989), 225–50.

16. Jacques Derrida, "The Law of Genre," in id., *Acts of Literature*, ed. Derek Attridge (New York: Routledge, 1992), 221–52; quotations from 224–25, 227. *Oxherding Tale* could be described as Derrida's "poster-text" for the "law of genre." Although contemporary theorists, and Derrida specifically, are conspicuously missing from Johnson's intertextual repertory, one of my claims here is that reading these two texts in light of each other has illuminating effects on both.

17. The strong parallels between postmodern poetics and the self-conscious, performative, playful mode of eighteenth-century ironists have been recognized by critics, especially those interested in generic innovation. In "Do Postmodern Genres Exist?" Ralph Cohen offers insights into the nature of those shared features, as well as a helpful discussion of how parodic attacks on genre simultaneously reinforce generic conventions and undermine them. In fact, he argues, it is part of the very discourse of genre, and, particularly, of satire and parody, to do so (11–27, esp. 17–20). See also Marjorie Perloff's introduction to *Postmodern Genres* (Norman: University of Oklahoma Press, 1989), 3–10.

18. Johnson, *Oxherding Tale*, 118, 119. Fritz Gysin locates "moments" of crossing and transgressing boundaries and their multicultural implications in the works of Johnson and John Edgar Wideman in "Predicaments of Skin: Boundaries in Recent African American Fiction," in *The Black Columbiad: Defining Moments in African American Literature and Culture* (Cambridge, Mass.: Harvard University Press, 1994), 286–97.

19. Regarding the politics of passing in literary history—whether ambiguous identities are to be celebrated or not, and under what conditions—see Elaine Ginzberg, *Passing and the Fictions of Identity* (Durham, N.C.: Duke University Press, 1996), esp. 2–18. In his book-length study of Johnson, Rudolf P. Byrd argues that "the mulatto Andrew Hawkins/William Harris is . . . the incarnation . . . of the emancipatory potential of hybridity": *Charles Johnson's Novels: Writing the American Palimpsest* (Bloomington: Indiana University Press, 2005), 96. On ontological and epidermal indeterminacy, Steven Weisenberger says in a review of *Oxherding Tale* that it "translates the Zen enigma of in-betweenness to the ante-bellum South" ("In-Between," *Callaloo* 20 (Winter 1984): 153–56). For a detailed analysis of how Johnson cross-fertilizes the "Afro-American tradition and Zen Buddhist philosophy" in this novel that is structured like an Eastern parable, see William Gleason, "The Liberation of Perception: Charles Johnson's *Oxherding Tale*," in *Black American Literature Forum* 25.4 (Winter 1991): 725–28. Gleason explicates the correlation between the quest for liberation, oxherding, and the phase-by-phase ascent to spiritual enlightenment.

20. See Charles H. Nichols, "The Slave Narrators and the Picaresque Mode: Archetypes for Modern Black Personae," in *Slave's Narrative*, ed. Davis and Gates, 284–98, for an illuminating discussion of the parallels between the picaro and slave narrators, both of whom are "engaged in a desperate struggle for survival" and employ a range of discursive strategies to describe their plights and plot their escapes. Nichols's analysis of how contemporary black fiction and autobiography have ingeniously used the picaresque in such complex comic modes as "anachronisms, contradictions, and absurdities" (298) applies perfectly to Johnson.

21. For an extremely interesting perspective on the notion of generic and temporal excess and the intersections between postmodernism, romance, and feminism (especially regarding the figure of woman), see Diane Elam, *Romancing the Postmodern* (London: Routledge, 1992).

22. See the analysis of Nancy Leys Stepan and Sander Gilman on the process of identification and introjection of the dominant discourses of "otherness" in "Appropriating the Idioms of Science: The Rejection of Scientific Racism," in *The Bounds of Race: Perspectives on Hegemony and Resistance*, ed. Dominick LaCapra (Ithaca, N.Y.: Cornell University Press, 1991), 72–103.

23. *The Slave Girl* is situated between two other novels by Emecheta in which slavery is intrinsically related to the status of women as wives and mothers, *The Bride Price* (1976) and *The Joys of Motherhood* (1979).

24. See Suzanne Miers and Igor Kopytoff's "African 'Slavery' as an Institution of Marginality," in *Slavery in Africa: Historical and Anthropological Perspectives* (Madison: University of Wisconsin Press, 1977), 3–84; also Paul Lovejoy's *Transformations in Slavery: A History of Slavery in Africa* (Cambridge: Cambridge University Press, 1983). As Claire Robertson and Martin Klein explain in their groundbreaking study of women as central figures in African slavery, "many accounts of African slavery are written as though the slaves were exclusively men." See "Women's Importance in African Slave Systems," in *Women and Slavery in Africa* (Madison: University of Wisconsin Press, 1983), 3–25.

25. Cynthia Ward, "What They Told Buchi Emecheta: Oral Subjectivity and the Joys of Otherhood," *PMLA* 105, no. 1 (1990): 84–85.

26. M. Keith Booker, *The African Novel in English* (Portsmouth, N.H.: Heinemann, 1998), 85. On the relationship between Igbo, Emecheta's "emotional language," and English as an international literary language, see *Interviews with Writers of the Post-Colonial World*, ed. Feroza Jussawalla and Reed Way Dasenbrock (Jackson: University Press of Mississippi, 1992), 82–99.

27. Abdul R. JanMohamed, "The Economy of Manichean Allegory: The Function of Racial Difference in Colonialist Literature," in *"Race," Writing, and Difference*, ed. Henry Louis Gates Jr. (Chicago: University of Chicago Press, 1985), 80–81.

28. Florence Stratton, "The Shallow Grave: Archetypes of Female Experience in African Fiction," *Research in African Literatures*, Special Issue on Women's Writing,

ed. Rhonda Cobham and Chikwenye Okonjo Ogunyemi, 19, no. 2 (1988): 148–50, at 148. Stratton argues that Emecheta's identification of Ojebete as an *ogbanje*, the Igbo term for spirit child—"believed to be destined to die and be reborn repeatedly to the same mother unless a means can be found to break the cycle"—signifies ambiguous status on two levels. The myth functions as a way to explain infant mortality in many West African societies, and it emblematizes the limitations of female destiny.

29. Ibid. For an interesting reflection on "issues of maternal identification for slave girls under the conditions of slavery," see Jennifer Fleischner, *Mastering Slavery: Slavery, Memory, Family and Identity* (New York: New York University Press, 1996). Although Fleischner examines family dynamics and personal identity in U.S. women's antebellum slave narratives, the reader of *The Slave Girl* will recognize the structures of mother-loss and mother-substitution across all these texts.

30. Susan Andrade, "Rewriting History," reads the central drama of Ma Palagada's mysterious "sudden illness" and subsequent death, in which the 1929 Igbo Women's War is marginally inscribed, as an example of Emecheta's "dialogizing of oppositional behavior." This strategy provides a historical context for interpreting women's complicity and resistance/rebellion in which the latter is represented so marginally as to be constructed as "un-inscribable."

31. In "Cracking the Code: Strategies in African Women's Writing" (MS, 1990), Chikwenye Ogunyemi identifies such a figurative strategy in many postcolonial texts by African women: "The continuing independence struggles underscored the need to obtain genuine freedom for all including the nations, who, like women, were still subjugated. The writers see woman's destiny and the motherland's as intertwined, a crucial point realized in some texts allegorically and symbolically" (1).

32. Epigraph: Maurice Blanchot, *The Writing of the Disaster*, trans. Ann Smock (Lincoln: University of Nebraska Press, 1986), 28. Although the English translation of the title *La mulâtresse Solitude* retains her proper name, unfortunately it reduces the historical Solitude to an abstract and arbitrary, indefinitely modified, female subject. By contrast, the French original insists upon Solitude's identity being crucially inscribed in a racial category. Thus, I retain use of the French title, although all quotations are from *A Woman Named Solitude*, trans. Ralph Manheim (Donald S. Ellis: San Francisco, 1985). For an incisive critique of the connotations of racial categories and terminologies, and an argument for the use of "métissage" as an aesthetic concept and analytic tool, see the introduction to Françoise Lionnet's *Autobiographical Voices: Race, Gender, Self-Portraiture* (Ithaca, N.Y.: Cornell University Press, 1989), esp. 3–18.

33. For an influential analysis of the metaphorical character of the Holocaust, both its literalizing abuses by Nazi ideology and Jewish uses of metaphor in Holocaust history and literature, see James E. Young, *Writing and Rewriting the Holocaust:*

Narrative and the Consequences of Interpretation (Bloomington: Indiana University Press, 1988), esp. chaps. 5 and 6, 83–116.

34. Derrida, *Acts of Literature*, 68.

35. While the original Seuil edition names only André as author of *La mulâtresse Solitude*, as does the English translation published by Atheneum, Donald Herdeck's *Caribbean Writers: A Bio-Bibliographic Critical Encylopedia* lists *La mulâtresse Solitude* under Simone Schwarz-Bart, "with André Schwarz-Bart." The *Callaloo Bibliography of Francophone Women Writers from Sub-Saharan Africa and Its Diaspora* (Washington, D.C., 1985) also lists *La mulâtresse Solitude* under Simone Schwarz-Bart "and André Schwarz-Bart." As evidence of how identical facile reductionism of authorial identity to thematic content can serve different ideological interests, the Centre de documentation juive contemporaine in Paris considers André to have authored only *Le dernier des Justes*. As far as its bibliographers are concerned, Simone is the single author of *La mulâtresse Solitude*, as well as of the other "Caribbean" texts with which her name is associated. Critics on both side of the divide tend to follow suit, presuming that authorial identity determines thematic content, and vice versa.

36. André Schwarz-Bart, in *Le Figaro littéraire*, January 26, 1967.

37. Édouard Glissant, *Caribbean Discourse: Selected Essays*, trans. J. Michael Dash (Charlottesville: University Press of Virginia, 1989), 98.

38. This fascinating and inspiring collaboration has been examined with empathy and finesse by Ronnie Scharfman in two essays, "Significantly Other: Simone and André Schwartz-Bart," in *Significant Others: Creativity and Intimate Partnership*, ed. Whitney Chadwick and Isabelle de Courtivron (London: Thames & Hudson, 1993) and "Exiled from the Shoah: André and Simone Schwartz-Bart's *Un plat de porc aux bananes vertes*" in *Auschwitz and After: Race, Culture, and "the Jewish Question" in France*, ed. Larry Kritzman (New York: Routledge, 1995).

39. Glissant, *Caribbean Discourse*, 61–62.

40. Jean Meyer, *Esclaves et Négriers* (Paris: Gallimard, 1986), 21; my trans. For a succinct revisionary assessment of the massive research on this subject, especially on the symbolic vs. historical significance of the Middle Passage, for example, see Herbert S. Klein, *The Atlantic Slave Trade* (Cambridge: Cambridge University Press, 1999).

41. C. L. R. James's account of the Haitian Revolution (1791–1803), "the only successful slave revolt in history," had a dramatic effect on Third World liberation movements. See *The Black Jacobins: Toussaint L'Ouverture and the San Domingo Revolution* (New York: Vintage Books, 1963), preface to the first edition.

42. Friederich Nietzsche, *Beyond Good and Evil* (New York: Random House, 1966), 4.

43. See Selwyn R. Cudjoe, *Resistance and Caribbean Literature* (Athens, Ohio: Ohio University Press, 1980), especially pt. 1, which provides a brief history of

resistance in the Caribbean. For recent gender-inflected studies of Africans enslaved in the Western Hemisphere, see Jacqueline Jones, *Labor of Love, Labor of Sorrow: Black Women, Work and Family from Slavery to the Present* (New York: Basic Books, 1985); Rosalyn Terborg-Penn, "Black Women in Resistance: A Cross-Cultural Perspective," in *In Resistance: Studies in African, Caribbean, and Afro-Caribbean History*, ed. Gary Okihro (Amherst: University of Massachusetts Press, 1966), 188–209; Marietta Morrissey, *Slave Women in the New World: Gender Stratification in the Caribbean* (Lawrence: University Press of Kansas, 1989); Barbara Bush, *Slave Women in Caribbean Society, 1650–1838* (Bloomington: Indiana University Press, 1990); and, especially relevant to this text, Arlette Gautier, *Les soeurs de Solitude: La condition féminine dans l'esclav[ag]e aux Antilles, du XVIIe au XIXe siècle* (Paris: Éditions Caribéennes, 1985), and Bernard Moitt, *Women and Slavery in the French Antilles, 1635–1848* (Bloomington: Indiana University Press, 2001). Moitt devotes a chapter to women and all forms of resistance, including *marronnage*, making specific reference to Solitude and her role at Matouba (125–50).

44. Arlette Gautier, *Nouvelles questions féministes* 9–10 (1985): 5–8.

45. Pierre Nora, "Between Memory and History: Les Lieux de Mémoire," *Representations* 26 (Spring 1989): 7–25. In this special issue on Memory and Counter-Memory, the editors, Nathalie Zemon Davis and Randolph Starn, stress the seemingly opposed collective tendencies of amnesia and obsession, the conflictual but productive "interdependence of memory and history" (1–6). For a far-reaching study of the relationship between collective memory and national identity, see John Gillis, *Commemorations: The Politics of National Identity* (Princeton, N.J.: Princeton University Press, 1994); for a provocative analysis of memory politics in the late twentieth century, see Andreas Huyssen, *Present Pasts: Urban Palimpsests and the Politics of Memory* (Stanford: Stanford University Press, 2003). Any inquiry into the recent obsession with memory and representation, especially in regard to the Holocaust, should include Lawrence Langer's *Holocaust Testimonies: The Ruins of Memory* (New Haven, Conn.: Yale University Press, 1991); Geoffrey Hartman's edited collection *Holocaust Remembrance: The Shapes of Memory*; and Saul Friedlander's edited collection *Probing the Limits of Representation: Nazism and the "Final Solution"* (Cambridge, Mass.: Harvard University Press, 1992).

46. For a rich introduction to the intertextual commentary on this central problem in Jewish interpretation, see David G. Roskies, *Against the Apocalypse: Responses to Catastrophe in Modern Jewish Culture* (Cambridge, Mass.: Harvard University Press, 1984); Alan Mintz, *Hurban: Responses to Catastrophe in Hebrew Literature* (New York: Columbia University Press, 1984); and Yosef Hayim Yerushalmi, *Zakhor: Jewish History and Jewish Memory* (Seattle: University of Washington Press, 1982).

47. Although homosexuals and other social and political "deviants" and "undesirables" were deported, interned, worked to death, and killed, only Gypsies and Jews were destined for genocide because of their race.

48. Sidra DeKoven Ezrahi, *By Words Alone: The Holocaust in Literature* (Chicago: Chicago University Press, 1980), 132.

49. Lawrence Langer, *The Holocaust and the Literary Imagination* (New Haven, Conn.: Yale University Press, 1975), 263. See also James E. Young, *Writing and Rewriting the Holocaust: Narrative and the Consequences of Interpretation* (Bloomington: Indiana University Press); Berel Lang, *Writing and the Holocaust* (New York: Holmes & Meier, 1988). For an excellent study devoted entirely to *The Last of the Just*, see Francine Kaufmann, *Pour relire "Le dernier des Justes"* (Paris: Klincksieck, 1986).

50. See Oruno Lara, *Histoire de la Guadeloupe* (Paris: L'Harmattan, 1921). For other novelistic versions of this tragically eclipsed episode in Guadeloupean history, see Michèle Lacrosil, *Demain Jab-Herma* (Paris: Gallimard, 1967) and Daniel Maximin, *Isolé Soleil* (Paris: Seuil, 1981).

51. Almost two centuries after the Matouba slave revolt, a commemorative statue of the pregnant Solitude was erected in 1999 in Abymes, Guadeloupe, the second of three sculptures dedicated on the occasion of the 150th anniversary of the abolition of slavery (the other two figures memorialized along what is now called "le boulevard des héros" are Ignace and Delgrés). Given that Guadeloupe, like Martinique, is still an overseas department of France, the particular symbolic significance of this monument to female armed resistance against Napoleonic oppression in the Caribbean colonies and territories must be noted, but again we must ask how the gesture is to be interpreted and whose interests are being served. Although the initiative was organized locally by a group called Comité des Peuples Noirs, it required, of course, the support and sanction of the French government. Thus it could be argued, in light of the ongoing drive for independence throughout the region, "liberté, egalité, fraternité" have yet to be fully achieved. For a most relevant reflection on the "decontextualizing" and "recontextualizing" movements of commemoration, see F. R. Ankersmit, *Historical Representation* (Stanford: Stanford University Press, 2001). In contrast to testimony, which compels a "resurrection of the past," Ankersmit describes commemoration as "the ultimate attempt to master the past and to render it innocuous forever" (166). My gratitude to Maryse Condé and Jean-Pierre Sainton for their report on these events conveyed to me via e-mail.

52. Pierre Nora, "Between Memory and History: *Les Lieux de Mémoire*," trans. Marc Roudebush, *Representations* 26 (Spring 1989): 7.

53. See the illuminating introduction that accompanies Zimra's translation of Daniel Maximin's novel *Lone Sun* (Charlottesville: University Press of Virginia, 1989), xxxviii.

54. David Rousset, *The Other Kingdom*, trans. Ramon Guthrie (New York: Reynal & Hitchcock, 1947). It is impossible not to think once again of Nora's *lieux de mémoire*, as Schwarz-Bart's novel brings together these two haunted sites and the souls destined to wander them. Nora associates such sites with ghostliness, because

they are haunted as well by the need of the living "to recover their buried pasts" (15). These sites represent a state of in-betweenness and liminality: they are "mixed, hybrid, mutant, bound intimately with life and death" (19).

55. James E. Young, "The Biography of a Memorial Icon: Nathan Rapoport's Warsaw Ghetto Monument," in *Representations* 26 (Spring 1989): 79. For a fascinating account of the complex political history of the monument to the uprising, see the article in its entirety, 69–106. For a richly documented history of the Warsaw Ghetto from the outbreak of the war through the crushing of the revolt, see Yisrael Gutman, *The Jews of Warsaw, 1939–1943: Ghetto, Underground, Revolt* (Bloomington: Indiana University Press, 1982).

56. Young, "Biography of a Memorial Icon," 87–88.

57. Sander Gilman, *Difference and Pathology: Stereotypes of Sexuality, Race, and Madness* (Ithaca, N.Y.: Cornell University Press, 1985), 35. The qualities most strongly associated with both groups have been violent change and sexual excess; the images have, at points in history, been interrelated and even interchangeable. The analogy between blacks and Jews is a pervasive motif in Paul Gilroy's *Against Race: Imagining Political Culture Beyond the Color Line* (Cambridge, Mass.: Harvard University Press, 2000); see especially the chapters on modernity and infrahumanity and identity and belonging, 54–133. See also the introduction on stereotyping, 15–35; and for a discussion of the convergence of images of Otherness and its relationship to language as a sign of difference, see Sander Gilman, *Jewish Self-Hatred: Anti-Semitism and the Hidden Language of the Jews* (Baltimore: Johns Hopkins University Press, 1986), esp. 5–16.

58. André Schwarz-Bart, "Pourquoi j'ai écrit *La mulâtresse Solitude*," *Le Figaro littéraire*, January 26, 1967; my trans.

59. Glissant's analysis of "dispossession" of identity utilizes two models of exile. The first response, based on an obsession with return to a single origin, he calls "reversion"; the second, which involves "try[ing] to exorcise the impossibility of return," he calls "diversion" (16–26). He points to a significant "difference between the transplanting (by exile or dispersion) of a people who continue to survive elsewhere and the transfer (by the slave trade) of a population to another place where they change into something different, into a new set of possibilities. . . . This difference between a people that maintains its original nature and a population that is transformed elsewhere into another people . . . is what distinguishes, besides the persecution of one and the enslavement of the other, the Jewish Diaspora from the African slave trade" (15).

60. Maryse Condé, *La civilisation du bossale: Réflexions sur la littérature orale de la Guadeloupe et de la Martinique* (Paris: L'Harmattan, 1978), 7, classifies the bossale, créole, and marron in the following way: "the bossale is not simply the slave newly debarked from Africa, but s/he who develops in a slave universe. The créole, the black from the post-slavery colonial period. According to the same

logic, the marron is s/he who refuses the rules of colonial society as her/his ancestors had refused slavery"; my trans.

61. Glissant, *Caribbean Discourse*, 9.

62. For an essay that links translation and marronnage as dissident, transgres-
sive practices in colonial and postcolonial Caribbean texts, see Jean-Marc Gou-
vanic, "Legitimation, *Marronnage*, and the Power of Translation," in *Changing the
Terms*, ed. Simon and St. Pierre, 101–12.

63. Toni Morrison, *Beloved* (New York: Knopf, 1987).

CHAPTER 3. SCENES OF INHERITANCE: INTERGENERATIONAL
TRANSMISSION AND IMPERILED NARRATIVES

Epigraph: Maxine Hong Kingston, *The Woman Warrior: Memoir of a Girlhood
Among Ghosts* (New York: Vintage Books, 1989), 240.

1. Walter Benjamin, "The Task of the Translator," in *Illuminations*, trans.
Harry Zohn, ed. Hannah Arendt (New York: Schocken Books, 1968), 69–82.

2. Rodolphe Gasché, "Saturnine Vision and the Question of Difference: Re-
flections on Walter Benjamin's Theory of Language," in *Benjamin's Ground: New
Readings of Walter Benjamin*, ed. Rainer Nagele (Detroit: Wayne State University
Press, 1988), 83–104, quotation at 90.

3. Benjamin, "The Task of the Translator," in *Illuminations*, trans. Zohn, 74.

4. Jacques Derrida, "Des Tours de Babel," in *Difference in Translation*, ed.
Joseph F. Graham (Ithaca, N.Y.: Cornell University Press, 1985), 187.

5. Sigmund Freud, *Totem and Taboo: Some Points of Agreement Between the
Mental Lives of Savages and Neurotics*, trans. James Strachey (New York: Norton,
1990), 158.

6. Art Spiegelman's *Maus: A Survivor's Tale*, vol. 1, *My Father Bleeds History*;
vol. 2, *And Here My Troubles Began* (New York: Pantheon Books, 1978, 1986), is
the most spectacular act of translation by a child of survivors and an exemplary
text for this study (section epigram from 2: 16). Other memoirs by children of
Holocaust survivors originally written in English include Anne Karpf, *The War After: Living with the Holocaust* (London: Minerva, 1997); Sonia Pilcer, *The Holocaust Kid* (New York: Persea Books, 2001); Lisa Appignanesi, *Losing the Dead*
(London: Vintage Books, 2000). Excerpts from some of these texts and others, fiction and nonfiction, are collected in Melvin Bukiet's *Nothing Makes You Free: Writings by Descendants of Holocaust Survivors* (New York: Norton, 2002).

7. H. Barocas and C. Barocas, "Wounds of the Fathers: The Next Generation
of Holocaust Victims," *International Review of Psychoanalysis* 6 (1979): 331–41.

8. Shamai Davidson, "Transgenerational Transmission in the Families of Holocaust Survivors," *International Journal of Family Psychiatry* 1 (1980): 95–112.

9. For an insight into the existential implications of parental trauma for children of survivors, see Robert M. Prince, "Second Generation Effects of Historical

Trauma," *Psychoanalytic Review* 72 (Spring 1985). Prince contends that while "the transmission of the trauma . . . is an important consideration, it is secondary to coming to terms with the nature of Holocaust imagery" (27). As will be clear in the following discussion, these may not be so easily separated. For what is arguably the most broad-reaching presentation of "the survivor syndrome," see *Generations of the Holocaust*, ed. Martin Bergmann and Milton E. Jukovy (New York: Columbia University Press, 1990).

10. In her essay, Ellen Fine thematizes the history of memory in a number of "post-Holocaust" narratives. She applies the term "second generation" comprehensively, as a way to characterize not only children of survivors born after the war, but also those born during the Shoah, including "those who did not directly participate in the Holocaust, but have come to endure the psychic imprint of the trauma" (186). Although Fine and I tread some of the same ground—she discusses Morhange-Bégué's memoir, among others, as an illustration of the processes of "collective memory" and "absent memory"—I take issue precisely with her collapsing of what I see to be crucial conceptual and experiential differences among survivors and related victims of the Holocaust.

11. Claude Morhange-Bégué, *Chamberet: Recollections from an Ordinary Childhood*, trans. Austryn Wainhouse (Marlboro, Vt.: Marlboro Press, 1987). A partial list of other child survivor narratives written in or translated into English includes Saul Friedlander, *When Memory Comes*, trans. Helen R. Lane (New York: Farrar, Straus & Giroux, 1979); Nehama Tec, *Dry Tears: The Story of a Lost Childhood* (New York: Oxford University Press, 1982); Yehudah Nir, *The Lost Childhood: A Memoir* (New York: Berkley Books, 1989); Elie Wiesel, *Night* (New York: Bantam, 1982); Stacy Cretzmeyer, *Your Name is Renée: Ruth Hartz's Story as a Hidden Child in Nazi-Occupied France* (New York: Oxford University Press, 1999); Goldie Szachter Kalib, *The Last Selection: A Child's Journey Through the Holocaust* (Amherst: University of Massachusetts Press, 1991); Jack Kuper, *Child of the Holocaust* (New York: Berkley Books, 1967); Ruth Kluger, *Still Alive* (New York: Feminist Press, 2001); Evi Blaikie, *Magda's Daughter* (New York: Feminist Press, 2003); and Imre Kertész, *Fateless*, trans. Christopher C. Wilson and Katherina M. Wilson (Ann Arbor: University of Michigan Press, 1992). The most controversial and disturbing "child survivor narrative" to have appeared on the scene is Binjamin Wilkomirski's *Fragments*, trans. Carol Brown Janeway (New York: Schocken Books, 1995), which turned out not to be an account of the author's own childhood wartime experiences at all, but a deliberate misrepresentation or, perhaps, a remarkable fantasy based on an imagined identity. A novel about two children in the Holocaust that translates the classic fairy tale of Hansel and Gretel is Louise Murphy, *The True Story of Hansel and Gretel: A Novel of War and Survival* (New York: Penguin Books, 2003).

12. Morhange-Bégué's project resembles the kind of memory work variously called *memoire trouée*, "postmemory," and "vicarious or belated memory." For fuller elaboration, see Henry Raczymow, "Memory Shot Through With Holes,"

trans. Alan Astro, *Yale French Studies* 85 (1994); Marianne Hirsch, *Family Frames: Photography, Narrative, and Postmemory* (Cambridge, Mass.: Harvard University Press, 1994); and Froma Zeitlin, "The Vicarious Witness: Belated Memory and Authorial Presence in Recent Holocaust Literature," *History and Memory* 10.2 (Fall 1998).

13. Sigmund Freud, *The Standard Edition of the Complete Psychological Works of Sigmund Freud*, vol. 18, *Beyond the Pleasure Principle*, trans. and ed. James Strachey et al. (London: Hogarth Press, 1955), 15. Freud's other primary example of individual trauma is the repetitive nightmares about the battlefield suffered by soldiers of World War I. Since the Vietnam War, this has become the model for post-traumatic stress disorder (PTSD). For a history of the concept of trauma, see Ruth Leys, *Trauma: A Genealogy* (Chicago: University of Chicago Press, 2000).

14. Morhange-Bégué, *Chamberet*, 3, 60, 7. To gain an understanding of France's unique position among occupied western European nations in having adopted indigenous anti-Semitic measures, see Robert R. Marrus and Robert O. Paxton's groundbreaking exploration and analysis of the policies of Vichy, *Vichy, France, and the Jews* (Stanford: Stanford University Press, 1995), and to track its extenuating implications for French postwar politics, see Michael Curtis, *Verdict on Vichy: Power and Prejudice in the Vichy France Regime* (New York: Arcade, 2002).

15. Cathy Caruth, *Unclaimed Experience: Trauma, Narrative, and History* (Baltimore: Johns Hopkins University Press, 1996), 4.

16. Cathy Caruth, ed., *Trauma: Explorations in Memory* (Baltimore: Johns Hopkins University Press, 1995), 10.

17. Ibid., 153, 152.

18. Morhange-Bégué, *Chamberet*, 7.

19. Ibid., 20, 18.

20. Ibid., 26, 30.

21. Dori Laub and Marjorie Allard, "History, Memory and Truth: Defining the Place of the Survivor," in *Holocaust and History: The Known, the Unknown, the Disputed and the Reexamined*, ed. Michael Berenbaum and Abraham J. Peck (Bloomington: Indiana University Press, 1998), 808.

22. Morhange-Bégué, *Chamberet*, 45.

23. Ibid., 68, 84.

24. Ibid., 62–63.

25. Ibid.

26. Caruth, *Unclaimed Experience*, 64. Claude's chances of surviving were much better as a hidden child in France than if she had been a child deportee, which was a virtual death sentence. From the moment of their arrival on the selection ramp at Auschwitz, all children were ordered to remain with the women; it was the Nazi practice to send mothers and children immediately to the left, to the gas chambers. That Claude's mother was a doctor and had a skill crucial to the functioning of the

camp helped her survive, but her status would not have helped Claude. See *Women in the Holocaust*, ed. Dalia Ofer and Lenore Weitzman (New Haven, Conn.: Yale University Press, 1998), both the introduction and the essay by Myrna Goldenberg, "Memoirs of Auschwitz Survivors: The Burden of Gender," and Deborah Dwork, *Children with a Star: Jewish Youth in Nazi Europe* (New Haven, Conn.: Yale University Press, 1991), a comprehensive study of how Jewish children fared under the Third Reich.

27. Caruth, ed., *Trauma: Explorations in Memory*, 153.

28. Morhange-Bégué, *Chamberet*, 114–15.

29. Jean Laplanche, *Seduction, Translation and the Drives* (London: Institute of Contemporary Arts, 1992), 174, 204. Laplanche's examination of the centrality of translation in the psychoanalytic model depends to a great extent on Benjamin's theory of translation. See Laplanche's chapter "The Wall and the Arcade," 197–216.

30. Benjamin, "Task of the Translator," in *Illuminations*, trans. Zohn, 78; emphasis added. I prefer Carol Jacobs's translation of fragments as being "articulated together" to Harry Zohn's "glued together." See the chapter "The Monstrosity of Translation," in id., *In the Language of Walter Benjamin* (Baltimore: Johns Hopkins University Press, 1999). Regarding Benjamin's image of the broken vessel, Jacobs argues for a metonymical, rather than metaphorical, pattern (part to part, not part to whole) of fragments that have never constituted a totality and never will.

31. Paul de Man, *The Resistance to Theory* (Minneapolis: University of Minnesota Press, 1986), 84. De Man uses Jacobs in support of his critique of how "The Task of the Translator" has been repeatedly mistranslated and misread.

32. Benjamin, "Task of the Translator," in *Illuminations*, trans. Zohn, 71.

33. I am grateful to Janet Alexander of the Sarah Lawrence College Library; it was her idea to try and reach Austryn Wainhouse of Marlboro Press in France. Mr. Wainhouse proved to be extremely informative, not only about the history of the book, but also about Morhange-Bégué personally. I am no less grateful to Mr. Wainhouse for having suggested that I speak to Sidney Feshbach, who was kind enough to share his reminiscences of Morhange-Bégué with me. It was he who first passed on the manuscript to Wainhouse. From our first conversation he continued to be a source of encouragement and critical acuity and I owe him a great debt. Marlboro Press is now an imprint of Northwestern University Press; their new edition of the book appeared in 2001.

34. Admittedly, *Chamberet*, a deeply personal memoir, would hardly qualify as an indictment of Vichy collaboration; all its politics are just under the surface. And yet, this is exactly Henri Rousso's point in *The Vichy Syndrome: History and Memory in France Since 1944* (Cambridge, Mass.: Harvard University Press, 1991), which examines not "the history of Vichy, but the history of the *memory* of Vichy" (3). Rousso's study of collective memory in France is a study of neurosis of the na-

tion: "The Vichy syndrome consists of a diverse set of symptoms whereby the trauma of the Occupation, and particularly that trauma resulting from internal divisions within France, reveals itself in political, social, and cultural life. Since the end of the war, moreover, that trauma has been perpetuated and at times exacerbated" (11). For a more sharply focused study of the postwar politics of memory and memorialization in Germany and France, see Caroline Wiedner, *The Claims of Memory: Representations of the Holocaust in Contemporary Germany and France* (Ithaca, N.Y.: Cornell University Press, 1999).

35. T. Obinkaram Echewa, *I Saw the Sky Catch Fire* (New York: Dutton, 1992), 5; emphasis added.

36. For an incisive critique of postcolonial literary theory's tendency to "exaggerate and simplify the effects of the colonial imposition of European languages" on "post-Independence literary production in Africa," see Karin Barber, "African-Language Literature and Postcolonial Criticism." The effect of overemphasizing written literature in the English language, Barber argues, is the erasure of "other forms of expression—written literature in African languages, oral literature in African languages, and a whole domain of cultural forms which cross the boundaries between 'written' and 'oral,' between 'foreign' and 'indigenous'" (3).

37. R. Radhakrishnan, "Postcoloniality and the Boundaries of Identity," *Callaloo* 16 (1993): 750–71.

38. K. Anthony Appiah, *In My Father's House: Africa in the Philosophy of Culture* (New York: Oxford University Press, 1992), 54.

39. Homi K. Bhabha, *The Location of Culture* (New York: Routledge, 1994), 173.

40. It is interesting to note that, despite the conventional linking of female expression with orality and male expression with textuality here, other traditional gendered metaphors do not likewise obtain. As Sherry Simon shows in her extensive examination of feminist issues in translation theory and practice, *Gender in Translation*, "woman" and "translator" have been historically relegated to the same position of discursive inferiority, i.e., the "original" is coded strong, generative, and male, and the "translation" is coded weak, derivative, and female. Echewa's rendering scrambles this binary code.

41. Echewa, *I Saw the Sky Catch Fire*, 5. Randolph Starn, Introduction, *Representations* 26 (1989): 1–6, quoted from 2.

42. Chantal Zabus, *The African Palimpsest: Indigenization of Language in the West African Europhone Novel* (Atlanta, Ga.: Rodopi, 1991), 179, 7; and see esp. chap. 5 for an enriching discussion of this mode of indigenization and its implications for the role of African source languages in postcolonial West African Europhone texts. Throughout her analysis, Zabus tracks how otherness is revealed and refracted in the indigenized novel. Whether Echewa's translation practice or strategy here is consonant with a declared cultural political agenda is difficult to say; clearly, however, Echewa is conversant with traveling theories and their wide and ever-changing contexts.

43. Echewa, *I Saw the Sky Catch Fire*, 3.

44. See the paradigmatic study by Nina Emma Mba, *Nigerian Women Mobilized: Women's Political Activity in Southern Nigeria, 1900–1965* (Berkeley: University of California Press, 1982), especially the chapter devoted to the Women's War, 68–97.

45. Pierre Nora, "Between Memory and History: Les Lieux de Mémoire," trans. Marc Roudebush, *Representations* 26 (Spring 1989): 8.

46. Judith Van Allen's important analysis of the Women's War and its place in British colonialist discourse has enabled me to frame my understanding of this event in the novel (Van Allen, "Aba Riots or 'Women's War'? Ideology, Stratification, and the Invisibility of Women," in *Women in Africa: Studies in Social and Economic Change*, ed. Nancy J. Hafkin and Edna G. Bay [Stanford: Stanford University Press, 1976], 59–85). For a somewhat apologetic presentation of the events leading up to the war, of the colonial administration, and of the war's subsequent effects on British colonial policy, see Harry A. Gailey's *The Road to Aba: A Study of British Administrative Policy in Eastern Nigeria* (New York: New York University Press, 1970). Susan Andrade also draws heavily on Van Allen's work in tracing the inscription of female rebellion and the inscription of women into history in novels by the Nigerian writers Flora Nwapa and Buchi Emecheta in "Rewriting History, Motherhood, and Rebellion," *Research in African Literatures* 21.1 (1990): 91–110.

47. Van Allen, "Aba Riots or 'Women's War'?" 71–72.

48. Echewa, *I Saw the Sky Catch Fire*, 160, 163.

49. Ibid., 167.

50. Ibid., 56.

51. For a demonstration of how normalizing (universalizing) and estranging translation strategies are implicated in the construction of the unequal relationships between source- and target-language cultures, as well as the impact of recent developments in postmodern (reflexive) ethnography, see Kate Sturge, "Translation Strategies in Ethnography," *Translator* 3 (1997): 21–38.

52. Edmund Leach, *Social Anthropology* (London: Oxford University Press, 1982), 53.

53. Talal Asad, "The Concept of Cultural Translation in British Social Anthropology," in *Writing Culture: The Poetics and Politics of Ethnography*, ed. James Clifford and George E. Marcus (Berkeley: University of California Press, 1986), 160. Asad argues that the languages of "societies that social anthropologists have traditionally studied—are 'weaker' in relation to Western languages (and today, especially to English), they are more likely to submit to forcible transformation in the translation process than the other way around" (ibid., 157–58). On the historical complicity between translation studies and anthropology in the growth of European colonialism, and especially on the rhetoric of humanism in ethnographic representation, see Tejaswini Niranjana's *Siting Translation: History, Post-Structuralism*

and the Colonial Context (Berkeley: University of California, 1986), especially the chapter on translation theory, humanism and ethnographic representation, 47–86. In his dramatic study of translation as "the central act" of colonial and imperial conquest in the New World, Eric Cheyfitz asserts, "the models of intercultural communication that anthropology produces (and as allegory these intercultural models are intracultural) influence the actual contact between cultures, which is only to acknowledge that the models are political productions that produce politics." In a provocative departure from other postcolonial readings, Cheyfitz distinguishes between "the difficult politics of translation" and "the politics of translation that represses this difficult politics" (xix).

54. Echewa, *I Saw the Sky Catch Fire*, 96, 98, 99, 100, 109, 110, 111.

55. Ibid., 90.

56. Helen Callaway, *Gender, Culture, Empire: European Women in Colonial Nigeria* (Urbana: University of Illinois Press, 1987), 6, 7.

57. Echewa, *I Saw the Sky Catch Fire*, 192.

58. Ibid., 216–17.

59. Asad, "Concept of Cultural Translation in British Social Anthropology," in *Writing Culture*, ed. Clifford and Marcus, 159.

60. Pierre Nora, "Between Memory and History: *Les Lieux de Mémoire*," trans. Marc Roudebush, *Representations* 26 (Spring 1989): 8–9.

61. Gayatri Chakravorty Spivak, "The Politics of Translation," in *De-Stabilizing Theory: Contemporary Feminist Debates*, ed. Michelle Barrett and Anne Phillips (Stanford: Stanford University Press, 1992), 181. Spivak has translated Derrida's *De la grammatologie* (Paris: Minuit, 1966), under the title *Of Grammatology* (Baltimore: Johns Hopkins University Press, 1976; rev. ed., 1997), and a range of Bengali texts, including, most recently, three stories by Mahasweta Devi, in a volume entitled *Imaginary Maps* (New York: Routledge, 1995).

62. Spivak, "Politics of Translation," in *De-Stabilizing Theory*, ed. Barrett and Phillips, 190.

63. Bhabha, *Location of Culture*, 178.

64. Sherry Simon, *Gender in Translation: Cultural Identity and the Politics of Transmission* (London: Routledge, 1996), 36.

65. I am grateful to Jonathan Boyarin for this insight and for suggesting a more ironized reading of Ashby-Jones's function in the text.

66. Echewa, *I Saw the Sky Catch Fire*, 109–10.

67. Asad, "Concept of Cultural Translation in British Social Anthropology," in *Writing Culture*, ed. Clifford and Marcus, 163.

68. For a penetrating account of this phenomenon, see Johannes Fabian, *Time and the Other: How Anthropology Makes Its Object* (New York: Columbia University Press, 1983).

69. Dorothy Hammond and Alta Jablow, *The Myth of Africa* (New York: Library of Social Science, 1977), 124, 127.

234 Notes to Pages 142–48

70. Helen Lackner, "Colonial Administration and Social Anthropology: Eastern Nigeria, 1920–1940," in *Anthropology and the Colonial Encounter,* ed. Talal Asad (New York: Humanities Press, 1973), 127.

71. Ibid., 145. And see Sylvia Leith-Ross, *African Women: A Study of the Ibo of Nigeria,* with a foreword by Lord Lugard (London: Faber & Faber, 1939), and *Stepping-Stones: Memoirs of Colonial Nigeria, 1907–1960* (London: Peter Owen, 1983).

72. Echewa, *I Saw the Sky Catch Fire,* 311.

73. Ibid., 290.

74. Ibid., 5.

75. Lawrence Venuti, *Rethinking Translation: Discourse, Subjectivity, Ideology* (London: Routledge, 1992), 12–13.

76. Arnold Krupat, *The Turn to the Native: Studies in Criticism and Culture* (Lincoln: University of Nebraska Press, 1996). References to this strategy are found throughout his work.

77. Derrida, "Des Tours de Babel," 179.

78. Benjamin, "Theses on the Philosophy of History," in *Illuminations,* trans. Zohn, 254.

CHAPTER 4. THE MEMORIALIST AS TRANSLATOR: JORGE SEMPRÚN

Epigraph: Roy Pascal, *Design and Truth in Autobiography* (Cambridge, Mass.: Harvard University Press, 1960), 11.

1. The concerns of this chapter are directly related to what has been called "thanatropism," defined as "a complicated rhetorical sub-group that covers any figurative or rhetorical attempt to represent death, loss, and grief . . . in as much as death can never be a referent for language, all talk of death is ultimately tropic," by William Watkin in *On Mourning: Theories of Loss in Modern Literature* (Edinburgh: Edinburgh University Press, 2004), 58.

2. Jorge Semprún, *The Long Voyage,* trans. Richard Seaver (New York: Grove Press, 1964), 69. Published in England as *The Cattle Truck* (London: Serif, 1993). Originally published as *Le grand voyage* (Paris: Gallimard, 1963). Though I use the American title, my page numbers correspond to the British edition.

3. Although he ceaselessly interrogates the effects of his experience in Buchenwald in all of his writing, the only text in which Semprún documents life *in* the camp and meditates on the concentrationary camp universe is *Oh, What a Beautiful Sunday!* (New York: Harcourt, Brace, Jovanovich, 1980). In it, Semprún recounts a particular Sunday in Buchenwald in 1944 with all its terrors and terrible ironies and paradoxes. Most explicitly, he acknowledges that he was afforded protection by the underground Communist Party organization within the camp, in whose administration German communists held the key posts. Not only did his status as a political prisoner protect him from complete dehumanization, despite the brutal and efficient industry of death that surrounded him, it no doubt played a role in his actual survival.

4. Jorge Semprún, *Communism in Spain in the Franco Era: The Autobiography of Federico Sanchez*, trans. Helen R. Lane (Brighton, Eng.: Harvester Press, 1980); id., *Literature or Life*, trans. Linda Coverdale (New York: Viking Penguin, 1997).

5. In the introduction to a recent special issue of *Biography* entitled "Personal Effects: The Testimonial Uses of Life Writing," the editors assert: "Starting from the late 1980s . . . autobiography studies was redefined as 'life writing,' in order to accommodate . . . the emergence of new testimonial forms. . . . Testimonial genres have provided particularly important insights into the connections between stories and collective bodies. They remind us that telling one's story can be first and foremost a profoundly political act, rather than primarily one of self-expression and self-making." In "Bodies of Evidence and the Intricate Machines of Untruth," *Biography* 27.1, ed. Cynthia Franklin and Laura E. Lyons (Winter 2004), ix. Although I do not fully subscribe to the notion that there has been a "transformation of autobiography studies into life writing studies" (ix)—for example, slave narratives have always been at the center of autobiography studies—I concur that the field has expanded tremendously to formally encompass collective accounts as well as highly individualized narratives of personal suffering and political persecution and survival. Semprún's survival narrative merits our interest precisely because it operates at the conjunction of the personal and the collective and expressly explores that relation.

6. Semprún's desire to have the PCE listen carefully to the book's arguments was balanced by his concern that the Right not use or manipulate it during the electoral period. For an illuminating exchange on this book, political cinema, and other related matters, see "The Truth Is Always Revolutionary," Semprún's interview with Theo Bloomfield, *Cineaste* 25 (1979): 265–81.

7. Philippe Lejeune, "The Autobiographical Pact," in *On Autobiography*, ed. Paul John Eakin (Minneapolis: University of Minnesota Press, 1990).

8. Gertrude Stein, *Autobiography of Alice B. Toklas* (New York: Vintage Books, 1990).

9. Christa Wolf, *Patterns of Childhood*, trans. Ursule Molinaro and Hedwig Rappolt (New York: Farrar, Straus & Giroux, 1980).

10. The resurgence of interest in the politics of memory as an instrument of repression as well as reconciliation includes new reflections on the Civil War and assessments of the political and social legacy of the Franco regime and the transition to democracy in Spain. For an excellent collection of essays on a range of perspectives, including an essay on Semprún's role in contesting the *retórica de la desmemoria*, see Joan Ramon Resina, *Disremembering the Dictatorship: The Politics of Memory in the Spanish Transition to Democracy* (Atlanta, Ga.: Rodopi, 2000), especially Ofelia Ferrán, "Memory and Forgetting, Resistance and Noise in the Spanish Transition: Semprún and Vázquez Montalbán," 191–222. On the role of identifying bones in this current process, see Elizabeth Kolbert's article, "Looking for Lorca," *New Yorker*, December 22, 2003.

11. Dominick LaCapra, "Reflections on Trauma, Absence, and Loss," in *Whose Freud? The Place of Psychoanalysis in Contemporary Culture*, ed. Peter Brooks and Alex Woloch (New Haven, Conn.: Yale University Press, 2000), 232.

12. Eric Santner, "History Beyond the Pleasure Principle: Some Thoughts on the Representation of Trauma," in *Probing the Limits of Representation: Nazism and the "Final Solution,"* ed. Saul Friedlander (Cambridge, Mass.: Harvard University Press, 1992), 145.

13. Barbara Harlow, *Resistance Literature* (New York: Methuen, 1987), 7.

14. *Whose Freud? The Place of Psychoanalysis in Contemporary Culture*, ed. Peter Brooks and Alex Woloch (New Haven, Conn.: Yale University Press, 2000), 6.

15. Peter Brooks, *Reading for the Plot: Design and Intention in Narrative* (Cambridge, Mass.: Harvard University Press, 1984), 107–8.

16. Terrence Des Pres, *Survivor: An Anatomy of Life in the Death Camps* (New York: Oxford University Press, 1976), vi.

17. Brooks, *Reading for the Plot*, 107–8.

18. In every account of the Nazi camps—forced labor, concentration, and death camps—there is the underlying tension between the deported-resister narrative and the extermination or genocide narrative. Was death the by-product or the objective of the camp? As Donald Reid explains in an essay that focuses on Ravensbrück, but applies to all the camps, the determining factor is whether there were gas chambers, as well as crematoria, on the grounds. See Reid, "Germaine Tillion and Resistance to the Vichy Syndrome," *History and Memory* 15.2 (2003): 36–63.

19. The "Holocaust" applies to a series of policies and events that were initiated in 1933 and resulted "in the systematic extermination of approximately six million European Jews by the Nazis and their allies." See the editors' general introduction to *The Holocaust: Theoretical Readings*, ed. Neil Levy and Michael Rothberg (New Brunswick, N.J.: Rutgers University Press, 2003), 3.

20. It is interesting to note that Semprún's experience as a communist resister in Buchenwald placed him at the nexus of fascinating and rather tortured postwar debates in France regarding the collective remembrance of World War II. "Resistance" gave way to "martyrdom" as the metaphor for all forms of Nazi persecution, with the concentration camp as the symbolic depository of national martyrdom. As Peter Lagrou explains in his illuminating study *The Legacy of Nazi Occupation: Patriotic Memory and National Recovery in Western Europe, 1945–1965* (Cambridge: Cambridge University Press, 2000), competing claims to moral and political legitimacy after the war hinged on the answers to such questions as: What constitutes resistance? Are resisters who fight or die for a cause martyrs, and therefore victims? Are agency and victimization necessarily mutually exclusive? Recognition of the fact that there are different kinds of agents, just as there are different kinds of victims can be seen in the "radical reversal of memories" regarding the image of the combatant/hero-victim vs. the victims of genocide. In the 1960s, in the establish-

ment of the central symbol of the Mémorial de la Déportation was established the image of the *résistant*, which assumed archetypal significance in the early years— and which served to conceal the more conflictual and humiliating memories of Vichy—was subordinated to the dominant category of the *déporté*.

21. Lawrence Langer, *Holocaust Testimonies: The Ruins of Memory* (New Haven, Conn.: Yale University Press, 1991).

22. No theoretical debate on the Holocaust seems complete without expressions of its "ineffability," "unspeakability," and "unrepresentability." "Unrepresentability"—another word for "untranslatability"—connotes an order of difference excessive and uncontainable, such that it exceeds the means available to render the information. Whether cast as the extreme-case example of "the limits of representation" (Saul Friedlander, Geoffrey Hartman) or "the representation of limits" (Berel Lang), these expressions clearly serve a necessary rhetorical function, both for the testifier and the interpreter. See Friedlander, ed., *Probing the Limits of Representation*.

23. Hayden White, *The Content of the Form* (Baltimore: Johns Hopkins University Press, 1987), 1.

24. Robert Jay Lifton, *The Broken Connection: Death and the Continuity of Life* (New York: Simon & Schuster, 1979), 169.

25. Mentioned in *Literature or Life* and elaborated upon more fully in Semprún's *Le mort qu'il faut* (Paris: Grand livre du mois, 2001) in a paean to *Absalom, Absalom!* is the shocking, surprising "disclosure" that there was a well-stocked library at Buchenwald. Semprún explains, with no lack of facetiousness, that readers who cannot assimilate this information or for whom this casts doubt on the gruesome reality of life in a concentration camp should remember that Buchenwald was bucolically situated at Weimar, the city of Goethe, the symbol of Germany's highest cultural achievements (67–70). Semprún repeatedly reminds us that Goethe used to climb the Ettersburg and sit and work under a beech tree, which was the site chosen by the Nazis to establish the concentration camp of Buchenwald.

26. Jorge Semprún, *Mal et modernité suivi de "Vous avez une tombe aux creux des nuages . . ."* (Paris: Éditions Climats, 1994), 76–77; my trans.

27. The idea of language as a denationalized homeland has been expressed by a number of transnational intellectuals. Hélène Cixous states, "At a certain moment for the person who has lost everything, whether that means a being or a country, language becomes the country. One enters the country of words." Cixous, "Coming to Writing," in *"Coming to Writing" and Other Essays* (Cambridge, Mass.: Harvard University Press, 1991).

28. Wulf Kirsten, "Bleak Site: A Triptych," trans. Sabine Dollinger. In *Erdlebenbilder: Gedichte aus fünfzig Jahren, 1954–2004* (Zurich: Ammann, 2004). Kirsten's difficult landscape poems are generally unknown outside of Germany; most published translations are in Czech. My introduction to Kirsten's poetry was a presentation

in French by Stéphane Michaud at the International Comparative Literature Association in 2004. I am grateful to Professor Michaud for helping me pursue this connection. Holm Kirsten and Wulf Kirsten also edited *Stimmen aus Buchenwald: Ein Lesebuch* (Göttingen: Wallstein, 2002), a collection of sixty eyewitness accounts of Buchenwald by a range of writers and artists, including Semprún.

29. The esteemed Edward R. Murrow's taped report from Buchenwald, transmitted on April 15, 1945, remains one of the most moving and shocking eyewitness accounts of what outsiders discovered there along with the liberators. Several months later, at the Nuremberg trial, amid the mounds of documentary evidence presented there, the savage, perverse contrast between the idyllic location symbolizing the highest aspects of German civilization and the barbarism of what took place in its name, was spectacularly exhibited. Two iconic examples of Nazi culture were displayed as part of the prosecutors' case: a human head, "with the skull bone removed, shrunken, stuffed, and preserved" and "flayed human skin, covered with tattoos, which had been preserved as an ornament for Ilse Koch, the wife of the Buchenwald commandant," Lawrence Douglas notes in "The Shrunken Head of Buchenwald: Icons of Atrocity at Nuremberg," in *Visual Culture and the Holocaust*, ed. Barbie Zelizer (London: Athlone Press, 2001), 276. See also Ulrich Baer's *Spectral Evidence: The Photography of Trauma* (Cambridge, Mass.: MIT Press, 2002) for a consideration of the gap between seeing and knowing in relation to the traumatized landscape of Buchenwald, as seen through the eyes of photographer Mikael Levin.

30. For an introduction to "trauma" and the Holocaust, see my "Teaching Trauma and Transmission," in *Teaching Representations of the Holocaust* (New York: Modern Language Association, 2004). For a historical overview of how "[t]he literature of trauma in the West, exemplified by Holocaust narratives, has become the dominant paradigm for understanding the processes of victimization, remembering, witnessing, and recovery," see Kay Schaffer and Sidonie Smith, "Life Narratives in the Field of Human Rights," in *Biography* 27.1 (Winter 2004): 9.

31. J. L. Laplanche and J.-B. Pontalis, *The Language of Psycho-analysis*, trans. Donald Nicholson-Smith (New York: Norton, 1973), 469.

32. Sigmund Freud, *The Standard Edition of the Complete Psychological Works of Sigmund Freud*, vol. 18, *Beyond the Pleasure Principle*, trans. and ed. James Strachey et al. (London: Hogarth Press, 1955), 32.

33. A cursory glance at the titles of a few of the most thoughtful articles devoted to Semprún confirms this triangular association. See Kathleen M. Vernon, "The Trauma of History/The History of Trauma: Plotting Memory in Jorge Semprún," in *Cine-Lit III: Essays on Hispanic Film and Fiction*, ed. George Cabello-Castellet, Jaume Martí-Olivella, and Guy H. Wood (Corvallis, Oreg.: Oregon State University Press, 1998); Ofelia Ferrán, "'Quanto mas escribo, mas me queda por decir': Memory, Trauma, and Writing in the Work of Jorge Semprún," *MLN* 116.2 (March 2001): 266–94; David Carroll, "The Limits of Representation and

the Right to Fiction: Shame, Literature, and the Memory of the Shoah," *Esprit créateur* 39.4 (Winter 1999): 68–79; Patricia Gartland, "Three Holocaust Writers: Speaking the Unspeakable," *Critique: Studies in Contemporary Fiction* 25.1 (Fall 1983): 45–56 (which focuses on David Rousset, Semprún, and Charlotte Delbo); Susan Rubin Suleiman, "Historical Trauma and Literary Testimony: Writing and Repetition in the Buchenwald Memoirs of Jorge Semprún," *Journal of Romance Studies* 4.2 (2004): 1–19. The striking exception is also the most intricate and thorough examination of Semprún's life and work to date, Françoise Nicoladzé's *La deuxième vie de Jorge Semprún: Une écriture tressée aux spirales de l'histoire* (Castelnau-le-Lez: Climats, 1997).

34. Angel Loureiro, *The Ethics of Autobiography: Replacing the Subject in Modern Spain* (Nashville, Tenn.: Vanderbilt University Press, 2000), 158.

35. For a detailed account of the "crisis of commemoration" and the long-range postwar impact on German national identity, see Sarah Farmer, "Symbols That Face Two Ways: Commemorating the Victims of Nazism and Stalinism at Buchenwald and Sachsenhausen," *Representations* 49 (Winter 1995): 97–119.

36. Semprún, *Mal et modernité suivi de "Vous avez une tombe aux creux des nuages . . . ,"* 92; my trans.

37. Peter Homans, *The Ability to Mourn: Disillusionment and the Social Origins of Psychoanalysis* (Chicago: University of Chicago Press, 1989), 3–4.

38. Sigmund Freud, *The Standard Edition of the Complete Psychological Works of Sigmund Freud*, vol. 14, *Mourning and Melancholia*, trans. and ed. James Strachey et al. (London: Hogarth Press, 1957), 243.

39. See Dominick LaCapra, Eric L. Santner, and Robert J. Lifton, appearing in the section entitled "Psychoanalysis and the Historiography of Modern Culture" from the timely collection *Whose Freud? The Place of Psychoanalysis in Contemporary Culture* (New Haven, Conn.: Yale University Press, 2000).

40. Eric Santner, "History Beyond the Pleasure Principle: Some Thoughts on the Representation of Trauma," in *Probing the Limits of Representation: Nazism and the "Final Solution,"* ed. Saul Friedlander (Cambridge, Mass.: Harvard University Press, 1992), 143–54.

41. The primacy and universality of the trope of trauma has, of course, not gone unchallenged, but generally objections are conducted within a critique of the universal applicability of the psychoanalytic model to adequately and fairly account for the ways in which non-Western cultures understand and figure cataclysmic events. These arguments regarding the translation/transporting of theories to other discursive and cultural contexts are compelling. At the same time, as is evident throughout this entire study, I am sympathetic to the psychoanalytical model and am calling here for a more refined, sensitive use of the instrument.

42. Derrida mourns the death of the spirit of Marxism as a monumental loss that demands reevaluation in *Specters of Marx: The State of the Debt, the Work of Mourning, and the New International,* trans. Peggy Kamuf (New York: Routledge, 1994).

43. David Eng and David Kazanjian, *Loss: The Politics of Mourning* (Berkeley: University of California Press, 2003), 2. An extremely provocative analysis of the "devaluation" of mourning in postmodernity and its implications for remembering are explored in Alessi Ricciardi, *The Ends of Mourning: Psychoanalysis, Literature, Film* (Stanford: Stanford University Press, 2003). Ricciardi indicts postmodernism's inability or refusal to mourn as a failure to provide a critical, ethical response to the claims of the past.

44. Cathy Caruth, *Unclaimed Experience: Trauma, Narrative, and History* (Baltimore: Johns Hopkins University Press, 1996), 62.

45. Testimony is not only an act of bearing witness in a political or legal context; it is also at the center of a psychical process by which the survivor "comes to know" his or her own story of survival, and by doing so, is able to ideally achieve the therapeutic goal of "repossessing the act of witnessing." As formulated by Dori Laub, "the survivors did not only need to survive so that they could tell their story; they also needed to tell their story in order to survive. There is, in each survivor, an imperative need to *tell* and thus to come to *know* one's story, unimpeded by ghosts from the past against which one has to protect oneself. One has to know one's buried truth in order to be able to live one's life" (78). Shoshana Felman declares that "our era can precisely be defined as the age of testimony," remarking on the "growing predominance of testimony as a privileged mode of transmission and communication" (5–6). See *Testimony: Crises of Witnessing in Literature, Psychoanalysis and History*, ed. Shoshana Felman and Dori Laub (New York: Routledge, 1992).

46. Primo Levi, *The Drowned and the Saved* (New York: Vintage International, 1989), 83–84.

47. Jorge Semprún, *Le mort qu'il faut* (Paris: Gallimard, 2001), 16; my trans.

48. Unlike the English, the French word *chance* means both luck and chance. The interplay between the two should not be lost on the reader.

49. Cathy Caruth, *Trauma: Explorations in Memory* (Baltimore: Johns Hopkins University Press, 1995), 153.

50. Primo Levi, *Se questo è un uomo* (Turin: Einaudi, 1958), trans. Stuart Woolf as *If This Is a Man* (New York: Orion Press, 1959) and subsequently published as *Survival in Auschwitz: The Nazi Assault on Humanity* (1961; reprint, New York: Simon & Schuster, 1996).

51. Caruth, *Unclaimed Experience*, 7.

52. Michel de Certeau, *The Writing of History*, trans. Tom Conley (New York: Columbia University Press, 1988), 4.

53. See the introduction to Jacques Derrida's *The Work of Mourning*, ed. Pascale-Anne Brault and Michael Naas (Chicago: University of Chicago Press, 2001). Derrida died on October 8, 2004, as I was completing this chapter.

54. Jacques Derrida, "Living On: Border Lines," in *Deconstruction and Criticism*, ed. Harold Bloom et al. (New York: Continuum, 1979), 76, 79.

55. Ibid., 108.

56. Jacques Derrida, *The Ear of the Other: Otobiography, Transference, Translation* (Lincoln: University of Nebraska Press, 1985), 12.

57. Walter Benjamin, "The Task of the Translator," in *Illuminations*, trans. Harry Zohn, ed. Hannah Arendt (New York: Schocken Books, 1968), 71. That Benjamin—whose lifework proposed a political, historical, materialist, and mystical vision of the afterlife of texts—did not survive the war, that he took his own life at the Spanish border while in flight from the Gestapo, haunts the postmodern scene of translation.

EPILOGUE. "THE HOME OF THE PHOTOGRAPH IS THE CEMETERY":
A SECOND-GENERATION HOLOCAUST NARRATIVE

1. Susan Sontag, *On Photography* (New York: Farrar, Straus & Giroux, 1973), 70. "Photography is the medium in which we unconsciously encounter the dead. . . . Photographs are not signs of presence but evidence of absence," Jay Prosser writes in *Light in the Dark Room: Photography and Loss* (Minneapolis: University of Minnesota Press, 2005), 1.

2. Julia Hirsch, *Family Photographs: Content, Meaning and Effect* (New York: Oxford University Press, 1981), 3.

3. Sontag, *On Photography*, 8.

4. Marianne Hirsch, *Family Frames: Photography, Narrative and Postmemory* (Cambridge, Mass.: Harvard University Press, 1998), 20.

5. Nadine Fresco, "Remembering the Unknown," *International Review of Psycho-analysis* 2 (1984): 417–27; quoted from 420.

6. Regis Durand, "How to See (Photographically)," in *Fugitive Images: From Photography to Video*, ed. Patrice Petro (Bloomington: Indiana University Press, 1995), 147.

7. Linda Haverty Rugg, *Picturing Ourselves: Photography and Autobiography* (Chicago: University of Chicago Press, 1997), 25.

8. Sigmund Freud, *The Standard Edition of the Complete Psychological Works of Sigmund Freud*, vol. 14, *Mourning and Melancholia*, trans. and ed. James Strachey et al. (London: Hogarth Press, 1957).

9. Marsha Lynne Abrams, "Coping with Loss in the Human Sciences: A Reading At the Intersection of Psychoanalysis and Hermeneutics," *Diacritics* 23.1 (1993): 67–82; quoted from 71.

10. Shoshana Felman and Dori Laub, *Testimony: Crises of Witnessing in Literature, Psychoanalysis and History* (New York: Routledge, 1992), 160.

11. Eduardo Cadava, *Words of Light: Theses on the Photography of History* (Princeton, N.J.: Princeton University Press, 1997), 7–8.

Index

Abrams, Marsha Lynn, 205
Africa, 78, 85–89, 98–100, 106–9,
221n24, 226n59, 226n60; women in,
85–86, 91, 131, 143, 221n24, 222n31,
232n46; in Echewa, 130–32, 136–37,
140–43, 222n28. *See also* Caribbean;
Colonialism; Echewa, T. Obinkaram;
Emecheta, Buchi; Nigeria; Slave nar-
ratives; Slavery; Women's War
African Americans, 67, 69, 76, 84
African American slave narratives,
74–77, 79, 81, 86, 91ff, 95, 222n29. *See
also* Slave narratives
African literature, 71, 85–86, 94–95, 127,
131, 141, 231n36, 231n42, 232n46; and
postcolonialism, 13, 94, 127, 222n31,
231n36, 231n42. *See also* Echewa,
T. Obinkaram; Emecheta, Buchi;
Nigeria
Allard, Marjorie, 118
America, *see* United States
Andrade, Susan, 222n30, 232n46
Andrews, William, 69
Ankersmit, F. R., 225n51
Anthropology, 135, 137, 142–43, 156, 173,
232n53, 233n53; and ethnography,
134–36, 138–45. *See also* Colonialism;
Echewa, T. Obinkaram;
Postcolonialism
Appiah, K. Anthony, 127
Apter, Emily, 210n8
Asad, Talal, 135, 138, 141, 232n53
Auschwitz, 97, 102, 116, 119, 174, 181–82,
191, 193, 229n26. *See also* Holocaust

Austen, Jane, 56
Autobiography, 13f, 69, 75, 114f, 149f,
150–51, 157, 185, 221n20, 235n5; and
genre, 4, 37, 154, 218n3. *See also* Child
survivor narratives; Holocaust survivors; Memorialization; Memory;
Morhange-Bégué, Claude; Semprún,
Jorge; Slave narratives
Autobiography of Federico Sanchez, The,
see under Semprún, Jorge

Babel, 4, 23, 30, 36, 47, 54, 108, 215n25.
See also Derrida, Jacques
Bal, Mieke, 212n21
Barber, Karin, 231n36
Barcelona, 41–42, 44–45, 51, 54
Bassnett, Susan, 210n8
Benjamin, Walter, 1–2f, 4–5, 113, 123, 145,
206, 211n11, 230n30, 241n57; "The
Task of the Translator," 1, 111–12, 187;
"The Theses on the Philosophy of
History," 5, 145; and translation, 13,
21–23, 27–29, 122, 124, 138, 145, 203,
238n29. *See also* Translatability
Berman, Antoine, 211n20
Berman, Jeffrey, 216n34
Bernheimer, Charles, 210n8
Bhabha, Homi, 37, 140
Blanchot, Maurice, 95
Borders, 40, 58
Borges, Jorge Luis, 30
Brogan, Kathleen, 211n10
Brontë, Charlotte, 95
Brooks, Peter, 157–58

Cultural Memory | *in the Present*

Jacques Derrida, *Paper Machine*

Renaud Barbaras, *Desire and Distance: Introduction to a Phenomenology of Perception*

Jill Bennett, *Empathic Vision: Affect, Trauma, and Contemporary Art*

Ban Wang, *Illuminations from the Past: Trauma, Memory, and History in Modern China*

James Phillips, *Heidegger's* Volk: *Between National Socialism and Poetry*

Frank Ankersmit, *Sublime Historical Experience*

István Rév, *Retroactive Justice: Prehistory of Post-Communism*

Paola Marrati, *Genesis and Trace: Derrida Reading Husserl and Heidegger*

Krzysztof Ziarek, *The Force of Art*

Marie-José Mondzain, *Image, Icon, Economy: The Byzantine Origins of the Contemporary Imaginary*

Cecilia Sjöholm, *The Antigone Complex: Ethics and the Invention of Feminine Desire*

Jacques Derrida and Elisabeth Roudinesco, *For What Tomorrow . . . : A Dialogue*

Elisabeth Weber, *Questioning Judaism: Interviews by Elisabeth Weber*

Jacques Derrida and Catherine Malabou, *Counterpath: Traveling with Jacques Derrida*

Martin Seel, *Aesthetics of Appearing*

Nanette Salomon, *Shifting Priorities: Gender and Genre in Seventeenth-Century Dutch Painting*

Jacob Taubes, *The Political Theology of Paul*

Jean-Luc Marion, *The Crossing of the Visible*

Eric Michaud, *The Cult of Art in Nazi Germany*

Anne Freadman, *The Machinery of Talk: Charles Peirce and the Sign Hypothesis*

Stanley Cavell, *Emerson's Transcendental Etudes*

Stuart McLean, *The Event and its Terrors: Ireland, Famine, Modernity*

Beate Rössler, ed., *Privacies: Philosophical Evaluations*

Bernard Faure, *Double Exposure: Cutting Across Buddhist and Western Discourses*

Alessia Ricciardi, *The Ends Of Mourning: Psychoanalysis, Literature, Film*

Alain Badiou, *Saint Paul: The Foundation of Universalism*

Gil Anidjar, *The Jew, the Arab: A History of the Enemy*

Jonathan Culler and Kevin Lamb, eds., *Just Being Difficult? Academic Writing in the Public Arena*

Jean-Luc Nancy, *A Finite Thinking*, edited by Simon Sparks

Theodor W. Adorno, *Can One Live after Auschwitz? A Philosophical Reader*, edited by Rolf Tiedemann

Patricia Pisters, *The Matrix of Visual Culture: Working with Deleuze in Film Theory*

Andreas Huyssen, *Present Pasts: Urban Palimpsests and the Politics of Memory*

Talal Asad, *Formations of the Secular: Christianity, Islam, Modernity*

Dorothea von Mücke, *The Rise of the Fantastic Tale*

Marc Redfield, *The Politics of Aesthetics: Nationalism, Gender, Romanticism*

Emmanuel Levinas, *On Escape*

Dan Zahavi, *Husserl's Phenomenology*

Rodolphe Gasché, *The Idea of Form: Rethinking Kant's Aesthetics*

Michael Naas, *Taking on the Tradition: Jacques Derrida and the Legacies of Deconstruction*

Herlinde Pauer-Studer, ed., *Constructions of Practical Reason: Interviews on Moral and Political Philosophy*

Jean-Luc Nancy, *The Speculative Remark: (One of Hegel's bon mots)*

Jean-François Lyotard, *Soundproof Room: Malraux's Anti-Aesthetics*

Jan Patočka, *Plato and Europe*

Hubert Damisch, *Skyline: The Narcissistic City*

Isabel Hoving, *In Praise of New Travelers: Reading Caribbean Migrant Women Writers*

Richard Rand, ed., *Futures: Of Jacques Derrida*

William Rasch, *Niklas Luhmann's Modernity: The Paradoxes of Differentiation*

Jacques Derrida and Anne Dufourmantelle, *Of Hospitality*

Jean-François Lyotard, *The Confession of Augustine*

Kaja Silverman, *World Spectators*

Samuel Weber, *Institution and Interpretation: Expanded Edition*

Jeffrey S. Librett, *The Rhetoric of Cultural Dialogue: Jews and Germans in the Epoch of Emancipation*

Ulrich Baer, *Remnants of Song: Trauma and the Experience of Modernity in Charles Baudelaire and Paul Celan*

Samuel C. Wheeler III, *Deconstruction as Analytic Philosophy*

David S. Ferris, *Silent Urns: Romanticism, Hellenism, Modernity*

Rodolphe Gasché, *Of Minimal Things: Studies on the Notion of Relation*

Sarah Winter, *Freud and the Institution of Psychoanalytic Knowledge*

Samuel Weber, *The Legend of Freud: Expanded Edition*

Aris Fioretos, ed., *The Solid Letter: Readings of Friedrich Hölderlin*

J. Hillis Miller / Manuel Asensi, *Black Holes / J. Hillis Miller; or, Boustrophedonic Reading*

Miryam Sas, *Fault Lines: Cultural Memory and Japanese Surrealism*

Peter Schwenger, *Fantasm and Fiction: On Textual Envisioning*

Didier Maleuvre, *Museum Memories: History, Technology, Art*

Jacques Derrida, *Monolingualism of the Other; or, The Prosthesis of Origin*

Andrew Baruch Wachtel, *Making a Nation, Breaking a Nation: Literature and Cultural Politics in Yugoslavia*

Niklas Luhmann, *Love as Passion: The Codification of Intimacy*

Mieke Bal, ed., *The Practice of Cultural Analysis: Exposing Interdisciplinary Interpretation*

Jacques Derrida and Gianni Vattimo, eds., *Religion*